Secrets of Great

Secrets of Great Teachers

22 Strategies to Energize Middle and High School Classrooms

ELISHEVA ZEFFREN

with PERELLA PERLSTEIN

McFarland & Company, Inc., Publishers

Jefferson, North Carolina

ISBN (print) 978-1-4766-7030-0
ISBN (ebook) 978-1-4766-3054-0

LIBRARY OF CONGRESS CATALOGUING DATA ARE AVAILABLE

BRITISH LIBRARY CATALOGUING DATA ARE AVAILABLE

Front cover image © 2018 iStock

Printed in the United States of America

*McFarland & Company, Inc., Publishers
Box 611, Jefferson, North Carolina 28640
www.mcfarlandpub.com*

To Mama

In a completely rational society,
the best of us would be teachers
and the rest of us would have to settle for something else.
—Lee Iacocca

Table of Contents

Acknowledgments

First and foremost, I would like to thank God who makes all things possible. Without Him, I would not have a single thought or experience. I thank Him for my every breath, for guiding me in teaching and writing, and for showering me with manifest blessings.

Thank you to my father, Gavriel Zeffren, an educator by profession and example, who has given me the most honest feedback in my life. Thank you, Dada, for your everyday noble inspiration.

I would like to thank my mother, Linda Zeffren, of blessed memory, whose immortal spirit and teachings are ever-present in my days. You saw the rough draft of this book, Mama. I wish you could have witnessed its completion.

My gratitude goes to my siblings, Yocheved Cohen, Dovid Zeffren, Paltiel Zeffren, Matis Zeffren, Nechama Rosenberg, Miram Zeffren, Avigayil Wolf, and Sara Muller, for the greatest family bond imaginable. Thank you to the "boys" for saying the usual brotherly things. Thank you, Yocheved, for living the book with me and checking up on my progress with genuine, active delight. Thank you Nechama, Miriam, Avigayil, and Sara, my insightful first editors, for reviewing chapters as soon as I emailed them and sending me exuberant responses along with candid opinions and suggestions.

Thank you to my brothers-in-law, sisters-in-law, and all my nieces and nephews for being my biggest fans.

Thank you to my big nieces, Yehudis Zeffren and Rivka Zeffren, for your curiosity about the book and your weekly questions and comments.

I want to thank my eleven-year-old niece, Dina Rosenberg. She knows why.

Thank you, Aunt Roz Leffler, for calling me three days before my deadline, two days before my deadline, and on the day of my deadline to wish me luck. What would I do without your support and love!

My most heartfelt gratitude goes to my current employers, Rabbi Michoel and Mrs. Esther Levi, Mrs. Shoshana Herzka, Mrs. Yentee Sonnenschein, Mrs. Bracha Wrona, and Mrs. Miriam Ungar for the years I've spent teaching in your excellent schools. Thank you to the following colleagues for their contributions to this book: Mrs. Shavey Ephrahti, Ms. Penina Kramer, Mrs. Gitty Pultman, Mrs. Bruria Rubin, Miss Leah Rubin. Your expertise and friendship mean so much to me.

I owe a tremendous gratitude to my friend and "sister," Dr. Perella Perlstein. Thank you, Perella, for the research, for your on-target examples, for reading the manuscript and verifying its positive psychological impact. My appreciation to the following principals and deans for their hospitality, warm conversation, and invaluable input: Mrs. Miriam Weiss,

Dr. Morgan Koch, Dean Gerard Phillips, Dean Joseph McNight, Dr. George Cantu, Mr. Jeffrey Hinton, Mrs. Dorothy Vaughan.

Thank you, Yocheved Mahana, for your inspiration, tireless cheerful responses, vast research, and meticulous bibliography. I am forever indebted to you. Thank you, Adina Reichman, for the beautiful graphics. Thank you for allowing me to take advantage of your good nature during hectic days. My appreciation to Mrs. Vitty Moskowitz for her help throughout the years with troubleshooting, particularly with this book.

I would like to thank my former students, many of whom I keep up with today, for their camaraderie and reminiscences. Thanks for your contributions to this book.

A special thank you to my current wonderful students in Bais Yaakov D'rav Meir and Bnos Yaakov for a remarkable experience this school year. Thank you for listening avidly to all my teaching ideas with feigned or real interest. I marvel at your good nature, talent, and maturity. Often, I've been humbled by your quest for the truth, the honesty of your opinions. You keep pushing yourselves just a bit harder. I can't feel more privileged to know growing people like you who give their daily work (writing, homework, extra credit assignments, speeches) their all, never entertaining mediocrity.

Many thanks to Andrew Carnegie for establishing the first public libraries across the nation and the world. The Central Library (on Grand Army Plaza) in Brooklyn, New York, provided me with years of successful research in the SST (Society, Science, Technology) division and other departments. Aside from collecting statistical information and data on current issues, browsing through the Brooklyn Collection, Civil War Collection, cartoon books, and new books for inspiration, I have acquired robust ideas for teaching and writing.

Lastly, I would like to thank all readers of *Secrets of Great Teachers*! As educators, you have the most glorious job in the world. Thank you for your idealism. Thank you for your big heart. Thank you for picking up this book. I hope it makes a difference.

—Elisheva Zeffren

Preface

I remember a preschool graduation song that had the audience in tears. One of the children stepped up to the microphone and sang, "We had so much fun together! Oh, why can't we stay here forever?" And then the rest of the children responded in a chorus, "Because now we've grown so high, high, high, and it's time to say goodbye! Goodbye! Goodbye!"

Children grow up fast these days, faster than ever before. Parents send seven-year-olds to sports camp, sign up nine-year-olds for violin lessons, and stress about finding their children the right college before the kids are wearing braces on their teeth. Each year, parents send their young ones off to school with glossy folders, sharp pencils, healthy snacks, and a blessing, "Have a good day!" hoping that every school day will build their offsprings' skills so that they will eventually emerge from the school system into the world as well-educated, accomplished, independent adults. Parents have grand expectations, and rightfully so. But what kind of education are their children really getting? Is our educational system doing our children justice?

Throughout the ages, a great many scholars have maintained that the school system does not teach or prepare students for the real world. English statesman and author George Savile (1633–1695) said, "Education is what remains when we have forgotten all that we have been taught." Fast forward a couple centuries, to read renowned American author and poet Ralph Waldo Emerson (1803–1882) state, "We are shut up in schools and college recitation rooms for ten or fifteen years and come out at last with a bellyful of words & do not know a thing." Skip to the mid–1900s and notice how American educator John Gardner (1912–2002) pretty much echoes the first two men. "Much education today is monumentally ineffective," Gardner said. "All too often we are giving young people cut flowers when we should be teaching them to grow their own plants."

And these days, more educators than ever lament our failing schools. John Taylor Gatto, retired American teacher, says in his book *Dumbing Us Down* (2005): "I've noticed a fascinating phenomenon in my thirty years of teaching: schools and schooling are increasingly irrelevant to the great enterprises of the planet" (21).

Rest assured, you would have no trouble finding many more pages of discouraging comments about the failing education today spouted by reputable scholars (along with lists of failing schools). Their low opinion of the educational system should give us pause. How much of our teaching is useless? What are we doing wrong?

Clearly, the U.S. Department of Education has attempted to change the course of education for the better. America has improved labor laws, implemented No Child Left Behind, Race to the Top, and most recently: the Common Core Curriculum, school choice and charter schools, and increased standardized testing. Countless educational mavens have designed sophisticated curriculums and tests holding schools accountable to meet high standards. Teachers have toiled to satisfy these standards only to get poor results. Disappointment then spurs the boards of education to think of alternative ways for schools to buckle down along with more rigorous testing.

Do you get the feeling we are chasing our tails?

According to the National Center for Education Statistics (NCES), over 50.7 million students headed off to approximately 98,817 public schools for the 2017 fall term, and before the school year is out in 2018, an estimated $623.5 billion will be spent related to their education. The projected government expenditure per child is $12,300 for the year.

An additional 5.4 million students attend private schools: the national average of private school tuition is approximately $10,003 per year which makes the total average cost for a child's elementary and high school tuition in private schools $120,036. Whether a child attends public or private school, one has to wonder: How much of this money is going to waste? And here is indubitably the greater question: At what expense?

The outlook for our educational system doesn't seem promising. In the Third International Mathematics and Science Study (TIMSS), twelfth grade American students scored nearly the lowest in math and science compared to students in 41 other countries. According to mathematics and reading assessments administered to eighth graders in 2015 by the National Assessment of Educational Progress (NAEP), the average score declined since the last testing in 2013.

Today 8,652 schools across the nation have been dubbed "failing." In my home state of New York alone, there are 109,000 students attending 178 failing schools in 17 school districts. Of the 178 schools, 77 have been failed for a decade of teaching futilely. Certainly, an outstanding worry for our children is whether they stand a chance in the competitive professional and business markets once they graduate. Perhaps more worrisome is children's inability to calculate and think critically, a threat to their personal and social growth. What recourse then must educators take in the classroom?

Observing schools nationwide for more than a decade, I have seen educators do no more than regurgitate textbook material for standardized tests. Frequently, I have observed educators who mimic age-old rigid systems that don't work. Just as often, I have witnessed educators with poor teaching skills, who bribe, yell, or coerce students to listen, learn, and study without providing learning incentives. The responsibility for preventing student failure falls mainly on the educators. Therefore, educators today have become more tense; their future employment and certification depend on success (the definition of which is up for debate).

Most educators mean well but need better tools. Sadly, they may have lost their resourceful spirit. Uninspired by textbooks they studied back in college and a thousand fruitless school meetings, educators today don't have the patience to revisit their teaching style. Juggling work and home life, they lack the physical time to search journals for ideas, and they are tired of pseudo-intellectual books on education that speak on elusive, broad terms. Many educators, burnt out from teaching to the test and its pressure, have resigned their creative enthusiasm.

Secrets of Great Teachers is designed to give educators an immediate shot of hope. It revives the resolve to make a difference. The book's instruction guarantees instant, positive feedback. The book asserts that teachers cannot force-feed education. It adamantly rejects curriculums that create robotic classrooms. It clearly evinces how educators can support learning by getting involved in what students crave—to think for themselves, to learn what they want, to communicate, and to discover what they need to know for their survival and success outside school.

The book extends to the whole breadth of subjects taught in the middle and high school classroom. It presents a variety of resources to make lessons come to dramatic life with practical applications. It defends the need for pace and practice, suggesting ways of lending students autonomy in managing their work time. The book promotes discovery in diverse subjects such as math, English, computers, and writing.

Secrets of Great Teachers advocates Bloom's Taxonomy, an ageless guide, to inspire higher level thinking. This book introduces homework that challenges students' brain power and electrifies a task. Chapters highlight specific visual aids, undiscovered or over-looked, and show how they can fortify lessons. The book additionally endorses children's books as springboards for discussion and useful tools for explaining higher level concepts. Other chapters show how audio aids, sound, and music recordings run the gamut of intel-lectual and emotional conquest, and how the sporadic showing of video clips spark attention and spring lessons to life.

Keeping organization and structure in mind, *Secrets of Great Teachers* breaks down lesson planning into easy steps. With precise guidance, the book shows the reader how to help the student navigate his way through the labyrinth of learning struggles. For example, a chapter addresses the 10 main pitfalls of competition, debunks the myths that competition boosts teamwork, and finishes off with a series of non-competitive stimulating games and activities. As a whole, the book dwells on the value of intrinsic motivation and the impor-tance of students thinking and working of their own volition, doing a superb job because they can, and not for the promise of an award or recognition.

With hard-hitting research based statements, *Secrets of Great Teachers* enumerates the pitfalls of teacher-pleasing behavior and addresses ways to mitigate the behavior. The book offers concrete exercises to encourage independent thinking, which precludes the need for teacher-pleasing. Furthermore, a chapter demonstrates how to cultivate critical thinking in students so that they think for themselves and use a discerning eye before accepting something at face value.

Offering innovative ideas to whet the appetite for reading, *Secrets of Great Teachers* also launches an active reading campaign for all students. Furthermore, the book suggests ideas for strengthening and testing literacy. The last chapters propose ideas for making testing nonthreatening, while ensuring retention and catering to the creative spirit in every-one. The book endorses a method which greatly reduces the educator's marking time. Finally, the book provides myriad examples of specific praise and constructive criticism designed to make students proud of achievements and propel them forward in their quest to perfect skills.

My aspiration in writing this book is to contribute something positive toward our children's future education. With the implementation of ideas in this book, I'm hoping your classes will take on a winning ambition. Daily, I work on improving my teaching because there's always a lesson, an activity, or paradigm that needs sprucing up. I believe, if you have the gumption, the courage, and a bit of humor, you can always make your class a better place.

When children graduate preschool, they think they're so big and capable. Their parents are so hopeful. How can we better their chances at success? We can give them a meaningful education. Join me in leading older, perhaps less spirited students towards a more important ceremony. Let us work with the goal of helping our students cross the stage during their high school graduation with a fierce pride and sense of purpose. Let us watch with our own pride as students accept their diplomas, knowing we did them justice. Let us know that these graduates are well-educated, competent, and ready to face a life of opportunity.

Let's refashion education in America together.

Best wishes for making it happen!

—E.Z.

1

Finding the "Hot Spots"

"I have never let my schooling interfere with my education."—Mark Twain

Remember the thrill of a roller coaster ride? Even before the ride, you found yourself waiting on line reveling in its promise. Sitting in the car and beginning the ascent, you felt your anticipation mounting. By the time you reached the summit, you were cherishing your excitement, practically choking on it. You were primed for that lightning descent, and when the majesty of the moment happened, you couldn't control yourself from shrieking all the way down. Then before you knew it, you were riding the next loop, and the adventure began all over again. No part of the ride was a "let down." Even at the end, you trembled from the lingering excitement and were eager to ride the roller coaster once more.

I believe we can bring the intellectual roller coaster into the classroom. If we educators would work on each lesson so that no part of it would be anticlimactic, if we would imbue our lessons with intellectual thrills, substantial meaning, astounding revelations, or some kind of galvanizing beauty, we would captivate our students in the learning experience. Creative lessons are the solution to student apathy, to low test scores, student drop-out, to defiance or rebellion in the classroom—to virtually any student and school-related problem!

Our students want the roller coaster ride. Unfortunately, we put them on the merry-go-round when our lessons are too simple. Other times, we keep promising students the Cyclone but don't deliver. Occasionally, we bring in engaging rides, but limit them because of time constraints or expense, or merely because we are just too lazy to run them. Often, we bore students with the same old rides since that's what we know, and we don't have the patience or ambition to learn about newer models.

No matter whether you're a beginning or veteran teacher, you can reinvent your lessons without too much trouble. Here's how to teach lessons on roller coaster rides so that your students want to keep running back for more.

How do we begin designing the roller coaster? With one simple rule:

Find the "Hot Spots"

When intrigued, students retain information for its own sake. Teachers can accomplish great teaching by finding the intriguing elements within teaching material and building the lesson around it. Let's call these intriguing elements "hot spots." The "hot spots" transform lessons from humdrum to spectacular. Teachers can expound upon these "hot spots" with fascinating facts, enlightening media, adventuresome anecdotes, scintillating demonstrations, innovative experiments, profound discussions, and absorbing activities—all which guarantee a thrilling experience.

But here's the caveat. We have to keep in mind students' interests, not merely our own.

For instance, let's say Mrs. Jarvis is preparing lessons on *The Old Man and the Sea* by Ernest Hemingway. In Mrs. Jarvis's opinion, Hemingway's ability to attain mood through dialogue, his penchant for portraying his characters as realistic human beings, and his gift for creating sentences rich in imagery, give a teacher plenty to discuss within lessons. Somehow, though, Mrs. Jarvis gets the gut instinct that her class won't kick up their heels in joy if she begins a lesson with a discussion about Hemingway's writing style. The writing style is not a choice "hot spot" for now.

Therefore Mrs. Jarvis ventures to find the "hot spots" that will engage her class. She asks herself what will get her students invested in this old man, Santiago, who is sailing along on the sea for almost the entire book doing nothing at all but speaking to himself and to a marlin he caught. Aha! The marlin! Now, that's an impressive fish. Maybe the class will show interest in marlins! But what does Mrs. Jarvis know about marlins? Not much. So, she sets to find out.

A marlin, so that you know, is one of the biggest and fastest fish in the ocean, known to put up a fearsome fight when hooked. Capable of growing twice the size of a man, with its rapier at least a foot long, the marlin is a worthy adversary! Perusing YouTube, Mrs. Jarvis finds a video clip that shows fishermen grappling with a 1,200-pound marlin (https://youtu.be/OmdBbTNdwR8) and another clip in which Matt Watson, the "madman of the sea," catches and tags a marlin from a surfboard (https://youtu.be/904hlyK5glQ). These clips will give Mrs. Jarvis's students visual insight into the skill and patience necessary in catching a marlin. Seeing the actual size and strength of the marlin, Mrs. Jarvis's class will appreciate Santiago's physical pain when they read about his struggle with a marlin. They will better imagine the strain of holding onto a line with a hooked marlin; how doing so hurts the old man's shoulders and back, and cramps Santiago's left hand, cutting into it. After viewing these clips, students might consider why Santiago doesn't feel enmity toward his opponent, why he has empathy for the marlin, even admiration.

Onward in the book, the next "hot spot" jumps out at Mrs. Jarvis with Santiago's sudden encounter with sharks. Aha! Sharks! Everyone is interested in sharks—and so Mrs. Jarvis does research on sharks which she plans to share with the class. She learns that of the four hundred species of sharks in the world's oceans, only thirty-two species are known to attack humans. Mrs. Jarvis reads that sharks attack most often when provoked or when their senses make them mistake a person for a sea lion or sea turtle. In fact, studies indicate that sharks do not like the taste of human beings, and often spit them out after the initial chomp (http://adventure.howstuffworks.com/shark-attack.htm).

Another interesting fact: The shark's razor-sharp scales ward off predators and generate whirlpools which help propel them through the water. Investigating distinctive sharks, Mrs. Jarvis learns that the whale shark, the largest fish in the world, measures up to fifty feet long! Like the whale shark, the megamouth shark swims with its mouth open, but has a much larger mouth (as its name suggests), and curiously, the megamouth was discovered only in 1976! And here's more: Known as the garbage cans of the seas, tiger sharks have proven to eat anything from medieval armor to dogs and shoes!

Possibilities for classroom discussion mushroom as Mrs. Jarvis gets more curious about other fish and their existence in the depths of the sea. She finds that species of fish migrate at different fathoms. This information explains the strategy behind Santiago's fishing techniques as he lowers his fishing lines at various fathoms. (Santiago's marlin takes the bait at 100 fathoms—which means 600 feet deep!) Maybe if the class is interested, Mrs. Jarvis will discuss other hook-and-line fishing techniques and deep-sea fishing. Perhaps her class will take a trip to a local fishermen's wharf and get some hands-on fishing lessons. Mrs. Jarvis can imagine the novice anglers among the class would also love a demo on filleting fish! After experiencing the fishing process, the class will understand the importance of a process and can write process papers about fishing or another skill.

By now, Mrs. Jarvis realizes the title of the book *The Old Man and the Sea* presents a great contrast in power. After all, an old man is feeble, the sea powerful. Mrs. Jarvis asks herself—what do I know about the sea besides scant information on a few of its inhabitants? To investigate, she turns to *National Geographic*. Once Mrs. Jarvis gets started, she can't stop gathering incredible facts and photos about the depth of the ocean. Mrs. Jarvis can't wait to stun her class with "Did you know" questions like: Did you know that the vast majority of the ocean is completely dark? Did you hear about underwater mountain ranges that go on for dozens of miles? Did you know the average depth of the world's oceans is about three miles? Did you know that Mount Everest, Earth's tallest peak, could be sunk without a trace in the Marianas Trench, the deepest part of the ocean? Did you know it would take a stack of twenty-nine Empire State Buildings to reach the surface of the Marianas Trench? Did you know that Hawaii is really the summit of the tallest mountain in the ocean, Mauna Kea, which rises up 33,480 feet from the floor of the Pacific Ocean?

From there, Mrs. Jarvis decides to present "The Ocean Song," which introduces the world's oceans and depicts their size, beauty, and power. For example, the Pacific Ocean is larger than the whole world's countries combined, over 60 million square miles wide. Now is an opportune moment for Mrs. Jarvis to direct students' attention to a part earlier in the book where Santiago travels out to the great well 700 fathoms deep (4,200 feet) in hope of catching a dolphin. It's a dangerous spot that can easily snatch up his skiff. Kids love danger, so Mrs. Jarvis finds reading material for the class about the dangers of whirlpools. This topic reminds Mrs. Jarvis of the time a family member nearly drowned in the midst of a whirlpool while whitewater rafting on Moose River in New York. She jots down this anecdote to tell the class.

Afterwards, Mrs. Jarvis might prompt the class to discuss Hemingway's metaphor of the ocean's unpredictable nature to symbolize life. Perhaps she can challenge the class to think of another object they can use as a metaphor for life. In addition, the class can dwell a bit on the personal symbols in the book such as the reference to Joe DiMaggio and his heel spur and to the lions playing on the beaches in Santiago's dreams. Next, students might want to discuss personal symbols of their own and/or bring in tangible symbols from home for an older kids' version of "show and tell."

In her quest for sea facts, Mrs. Jarvis keeps stumbling upon great visual materials her students will clamor to see: a photograph of Ernest Hemingway in 1956 posing in Peru with a marlin he caught. Photographs of Hemingway's home in Havana, Cuba, from 1939 to 1960 where he wrote *For Whom the Bell Tolls* and *To Have and Have Not* in addition to *The Old Man and the Sea* and other works. Mrs. Jarvis comes across pictures of icebergs, the *Titanic*, sunken treasures and shipwrecks, submersibles, underwater robots, underwater photographers taking pictures of sharks, a picture of a JIM suit that protects the deep-sea diver from crushing water pressure, photographs of the sediment that cover the ocean floor, the black sand beaches of Hawaii created by black lava that burst forth from the ocean, a beach damaged by wave action, a shark feeding frenzy. Mrs. Jarvis jots down an idea to coach students to research and produce their own collages, slides, or video representations of awesome sea delights.

By now, the class is sure to realize Santiago's great risk in venturing out to the sea by himself to take on marlins and possibly encounter his rivals—sharks. Maybe how will be a good time to promote a discussion about risk taking. To this end, Mrs. Jarvis plans to talk about the reasons people take risks. For instance, why Russian and German children (and others across the world) "train surf" on top of speeding trains, and why it's so popular for people in California to go skydiving headfirst at over 180 miles per hour. Mrs. Jarvis's mind races as she writes down other audacious, risky hobbies the class can evaluate such as motor racing, rock climbing, or high-stakes gambling. She also decides to discuss the Lewis and Clark Expedition across North America and other expeditions. Her class can consider whether all these risks are worth it, weighing the gains against the potential losses. Some questions to explore along these risk-taking lines include: Are boys greater risk takers than girls? Men greater risk takers than women? Do powerful people take more risks? To stimulate reflection about their own risk-taking styles, Mrs. Jarvis plans to have the class take a risk-taking assessment quiz. With results at hand, the class can discuss the fine line between adventure and recklessness, how to take calculated risks and the drawbacks of always playing it safe.

After this discussion, Mrs. Jarvis might challenge students to prove another one of Santiago's attributes, his perseverance. Then the class can discuss how Santiago's perseverance served him. Mrs. Jarvis plans to ask questions such as why did Santiago set out again to the sea after 84 days without catching a fish? If you were in Santiago's shoes, would you have given up? Why or why not? Did you think Santiago would catch a marlin? Fight off the sharks? Make it home alive? Do you think Santiago's perseverance praiseworthy? Were you rooting for him? Why? Do you think Santiago's perseverance paid off? Did you ever attempt to do something and persevere despite the odds?

Along this theme of perseverance in the book, Mrs. Jarvis plans to introduce the Hemingway Code and ask whether the class agrees with Ernest Hemingway's conviction that will, pride and endurance define man in both the early and later stages of life. The class can examine Santiago's statement, "A man can be destroyed but not defeated," and his triumph at the end of the story. They can contemplate why Hemingway allowed the marlin to emerge as a skeletal carcass at the end, after Santiago worked so hard to catch it and ward off the sharks. Maybe the class could relate the old man's fishing experience to a real-life challenge in their own lives. Perhaps the class could interview someone who lost something significant but remained undefeated.

Furthermore, Mrs. Jarvis might have students devise a survey with items to test people's perseverance quotient. She might have students take on a task to test their perseverance and have them plot their successes and obstacles along the way. She might have the class as a whole take on a worthwhile project to prove their perseverance. Afterward, the class can write "Tips for Persevering" based on their experiences (whether or not they conquered the cumbersome task).

Also worthy of contemplation is Santiago's humility throughout the book. With this idea brewing, Mrs. Jarvis plots the following questions in her notes to ask the class: Why doesn't Santiago get angry at the fishermen who make fun of him? What does Hemingway mean when he says Santiago didn't know when he had attained humility? What is humility? How do you attain it? Do you agree with Santiago that humility carries no loss of true pride?

At this point, deeply drawn into the book, Mrs. Jarvis's class is ready to appreciate a chat about Hemingway's writing prowess. They can take a critical look at the mood Hemingway creates with dialogue and what this mood conveys about the relationship between Santiago and the boy, Manolin. Students can find dialogue in other works that sets a mood and discloses something about relationships between characters. Peers might enjoy acting out the dialogues before the class (with a partner or partners) to have the class detect the quality of the relationship. For extra credit, students can write a fictional dialogue of their own that establishes a mood.

Additionally, students can reflect upon other techniques in the book that lend the story its realistic atmosphere. Students can search the book for sensory details that appeal to them. They can take down their favorite sentences and compare their lists with peers. They can sketch or paint the meaning of a favorite sentence to depict its imagery. They can delve into Hemingway's profound analogies, such as the comparison between Santiago's scars and erosions in a desert. They can discuss Hemingway's "iceberg principle" of writing in relation to *The Old Man and the Sea.* They can demonstrate this principle with examples of how Hemingway says so much by saying so little.

As it usually happens while doing research on a book, Mrs. Jarvis chances upon some related reading: *Soul Surfer,* a true story told by Bethany Hamilton, who at thirteen was attacked by a fifteen-foot tiger shark that bit off her left arm while she was surfing in Kauai, Hawaii, but despite her handicap ultimately returned to professional surfing. Mrs. Jarvis decides to buy the book for the class library, confident her students will find the book inspirational. On a lighter note, Mrs. Jarvis hits upon entertaining ocean stories in *Chicken Soup for the Ocean Lover's Soul,* bona fide stories about a swimmer's encounter with a white whale, a dolphin that paints on canvas at the Dolphin Research Center in the Florida Keys, a woman who fosters an abandoned pup on Mount Desert Island, Maine. Mrs. Jarvis is positive students will read this book for pleasure, so she slips it in with her other materials.

Walking into class with all these materials before teaching *The Old Man and the Sea,* Mrs. Jarvis knows her preparation will pay off. She has a solid plan for making the most dreaded story on the curriculum irresistible. With her lesson plan, the sea comes alive. The old man transforms from the stereotype of a decrepit, fragile minded human being into a fierce warrior. The story carries meaning beyond its deceptive simplicity. Students are sure to look back at the plot and the time they spent on it with fondness.

What if Mrs. Jarvis doesn't get to all the material she prepared?

Practically speaking, Mrs. Jarvis won't carry out all her preparation for *The Old Man and the Sea,* but because she has a bursting arsenal ready for sharing, Mrs. Jarvis's excitement spills over to her students. They anticipate the video clips, photographs, and general knowledge, and activities she has in store for them. Inspired to think more broadly during the book's lessons, the class begins to view required reading as an adventure. Mrs. Jarvis's students imbibe the book's pages, trying to predict what the discussions will be. Soon, apart from their assigned work, they bring their own "surprises" into class based on the story and delight in presenting their newfound information.

As you can see, finding the "hot spots" leads the educator on a whirlwind journey. The goal is to draw students into that experience and leave them breathless at the end of class. Mrs. Jarvis prepares a thorough plan and you can too. Every book, every subject, every topic contains intriguing stimuli. The challenge is to look for it. The joy is in finding and sharing it.

2

Blending and
Broadening Teaching

"We need to have as broad a range as possible because life itself has that kind of range."—John Eaton

Raise your hand if you think departmental teachers should stick strictly to the information in their subject. Meaning math teachers should teach math, science teachers should teach science, and so on. Although a few of you may be waving your hands emphatically, I believe the majority would agree that teachers should play the curriculum partly "by ear," taking into account how other subjects might influence its direction.

Let me explain in concrete terms how educators might take the opportunity to blend or broaden subjects.

Blending Subjects

To properly acquaint students with any reading material, from fiction to nonfiction, historical fiction to science fiction, teachers might step away momentarily from the plot to teach relevant information. As you saw in *The Old Man and the Sea*, the lesson took detours, for instance with its portrayal of ocean facts. Discussing the depth of the ocean and the creatures found there, outside the storyline, strengthened important concepts within the plot. Similarly, other novels deal with scientific terms or foreign concepts to the student that the teacher needs to clarify for the integrity of the story. In discussing Mark Twain's book *The Connecticut Yankee in King Arthur's Court,* for example, where a nineteenth-century protagonist is transported to early medieval England, the teacher needs to familiarize students with medieval practices and superstitions, and with the way things work, such as the solar eclipse, explosives, torpedoes, and lassos. Otherwise, the student misses out on the genius strategies Twain's protagonist brings to the plot.

Likewise, a teacher might blend literature with history by having the class research particular time periods where the historical setting has a major bearing on the plot of a story. In discussing the nonfiction short story "I Stand Here Ironing" by Tillie Olsen, for instance, students cannot properly empathize with the characters without exploring the difficulty of living through the Great Depression. By the same token, the flavor of a great novel, such *The Great Gatsby* by F. Scott Fitzgerald gets lost without a historical blurb of the 1920s time period to depict the emergence of the Prohibition, the proliferation of the automobile and Jazz Age. Then, of course, historical novels by definition deal with characters whose struggles for societal ideals intertwine with historical periods. The educator must immerse students in these time periods to impart the proper message of the story. For instance, students can't adequately appreciate the characters' fight in a historical novel such as Dickens' *A Tale of Two Cities* without a solid background on the French Revolution.

Furthermore, a literature teacher might even incorporate a little mathematics to make a concept more relevant to students. Here's a case in point. In Guy de Maupassant's short story "The Necklace," set in the late 1800s, students can't empathize fully with Madame Loisel for losing her friend's necklace without knowing the cost of a 36,000-franc necklace today. To figure out the dollar cost, a colleague, Mrs. Webster, has students research how much a franc was equivalent to in American money. They find out that one franc was equal to 19 American cents during the late nineteenth century. So then Mrs. Webster poses the following question: How much would a 36,000-franc necklace cost in the late nineteenth century in American dollars? The answer: $6,840. Good.

Now students have a number they can imagine, but how much would $6,840 amount to today? With the help of the Consumer Price Index inflation calculator, students find out that a dollar in the late nineteenth century is roughly equal to $24.78. The last step: If a dollar in the late nineteenth century was approximately $24.78, what would the current dollar value of the necklace be today? The answer? $169,468.99.

Once they have figured out this answer, students can appreciate how much money Madame Loisel sacrificed to buy her friend, Madame Forestier, a replacement necklace. After all, 36,000 francs in those days was equivalent to $6,840 which is equivalent to $169,468.99 today! With this information, the irony of the story's ending hits students extra hard when Madame Loisel finds out that the necklace she lost was fake!

As soon as you adopt the mindset to teach the lesson with depth and clarity, you'll train yourself to explore ideas outside your current subject. All of a sudden, your lessons turn into a blend of subjects! It's great when you peer into a classroom and don't know off the bat what subject is being taught.

What I'm imparting is that it shouldn't be unusual for students in music class to work on equivalent fractions while enhancing their understanding of the relative value of notes. Likewise, it makes sense for students in a social science class to use mathematic knowledge and skills when exploring ideas such as probability, risk, and chance. Furthermore, a science teacher can absorb students in designing and drawing; the art teacher, in a timeline of architectural styles. A writing teacher might choose to teach graphic design and photography for composition writing. A health teacher might teach health in conjunction with talks about fashion or psychology. By deviating from the subject at hand, you show students that learning covers many fields of interest. You also give them the message that all learning is important and as a well-rounded person, you are interested in teaching more than the required subject at hand.

Broadening Subjects

Educators can broaden subjects by expanding the student's knowledge of topics. For instance, a teacher can expand a topic geographically. In teaching about the history of the

Brooklyn Bridge, a teacher can broaden the topic to explore the history of other bridges in New York City or bridges in other states. Likewise, a writing teacher might expand the writing craft by teaching many genres of writing. In a similar vein, a teacher might expand a topic chronologically, for example, not only teaching about the Civil Rights Movement in the 1960s but going back to the NAACP's anti-lynching campaign of the 1930s, the foundation of earlier struggles.

What does broadening a subject accomplish? It gives students a complete picture that they're more apt to remember than if you teach singular concepts. Let's ascertain how with just a little research, educators can cover topics in their curriculum while simultaneously opening a bit of the world to their students.

For example, let's take one of the most epochal topics of American history, the American Civil War. The average teacher who covers the American Civil War, which lasted from 1861 to 1865, certainly spends time discussing the causes and effects of the war and the crucial events encompassing the war, such as the Confederates firing upon Fort Sumter, the Battles of Bull Run, the Battle of Gettysburg, the Gettysburg Address, and the surrendering of General Robert E. Lee to General Grant. From there, the teacher typically moves on to the Reconstruction Era, 1865–1877, and that's about it for the 1860s. But curious students can't help but wonder what happened outside the political arena that surrounds the Civil War and Reconstruction.

A superior teacher, Mr. Scott, taps into the educational, social, industrial, economical, and cultural atmosphere within America and abroad during this era. And so much is happening! Mr. Scott peruses literature on the Civil War, biographies, and web sites. He finds so much happening during the 1860s at his fingertips, literally!

Let's first take a look at the material Mr. Scott decides to share about the Civil War era during the 1860s in America outside the battlefield. Putting himself in his students' shoes, Mr. Scott comes up with the following questions students may have about the time period.

Students' proposed questions for what's happening in America during the 1860s:

- What type of schooling existed during this time?
- What subjects did children learn?
- What style clothing did people wear?
- Did people have enough money?
- How did people communicate and travel?
- What are some interesting facts about the Civil War era?
- What did people do for fun?
- What American literature did people read?
- What inventions came to town?

Mr. Scott prepares the answers to each question.

What type of schooling existed during this time? Various types of schools existed in the North. In rural communities, children learned in one-room schoolhouses. In many Northern cities, classrooms along with grade divisions replaced the one-room schoolhouse. By the beginning of the Civil War, public education for elementary schoolchildren was available in most Northern cities. Many wealthy children attended private academies. Freed African American children attended separate schools from white children. These schools received little funding and students studied from books handed down from white public schools.

In the South, school was still a privilege of the wealthy. Most plantation owners hired private tutors to teach their children at home. Others chipped in and hired teachers to teach their children in one-room schoolhouses. Many sent children to private academies in large cities in the South. Most Southern families, though, owned small farms and couldn't afford to buy slaves or send their children to school. While some children attended one-room schoolhouses, most parents taught their children at home.

What subjects did the children learn? The curriculum depended greatly on what the particular teacher knew. Children learned basic subjects such as reading, writing, arithmetic, geography, and spelling. Learning was done through memorization and recitation. Children wrote with chalk on slate boards. They practiced their penmanship with ink and quill. Grades and report cards were uncommon.

With the commencement of aggressions between the North and South, the two divisions biased their school textbooks. *The Union ABC* promoted the Union Army with rhymes such as "O is an Officer, proud of his station. P is the President, who rules this great nation." Johnson's *Elementary Arithmetic,* published in 1864, put forth the following arithmetic problem to Southern schoolchildren: "If one Confederate soldier kills 90 Yankees, how many Yankees can 10 Confederate soldiers kill?"

What style clothing did people wear? Women wore corsets and dresses with full hoop skirts. (Daring women smuggled army supplies past enemy lines by attaching them to their crinolines.) Wealthy women wore several dresses each day. Widows were expected to wear dull black fabric for a full year of mourning. Women's dresses buttoned up the front. Girls wore multi-layered dresses, which buttoned up the back. Their dresses fell below the knee and gradually lengthened as they grew up. Full-length trousers came into fashion for men. Men wore hats whenever they went outside. Facial hair was considered handsome and men began to wear beards. Levi Strauss and Co. began to manufacture durable/sturdier canvas-cloth work pants for miners—the first Levi's brand of jeans. Boys' jackets and trousers were shorter than their father's and they wore caps.

Did people have enough money? The North did pretty well economically during the 1860s. By 1860, 90 percent of the nation's manufacturing came from Northern states. The North produced 32 times more firearms, 30 times more leather goods, and 17 times more cotton and woolen textiles than the South. In 1861, the first national income tax was issued in the U.S. to help the North pay for the cost of war.

By 1860, 26 percent of the North lived in urban areas, influenced by the notable growth of cities such as Chicago, Cincinnati, Cleveland, and Detroit, with their farm-machinery, food-processing, machine-tool, and railroad-equipment factories. The economy in the postwar North also thrived due to wartime manufacturing and spending.

The South didn't fare well economically during the war. By 1860, 84 percent of the South was engaged in agriculture. Only about a tenth of the Southern population lived in urban areas. The Northern blockade on all Southern ports, beginning in 1861, cut off overseas trade, which left the South with food deprivation and the lack of vital supplies such as candles and shoes. Postwar, the economy also suffered in the South. In fact, lack of food crops played a big role in the South's final surrender since Confederate soldiers were dying from starvation. Preserving food from homegrown gardens helped many families stave off hunger during the winter.

How did people communicate and travel? Telegraphy was the main form of communication. The telegraph line from Missouri to California was completed in 1861. The building of the first Transcontinental Railroad, starting from 1863 and finished in 1869, cut travel time across the country from months to days!

What are some interesting facts of the Civil War era?

- The U.S. printed its first paper bills, called "greenbacks," in 1861.
- Postage stamps were also accepted currency.
- The U.S. Mint engraved "In God we trust" on coins in 1863.
- In 1865, the nickel was born.
- President Lincoln signed the Homestead Act in 1862, one of the most vital pieces of legislation in history, granting 160 acres of land free to any person who wanted to settle the frontier.
- Without an organized government, the frontier would soon gain its reputation as the "Wild West" as range wars developed between farmers and ranchers.
- President Lincoln proclaimed Thanksgiving a national holiday in 1863.
- John Wilkes Booth murdered President Lincoln on April 14, 1865, in Ford's Theater.
- The first ambulance went into service in 1866 in Cincinnati, Ohio.
- The Ku Klux Klan materialized in 1866.
- The Jesse James gang robbed banks in the U.S. in 1867.
- The U.S. purchased Alaska from Russia for $7.2 million in 1867.
- Uncle Sam made his first appearance in 1869, in a magazine called *Harper's Weekly*.
- Elizabeth Cady Stanton and Susan B. Anthony established the National Woman Suffrage Association in 1869. For the first time in the U.S., women had the right to vote in Wyoming. (It would take at least another fifty years for women to obtain voting rights throughout America.)
- The American Museum of Natural History opened in New York City in 1869.

What did people do for fun? What's the recreational lifestyle during the 1860s? Northern cities were more bustling than their Southern counterparts. Entertainment, though, was aplenty in cities of both regions, ranging from musical concerts, operas, and stage plays. Still the New World, America had not yet established "American sports." European sports remained popular. These included rugby, soccer, chess, tennis, fencing, and cricket. Croquet, a very popular outdoor game, was played even after dark. Soccer was quickly growing into the world's most popular sport after the formation of the Football Association in Great Britain in 1863. Baseball became a common sport, and in 1869 the Cincinnati Red Stockings were the first team to pay salaries to their players. Milton Bradley began making board games in 1860. *The Checkered Game of Life* (which later was simplified as *Life*) sold 45,000 copies and was a popular parlor game. People also spent free time pitching horseshoes, playing card games, and racing horses.

What American literature did people read? The United States boasted prolific authors like Herman Melville, Ralph Waldo Emerson, Henry David Thoreau, and Nathaniel Hawthorne. Henry Wadsworth Longfellow in 1861 composed his famous poem "Paul Revere's Ride": "Listen my children and you shall hear…." In 1864, Mark Twain published his classic *Adventures of Huckleberry Finn*. Walt Whitman responded to slavery in *Leaves of Grass* and voiced his grief over Lincoln's death in "O Captain My Captain." Louisa May

Alcott published her novel *Little Women* in 1868, the tale of four Northern sisters at home during the Civil War.

What inventions came to town? Inventions in U.S. during this decade ran the gamut. Here are several worthy of mention: the machine gun by Richard J. Gatling of the U.S. in 1861. James L. Plimpton patented roller skates in 1863, which he called the "rocking skate," and opened roller-skating rinks in New York City and Newport, Rhode Island. James H. Mason of Massachusetts patented the first U.S. coffee percolator in 1865. American Christopher Sholes first patented the typewriter in 1868, though it didn't become a commercial success until 1874 because people thought typing rude; it lacked the personal touch. American inventor Thomas Edison patented his first invention: the electric vote recorder in 1869. I.W. McGaffers from Chicago invented the vacuum cleaner in 1869.

Now to further expand students' knowledge of the Civil War era during the 1860s, Mr. Scott plots the rest of his Civil War lessons around questions students might have about the world at large during that time. Once again, he predicts students' questions and goes to work finding the information.

Students' proposed questions for what's happening abroad during the 1860s:

- Are there any wars going on outside America?
- How did people travel outside America?
- Were there any breakthroughs in science or medicine?
- Were there any advancements in technology?
- What inventions came into the world?
- Who were the famous artists and writers during that time?

Mr. Scott prepares the answers to these questions about the world at large.

Are there any wars going on outside America? Political strife had no monopoly over the United States during the 1860s. Some of the conflicts that happened during this time period: The French captured Mexico City in 1863. The King of Prussia invaded Denmark in 1864. The deadliest war in Latin America, the Paraguayan War, 1864–1867, began with the invasion of the Triple Alliance and killed almost 60 percent of Paraguay's population. Italy declared war on Austria-Hungary in 1866. A large number of Civil War veterans, the Fenians, also known as the Irish Republican Brotherhood, invaded Canada in 1866 to pressure Britain to free Ireland. The Spanish Revolution began in 1868; the deposed Queen Isabella fled to France.

How do people travel outside America? The first underground railway opened in London in 1865. Linking the Mediterranean and Red seas, the Suez Canal in Egypt opened for travel in 1869, providing shortcuts between North America and Europe to eastern Africa and Asia. This had a dramatic effect on world trade; the Suez Canal combined with the Transcontinental Railroad allowed the world to be navigated in no time.

Were there any breakthroughs in science or medicine? Florence Nightingale opened the first school for nurses in St. Thomas' Hospital in Lambeth, London, in 1860. Frenchmen Louis Pasteur and Claude Bernard completed the first pasteurization test in 1862. In 1864, Dutch ophthalmologist Franciscus Cornelis Donders discovered the astigmatism, an uneven curvature of the cornea or lens of the eye. The worldwide Red Cross is organized in Geneva in 1863. William Booth founded the Salvation Army in London in 1865. Austrian Gregor Mendel, "the father of modern genetics," published his findings in *Mendel's Law of Inheritance* in 1866.

Were there any advancements in technology? The Toronto Stock Exchange opened in 1861. Tokyo opened for foreign trade in 1867. The first traffic signals, semaphores using red and green lenses, were installed near the Parliament in London in 1868. The famous Russian scientist Dmitri Mendeleev developed the Periodic Table of Elements in 1869.

What inventions came into the world? Englishman Fredrick Walton invented linoleum in 1860. English photographer Thomas Sutton took the first color photograph in 1861. Frenchman Pierre Lallement invented the first bicycle with pedals in 1862. Frenchman Louis Jannin invented barbed wire in 1865. Swedishman Alfred Nobel invented dynamite in 1866. Robert Whitehead invented the torpedo in 1866. British engineer James Anderton invented the first machine to cut coal in 1868, and C.H. Gould patented the stapler in 1868.

Who were the famous artists and writers during that time? Claude Monet, French impressionist painter, gained recognition for *The Woman in a Green Dress* also known as *Camille.* English author George Eliot published *Silas Marner* in 1861. English author Charles Dickens published *Great Expectations* in 1861. French writer Victor Hugo published *Les Miserables* in 1862. Russian novelist Leo Tolstoy authored *War and Peace* in 1865 and English satirist Lewis Carroll published *Alice's Adventures in Wonderland* that same year. French writer and pioneer of science fiction Jules Verne wrote *Twenty Thousand Leagues Under the Sea* in 1869.

Now, what happens if the teacher just dwells upon the battles of the Civil War and Reconstruction? Without the broader picture, the Civil War becomes an isolated event in history. Students don't get to feel or know the time period. Events drift apart, never remaining secure within an era. You have a bunch of rootless trees in a nameless forest. To retain knowledge, students need to place it somewhere, to have it stick together with something else. Otherwise, students quickly forget what they've learned.

This is sadly the reason so many adults are weak with their world knowledge. As students, they learned about events singularly, not as part of a bigger picture. Without an expanded global picture, historical events float about aimlessly, never staying fixed in any time period in the students' minds. Consequently, given terms like the Emancipation Proclamation, the Renaissance, the Spanish Armada, and the Cold War, many adults do not know where the terms belong in world history, how to place them chronologically, or worse, have forgotten them altogether.

Amid the reforms directed toward the educational system, I propose that educators set up timelines on the walls in their classrooms and plot the notable events that occurred across the globe, working with decades, half centuries, and centuries. In this way, as they touch upon one aspect of history, students can cross-reference events regionally and globally and gain much more understanding of the broader history.

I also suggest students create timelines themselves. Pictorial timelines make for magnificent group projects where each group finds pictures, photographs, or drawings which are focal points to their assigned time period. Teachers can direct students to sources. If they wish, teachers can assign specific tasks to members of the group, for example, one student can check out technological advancement of the decade; another, culture and recreation; yet another, government politics. Then groups can organize their material and write catchy titles for each visual along with appropriate captions. Once the teacher gives the go ahead, groups get to hang up their findings in the proper space on the timeline.

On an even grander scale, the timeline can be a school-wide project where each class works on a different decade or era. I have often thought it an awesome idea for a school building to turn its corridors into a museum, featuring a global timeline replete with drawings, maps, photographs, and relics of notable incidents from 1500 to the present day. Imagine walking through those corridors!

With this kind of global connection, students would feel a part of history. They'd learn from events and connect to time periods and ancestral backgrounds. They'd feel obligated to carry on legacies and to make their own mark in the world.

Are you sold on blending and broadening subjects? To review, blending and broadening subjects enhances students' comprehension of material to an extensive degree. Blending subjects sometimes requires you to digress from the subject at hand to teach a concept so that students can come back to the current subject more enlightened than before. Other times blending subjects means intertwining subjects for the sake of effecting a deeper understanding of concepts. Broadening a subject means expanding on a topic to give a more complete picture. Both techniques improve understanding and ensure retention. True, blending and broadening takes more preparation and often, more class time, but they also make a lasting difference.

3

Moving Away
from Useless Teaching

"I am always ready to learn although I do not always like being taught."
—Winston Churchill

"What did you learn today at school, Alexa?"

"Nothing."

"What do you mean, 'Nothing'? You sat in seven classes today. You must have learned something."

"We don't learn anything, Mom, really. It's just a whole lot of names and places. Nothing that matters."

Does this dialogue sound familiar? Do you think students in your school feel like Alexa? Do they find their learning useless? This past year, I couldn't help but wonder if mature students might shed some light on what's not working for them. Curious to find out, I conducted a survey asking high school seniors across the country to define useless learning. The survey question read, "In your career as a student, what do you consider useless learning? Can you give a particular example?"

Immediately, I was inundated with replies. Here is a sampling of responses from high school seniors in 2017.

- "Learning about governments, politics, or organizations. I don't think there's anything my friends and I could care about less."
- "Having the teacher go on about abstract concepts like *collateral damage* and having no idea what he's talking about."
- "The teacher circling errors on my paper and writing, 'Maintain parallel structure' or 'Revise misplaced modifier' and not knowing what those terms mean."
- "Doing something without understanding why, for example, papier-mâché."
- "Memorizing names and dates in history. Why do we need to know names, dates, and towns of non-important people or events? It is just a waste of brain space."
- "Memorizing senseless charts—the name of the artwork: Guernica. The type: painting. The date: 1937. The museum: MOMA."
- "Memorizing texts. In the seventh grade, we had to know the preamble of the Constitution word for word. I remember it till today and still have no use for it."
- "All the practice work on math examples when we have calculators on our phones."
- "Trying to figure out grammar. Every year we review the same rules and still don't

19

know them. And for what purpose? What is going to happen if someone puts a comma in the wrong place?"

- "Filling in blanks on review sheets. It is mindless work. If you don't know the information, you have to look it up or wait for someone to say it, so you can fill it in."
- "Studying Shakespeare and other olden day classics. Is anyone going to be the next Shakespeare? Do we really need to read old English? Does anyone speak or write like that?"
- "All the confusing group activities that give one anxiety. I never knew what I was supposed to be doing. I just hung around on the outskirts until the activity was over."
- "Writing classes. I was never a good writer. Why keep at something you can't improve?"
- "Reading boring books like *The Call of the Wild*. I can place no value in reading about survival from a dog's point of view."

What do you think of these testimonies? Might these students have a point? Have they missed the point? More importantly, have we educators missed the point?

Where Do We Go from Here?

A common thread running through these seniors' comments is the complaint of having to deal with what they consider confusing or pointless lessons and tasks. I believe these lamentations reflect those of many across a vast swath of students currently attending elementary to high school. Uninspired with the learning content, our students resign themselves to meaningless work and as a result, perform badly. Others, even less motivated, don't bother at all. You know the old maxim, "You can lead a horse to the water but can't make it drink"? Surely it applies here. So, do these students have a point? Yes. Can we be teaching better? I would think so. Therefore, I offer the following logical suggestion: Perhaps in place of educational reforms that demand more sophisticated work, we should revamp our current lessons to communicate useful learning.

How do we do that? With a little more conscientiousness and a bit of creativity. The guidelines below will ensure you success in teaching students the value of information.

How to Make Learning Worthwhile

PREPARE WITH THE STUDENTS' INTERESTS IN MIND

Here's the deal: Whenever a teacher launches a topic, students begin thinking, "What's in it for me?" They want to know directly how they can use this new knowledge either to create something (useful or beautiful), understand the world (or themselves) better, make money, improve their skills or lifestyle, communicate better, solve problems, help others, or even keep out of trouble. Otherwise, the learning of information has no value to them. Bear this in mind and you'll find yourself gearing lessons to communicate useful learning.

MENTION WHAT'S IN IT FOR THEM

Are you introducing a task without mentioning its purpose? Sometimes teachers think they have expressed the purpose without actually doing so. Always include a personal incentive in your instruction.

Instruction without Personal Incentive	*Instruction with Personal Incentive*
Let's begin learning fractions. Please turn to page 82.	Let's figure out how fractions can help us wallpaper the bulletin board. Please turn to page 82.
Watch how I shade my apple in this demonstration.	Watch how I shade my apple so that you can copy the skill to make your apple look three-dimensional.
Let's view this film to see what the fashion industry is all about.	Let's view this film to decide whether the fashion industry exploits us.
I want everyone to join this exciting activity.	Please join this activity to discover if you're a leader or follower.
Criticize the following dialogue to see how Noah could have negotiated a better salary.	Read the following dialogue and tell me how you might have negotiated a better salary.
Please listen to this fabulous talk about diet food.	Please listen to this dietician explain how diet food can make you gain weight.
Read these children's books to see great examples of double-spread illustrations.	Read these children's books to see the purpose of using double-spread illustrations in your stories.
Practice your typing with these games.	Practice your typing with these games to improve your speed and accuracy by 20 percent!
Follow these writing rules on strong verbs.	Follow these rules on strong verbs to make your sentences precise and vivid.
Let's study these survey responses.	Let's study these survey responses to determine how we can eliminate crime in this neighborhood.
Let's explore the latest technology while using Mac laptops.	Let's explore the latest technology on Mac laptops to see how you can put yourself on the cover of a fashion magazine.

PLAN THE PERFECT ORDER

Order is imperative in teaching. By teaching capital letters first to kindergarten children, we prepare them for nearly half of the lowercase letters that are similar in formation. Letting kids "shop" with fake money serves as a logical preliminary for lessons on money management. Sometimes, though, a practical order is less obvious. For instance, when reviewing literary works, you might think it makes sense to discuss characters' motivations and behavior before the author's themes. Yet, for particular books, discussing themes first and referring back to characters in the story may invoke more meaningful discussion. What do we learn from here? Just this. Before teaching lessons, we must consider the order carefully for its effectiveness. We want our class to recognize and follow the logic of our lessons.

Even when the topic seems to call for no particular order, study the material to determine a more perfect order than the one you've originally planned. For example, first Mr. Lopez thought he could teach the eight parts of speech any old way. Yet, after analyzing the parts of speech and their relationship to writing, he realized he had to plan a precise order if his students were to use the knowledge to build sentences, maintain subject-verb agreement, and pronoun-antecedent agreement. How did he come to this conclusion?

First, Mr. Lopez figured that in preparation for teaching sentence construction, he needed to address the core of all sentences: subjects and predicates. This propelled him to introduce the eight parts of speech with the noun, pronoun, and verb. Next, Mr. Lopez realized he had to teach the preposition or students might confuse nouns or pronouns within prepositional phrases for the subject of the sentence when checking for agreement. From there, Mr. Lopez chose to teach the adjective and adverb—the difference between them, when to use them, and when to lose them. It didn't make sense to teach these modifiers beforehand since students first need to recognize the parts of speech the adjective and adverb modify. (Adjectives modify nouns and pronouns, and adverbs modify adjectives, verbs and adverbs.)

Last on the list, Mr. Lopez saved conjunctions for teaching more complex sentence structures involving all the aforementioned parts of speech. (In case you're an English teacher thinking, "Hey, Mr. Lopez didn't teach the interjection!" it's because Mr. Lopez teaches the interjection along with punctuating dialogue.)

Never underestimate the significance of mapping out your lesson in the most workable form. The reason students exhibit poor grammar in their writing is for this reason. They've never learned grammar in a practical sequence. When the student doesn't see a direct relationship between grammar and writing, grammar becomes useless. Yet when the educator teaches grammar in a sensible order, its application becomes obvious.

FOCUS ON TEACHING CONCEPTS

Teach concepts behind organizations, programs and practices to give them meaning and relevance to students.

For example, let's say a teacher wants to teach about the United Nations. To have her students fully appreciate the significance of the UN's establishment, she need not focus only on the organization but on the concept of peace. She might ask her class questions like, when do you feel at peace? What disturbs your peace? What do peace and freedom have in common? Then she might channel the discussion outward by asking: How do we find peace? How do we promote peace? Why is there so much violence in the world? What can we do to safeguard peace? Is a democracy integral to the peace of a nation? Is war inevitable in some countries? Do you think world peace will ever become a reality?

With the concept of peace understood, the importance of the establishment of the United Nations after World War II, and its peace operations, becomes manifest to the class. The United Nations is no longer just another organization but a symbol of peace vital in maintaining our personal safety. At this point, the teacher can discuss why the United Nations was awarded the Nobel Peace Prize eleven times in the past seventy years. Looking at circumstances in the world today, students can judge whether the United Nations is still doing its job. They can look at the reasons the UN is severely criticized. They can discuss what UN leaders might do differently and whether any current members deserve the Nobel Peace Prize.

Setting the concept of peace aside, the teacher might then discuss other roles integral to the UN. After all, besides its main role in dealing with international conflicts, the UN also has an important role in promoting social progress. Once again, to make this goal real, the teacher might focus on a concept identifiable to children. In addressing UNICEF (the

United Nations International Children's Emergency Fund), for example, the teacher might broach a discussion on poverty.

While some students might already know about poverty or have heard about it in adjacent neighborhoods, others might have little knowledge of how children worldwide lack basic needs. Depending on the grade, the teacher can introduce poverty and ask students to imagine living daily with little food and no time for play because they must work to survive. The teacher can acquaint students with photographs of impoverished children and their circumstances.

Students might then be much more interested in learning about how UNICEF helped more than 1.2 billion impoverished children worldwide get clean access to water or how UNICEF vaccinates children against deadly diseases, buying half the vaccines produced worldwide. Students might be interested further in reading and watching video clips of UNICEF helping countries rebuild schools, hospitals, and communities in the aftermath of floods, earthquakes, and tsunamis.

The bottom line: To make an organization, agency, institution, program or movement matter, educators should teach concepts inherent to the organization. Once students understand these concepts, organizations will resonate with substance and meaning, and students will want to learn more about the organizations. Students can then decide whether they want to get involved in the movement/program; socially, politically, or otherwise. They might emulate the organization by starting a prototype of their own. At the very least, students can speak knowledgeably about the organization in future discussion or debate. Nothing feels better than understanding one's world and feeling connected to it.

MAKE ABSTRACT IDEAS CONCRETE

Once while I was working on my laptop, my then four-year-old niece, Molly, sidled up to me and asked shyly, "What does it mean that a computer comes with a mouse?" She knew in her little heart that a computer didn't come with an actual mouse but still had to muster the courage to ask me what the term meant in connection with computers. Like most kids, she thought she was expected to understand the confusing things in the adult world.

Thrown off by abstract ideas, older children (less brave than four-year-olds) seldom seek clarification, and in consequence, give up on understanding many crucial concepts.

For instance, when Braden's fifth grade teacher draws a ladder on the board to explain DNA, Braden envisions a ladder propped up somewhere in his body. He knows it's not an actual ladder people use for climbing, but thinks of the ladder as an organ. Now if the teacher would have explained that our DNA is stored in nearly all the cells in the body, Braden would have gotten the idea that DNA is not an organ, but a microscopic structure we can't see.

It would do us educators good to pause in our teaching to explain possibly perplexing terms so that students don't struggle with them.

Here are several confusing abstract concepts that commonly baffle children of all ages:

- How inflation happens and why the government can't just produce more money when citizens need it.
- How politics cause commodities such as gold and silver to fluctuate in value.

- Negative numbers—How can you take 5 apples from 4? How can you have less than nothing?
- Globes and maps—How can countries on the globe hang upside down without falling off? Is it possible to dig a hole to China? How does one turn the globe into a flat map or vice versa?
- The difference between character traits such as self-esteem, pride, and arrogance.
- How can we be in danger of overpopulation? There seems to be so much empty space, especially in the countryside.
- Why should the United States care about people in other countries? Why not just concentrate on taking care of its own?
- Free verse poetry—What makes a poem good if it doesn't rhyme? Why can't anyone just write half sentences and call it poetry?
- Global warming—How can the world be in danger of global warming if we had so much snow this winter?
- Abstract Art—What's the big deal? It looks like a bunch of splotches and scribbles.

How do educators make abstract concepts concrete for students?

When reading this list, did you challenge yourself to answer these questions in simple concrete terms? If not, try doing so now. How would you make these abstract concepts understandable to your students? The next time you enter into class to discuss inflation, or negative numbers or abstract art, what will you do differently? This is an important question. While preparing a lesson, think of the less sophisticated thinkers in your classroom. What might bewilder them?

Then try this. Play a game with yourself imagining how you might explain a difficult concept to your 10-year-old neighbor, Sam. That really helps. We get very creative when trying to break down a concept into simple dimensions. Once you come up with an explanation for Sam (which might involve an analogy), use it in class and your students will readily acknowledge what you mean.

Here is a case in point: Let's say Mr. Sullivan wants to define abstract art in terms students can comprehend. He explains that this type of art exhibits what an artist thinks and feels rather than what he sees. The artist uses designs, colors, and shapes to express himself. Abstract art is open to interpretation. The viewer isn't supposed to see specific objects but enter the painting and experience where it takes him. Mr. Sullivan tells the class to imagine listening to their favorite songs. They don't have to define the instruments or the notes. They can just let the music wash over them. Similarly, to appreciate abstract art, they can relax and examine how the colors, texture, and design affect them. What sensations or emotions does the painting evoke? Can they feel the strength of the painting? The best abstract artists have incredible drawing skills, Mr. Sullivan informs the class, so they're not imposters. Abstract artists have the ability to draw realistic portraits but choose not to.

Mr. Sullivan then shows the class an abstract painting and lets them experience it on their own. Soon he asks: How does the painting make you feel? What did you look at first in this painting? Is there movement in this painting? Imagine the painting as a map. What kind of tour is it giving? Is it an adventure? What do you think the artist had in mind? Do you like it? Why? Does it disturb you? Why?

Whether or not students begin to acquire a taste for this art form isn't Mr. Sullivan's goal here. The aim is to successfully communicate to students that abstract art is not random splotches on canvas.

DEFINE MEANINGS

How often do we expect students to follow our train of thought while they get lost on the meaning of a word, phrase, or expression? Better to stop and see if students follow than forge ahead and leave them behind in the dust of unexplained verbiage.

Define vocabulary words. We want our students to build a rich vocabulary. That's why we use advanced vocabulary words in our daily language. Children identify the meaning of the words based on the context of our sentences. The problem occurs, though, when we use these words without context clues. The vocabulary words then become ambiguous and interpreting them a guessing game for students.

To illustrate: Once when substituting a fifth-grade class, Ms. Perez makes the mistake of asking Becca to *distribute* the markers. Not knowing what *distribute* means, Becca stands there looking uncomfortable. Catching on to the source of her confusion, Mr. Perez explains, "To *distribute* means to hand out. I'd like you to hand out the markers." With noticeable relief, the student sets off to do the task.

My point? We have to define vocabulary words when their definitions aren't apparent. Otherwise students can't possibly know what we're talking about.

Define key words. Don't take for granted students know definitions of the key words within your discussion. Write the word and definition on the board. Otherwise you may be speaking about organic foods for a week and have kids wondering, "What's organic?"

Define subjective terminology. To you, the American Dream might mean owning a home, raising a family, and having a good job. To your students, based on their background and what they've read or heard, the American Dream can simply mean paying the bills without bouncing checks. Confusion arises when people's definitions don't agree. Therefore, it's crucial to define what you mean when using subjective terms. This clarification keeps you and your students on the same page.

For example:

- "When I speak about the *American Dream,* I'm talking about living the good life: owning a home, raising a family, having a good job."
- "When I refer to a *healthy relationship*, I mean that the parties involved think of each other on equal terms and cater to each other's needs."
- "My definition of a *good education* is one that prepares you to make a good living."
- "When I mention a *slim body*, I mean one that falls within the normal weight of the Body Mass Index (BMI)."
- "My definition of a *workaholic* is someone who allows his work to consume his complete focus in life."

CONSIDER THE ABSURDITY OF ROTE LEARNING

The psychiatrist Edward Hallowell said, "The opposite of play isn't work, it's rote." He's quite right. Rote learning involves mechanical memorization and practice of a skill. Definitely the opposite of fun; more pointedly, the opposite of valuable learning.

A former "victim" of conventional mathematic teaching, I commiserate with students who are coerced to engage in rote learning. Particularly in math, rote learning was an enigma to me. I have a vague remembrance of using formulas to construct shapes (squares, rectangles, triangles, parallelograms, and circles) and finding the perimeter and area of these shapes, wondering all the while how the constructions and calculations came into practical use. Busy as we were in the seventh grade, the teacher brushed off my requests for explanations with something like, "It sharpens the brain." And so, I went on memorizing and practicing formulas, and trying my best not to poke myself with the point of the compass. Eventually, we were finished with geometry and onto algebra. There, too, I became quite competent in following instructions—this time plotting integers on a graph, but still not knowing what working with the coordinate planes or any of this math had to do with my future as a productive human being.

And does all this rote instruction stick? Let's see. Offhand, can you tell me the formula for a radius, diameter, circumference, area, or chord of a circle? Probably not. Why? Because like me, you weren't taught the practical application of your geometric constructions in a way that mattered. Back in junior high, if you were a diligent kid, you could probably spew forth a bunch of formulas and apply them for the sake of constructing parts of a circle. You never knew there was more to it.

Here's a guarantee: Give up rote instruction for practical application and your students will appreciate their learning.

Show the Practical Application

Consider the educator who teaches geometry to help students study and create package designs. Students study the geometric designs on ice cream cartons, board games, and hand soap, appraising the effect of the design based on shapes, their sizes, and placement. Next, students learn how to construct geometric patterns to create their own package designs for a chocolate bar. Using polygon, circle and sphere formulas, they practice tile patterns and then circle patterns—dividing the circumference of the circle into a number of equal parts— all with compass and straight edge.

Soon students see how complex shapes can be made from simple shapes. Their package designs include triangles, pyramids, polygons, and mosaics. To measure the design's success, students use different package designs to sell the same chocolate bar in a school sale. Once the best seller is apparent, the class discusses the design's attributes. From there, the artist of the design might want to patent his design, sell it to a candy company (a wallpaper, paper goods, upholstery, clothing, or jewelry company) or at least publish it in the school newspaper.

This teacher teaches students a practical application. Using their knowledge to draw and sell package designs gives their constructions meaning. Introduced to advertising and sales, the class learns a bit about attracting a potential buyer and gets a glimpse into the complexity of marketing.

But surely not all learning must dovetail with a business enterprise. Teachers can teach students information for the simple purpose of creating something useful or beautiful, for themselves, others, or society.

For instance, let's take a look at another teacher who teaches geometry for the sake of creating a geometric flower garden. First the teacher shows the class the garden space and they figure out its perimeter and area. Then students calculate how many feet of fence or brick is needed for borders and how much fertilizer and mulch to buy for the garden.

Next, students research which flowers grow best during the season and how much space different species need from each other. On scale grids, students learn how to construct different shapes and designs using their compass and straight edge. Cutting out their favorite constructions, students paste them on paper in symmetrical or asymmetrical patterns.

Finally, the teacher holds up various designs for the class's critique. After selecting the most appealing geometric garden and tweaking it to perfection, the class sets out to make the design a reality. Over the next few months (possibly with the aid of a hired landscaper), students work on planting their flowers and observing how the garden grows. Individuals can design their own garden at home and bring in photos or slides to show the class.

How refreshing to see children immersed in learning that matters to them. Whether the teacher chooses to embark upon bigger or smaller projects is up to her. A simple class project such as constructing geometric coloring pages for a children's or adult coloring book can prove a sensation with every child contributing one page to the coloring book. The point is to make the learning real and relevant for the student.

Rote teaching gets in the way of children's learning even in very young classes. Even small children want to know the logic of what they're doing. Problem solving in the classroom versus robotic figuring shows children the meaning behind numbers on paper. Figuring how many gummy bears each child can have so that everyone gets the same number makes more sense to the class than memorizing $20 \div 5 = 4$. Finding the mean, median, and mode of random numbers holds greater significance for students when they're trying to determine the class's average height and most common height so that they can work out practical poses for class photos. Likewise, figuring out inconsequential ratios and proportions on paper becomes meaningful when students know they're learning it for the sake of doing something real such as preparing appetizing food platters.

CONDUCT CLASSROOM EXPERIMENTS

Tell your class, "Let's do an experiment," and you'll get a favorable response. Well-designed experiments clarify concepts students can easily transfer to other learning situations. So, don't just depend on telling the class information, show it to them in progress. Try the following type of experiments with your class, and you'll see the purpose of your teaching come alive for the student!

Understanding the concept "the survival of the fittest." Let's say you want to teach the concept of survival of the fittest. Don't imitate the amateur teacher who explains the concept with words. Show the class what "the survival of the fittest" means. How so?

Using gripping tools such as pliers, tweezers, and tongs, let students experiment to see which tool is the most adept at transferring single lima beans from one plate to another. Have students time themselves to get an accurate count of the beans they pick up per minute with a particular tool. After students come up with the "fittest" tool for the job, tell them that the tools represent "beaks" of different species of finches. Now they can understand why a finch's beak size and shape often determines whether a particular finch will survive on an island in its competition for food. Darwin's idea of "the survival of the fittest" becomes clear. Students can easily apply this concept when the teacher speaks about the struggle for survival among other species of animals.

Understanding the value of economic exchange. Imagine telling your class, "Today we'll be discussing why countries trade with each other." You know what's going on in the children's heads? "Who cares? What's that got to do with me?" Here's an alternative idea.

Open a discussion about free trade with an experiment that lets the class experience the value of trade. For this purpose, hand each student a bag with a different assortment of small toys they may keep, let's say four toys per child. (Don't use fewer than 15 different types of toys for a class of 25, but keep to the school's budget.) Have students record on a chart the value each toy has for them from a scale of 0–5 and write the sum. Then tell the class they may check out other kids' toys and trade items if they want. The trade must be agreeable for both parties. No other rules apply. For example, they do not have to keep to a one-for-one ratio, meaning someone can trade a pack of baseball cards and a glitter pen for a bendable action figure.

After their final round of trading, have students record the value of items in their new stash and write the sum. Next, have students figure the difference between the tally of their first and second sum. That's how much the value of the toy rose for them. At this point, students realize the value of the exchange. Everyone's happier now with their new toys.

In a discussion, you might ask students why the classroom's overall satisfaction increased if the total number of toys available in the classroom didn't change. You can also discuss the reasoning behind the children's trades or negotiations. For example, maybe Caleb likes sports games so much that he went around the room trading his four toys for four different pocket sports games. Or maybe Annie agreed to exchange her rubber bracelet for Emily's earphones if Emily agreed to trade her yoyo for Annie's teddy bear key chain. Now students understand the basic benefits of economic exchange. They can apply their trading experience to understand how free trade between countries increases economic growth.

On occasion, you might come across an experiment that can live on outside the classroom. Why not run with it? Children gain deeper understanding when trying the experiment in new settings. Take the following experiment on bacteria.

Becoming mindful of harmful bacteria in the atmosphere. Let's say you want your students to beware of the harmful bacteria that lurks everywhere. After all, some bacteria can cause a life-threatening infection. Instead of merely informing students about harmful bacteria in their midst, why not let them see the danger for themselves?

To this end, you can have the class swab surfaces and test them for bacteria in petri dishes. Students can create their own hypothesis—for example that the doorknobs in the school carry more bacteria than the window sills. After observing the bacteria growth, students can come up with ways to prevent illness in school.

But the learning doesn't have to stop there. Encourage students to test other environments for bacteria—surfaces in public areas: elevator buttons, handrails of escalators, the poles on a train—or surfaces at home: the kitchen counter, the bathroom sink, the telephone. On their own, students might continue to test personal items for bacteria such as make-up, desk tops, used water bottles, or toothbrushes. They can even test which soaps or household cleaners work best against bacteria by swabbing and testing different cleaners on bacteria-ridden areas. With the awareness of bacterial growth in areas they test, students see the need for germ prevention in many environments.

MODEL PROFESSIONAL WORK

Experts at many skills, we think students will catch on to our instructions quickly, but most people don't fully comprehend what we mean without model examples. This bodes true especially when teaching writing skills.

For instance, hounding students to use smooth sentences won't get you anywhere. To imitate good writing, students must see clear-cut illustrations of a professional writer's craft. So, supposing you want your high school students to fashion smooth sentences, you might turn to David McCullough's Pulitzer Prize–winning biographies *John Adams* and *Truman,* which sport spectacular sentence variety worthy of emulation. Or perhaps you decide to teach the beauty of parallel structure. How about presenting Francis Bacon's essay "Of Studies," Abraham Lincoln's Gettysburg Address or an excerpt from Edward M. Kennedy's eulogy for his brother Robert F. Kennedy. These works contain remarkable examples of parallel structure. Keep the examples coming until students get the hang of the writing tool.

MODEL STUDENTS' WORK

Give your students samples of former students' exemplary work to show them the task is doable. Along with presenting professional pieces, you might portray how former students employ a particular skill or technique in their paragraphs or sentences. Astounded by their contemporaries' creativity, the class tends to buckle down to try the skill, feeling that mastery is within reach. They reason if these kids could do it, so can they.

If you haven't kept copies of students' model work, you might as well begin collecting them. You'll thank yourself in the future. For now, if possible, track down former students and ask them for their best papers. Otherwise, select good writing excerpts from current students' first and second drafts.

Here are excerpts from students' fantasy papers and memoirs that model writing techniques. These handouts portray good leads, specific language, and analogies. When given the chance, students revel in reviewing their peers' writing samples and gaining "know-how" from them.

Handout

Regarding: Good Leads
Subject: Fantasy papers
Instruction: Evaluate the following leads. Do they carry suspense? Do they make you want to read on? Why?

- "I'm sorry, Harold, you may have to die."
Harold stared at Professor Hilbert as if he were some Martian.
The professor hitched his glasses up his nose and crossed his legs. He continued, "It's her masterpiece. It's possibly the most instrumental novel in her already stunning career and it's absolutely no good unless you die at the end. I've been over it again and again."—Chaya Rivkin
- "Oh, gosh! Help me! I shot my pa! Help, my pa! I killed my pa!" I hear these garbled screams from somewhere in the distance. Only it isn't so distant; everything on this vast field seems distant. I recognize the voice of Aaron Murphy, a young private from the 34th regiment. Cradling the limp body of an older man who looks like him, Murphy is moaning and sobbing like no grown man ever should.—Zlaty Hertz
- Miss Pruzky was a fishing rod. She was tall and lanky, her nose was sharp and pointed upward. Her long, stringy hair hung down her back, limp like our national flag sulking on a windless day. She had a demanding attitude, and we liked her as much as we liked brussels sprouts.—Chayala Apfelbaum

Handout

Regarding: Specific Language
Subject: Fantasy papers
Instruction: Notice the specific language in the following paragraphs. Does it create vivid imagery? How so?

- Heaving a sigh, she hung her robe on a hook in the wardrobe beside a sack of arrows. On the dirt floor lay a heap of twigs and glass bottles, saddles and swords. As much as they liked to ignore what was happening, they both knew: Tim was dreaming again of witches and dwarfs, satyrs and marsh-wiggles, of fauns and talking beasts. And after every dream, something was found in his rumpled bed the next morning. A candle here, a bow there, an arrow or a horn…—Naomi Broker
- Grandma Willis stepped out of her grave and squinted as she looked up at the sun for the first time. On planet Nahapachu where Mrs. Willis was going to live, people were born at one hundred and twenty and died at age zero. Mrs. Willis clicked her dentures onto her gums, lifted her cane, mumbled about her arthritis in her shoulder, and went to look for her husband, Harry. Two rows down, she spotted Harry crawling out of his coffin, careful not to mess up the wreath of roses. He dusted off his tweed trousers and propped one foot on a tree stump to tie his Cole Haan "Colton" Wingtip.—Faigy Neiger

Handout

Regarding: Comparisons
Subject: Memoirs
Task: Use comparisons in your memoirs
Instruction: Discuss the comparisons in the following sentences with your partner. Which ones do you especially like? Why? What about the comparisons appeal to you?

Sentences using comparisons

- "What is it?" I croaked like a hermit who hadn't spoken in years.—Mashy Kaufman
- Aunt Sally was frozen in place like an ice cube stuck in its tray.—Ricki Schindler
- "Welcome," says the ghost, its voice tickling my neck like a Brillo pad.—Devoiry Sommer
- I was horrified as the edges of his lips curled upwards like the corners of burning parchment.—Hindy Berglas
- Two coins raced to the far edges of the sidewalk as if they were playing tag.—Raiza Lisker
- Sure enough, he was as calm as a lily pad on still waters.—Frady Wercberger
- The crowd was gushing with energy like an open fire hydrant.—Goldie Gleiberman
- I surveyed the area: rows and rows of tombstones, all in a straight line as if they were ready to march out to war.—Chaya Teitelbaum
- Her hands started to shake violently like a car engine sputtering to life.—Estie Klein
- The tension was as thick as a vat of concrete mix.—Rochel Malka Freund
- She hurried down the trail through the woods, the dense fog shrouding the trees like misty gowns.—Raizel Fordsham

Instruction: Incorporate two analogies into your memoir and ask three classmates to appraise them.

SHOW THEM HOW TO HONE SKILLS

Impatient for positive results, students lose enthusiasm when they don't see progress in their work. With this in mind, we educators need to constantly help students hone their skills. (This applies to all subjects, whether it's writing, math, science, art, gym, music, computers, etc.)

Find a skill your students lack in common, and address it on a handout, explaining why improvement is necessary. Give model examples of the skill—from professionals or students—and then put students to work incorporating the skill.

For instance, here's a handout I prepared to show students how to instill atmosphere in the second drafts of their short stories. Implementing the instruction, students delight in seeing a positive transformation in their writing.

Handout

Regarding: Atmosphere
Subject: Second draft short stories
Task: Create a better atmosphere in your second draft

One main element missing in your short stories was atmosphere. The vast majority ignored the atmosphere, letting their characters exist, talk, or move about in a vacuum. Others, just as cruel, teased the reader with the mention of a forest, building, or room, without providing the crucial detail necessary to make the atmosphere come alive.

How do you incorporate a good sense of atmosphere in your story? Remark upon what characters see, hear, feel, or smell in their surroundings. Show how characters relate to their surroundings—how they move about it, use it, enjoy it, relax in it, disturb it, run from it, or otherwise experience it. You need to describe surroundings. Mention specific things: a specific location (Prospect Park Zoo), name of a street (West 131st Street), species of a tree (birch), make and model of a vehicle (Honda Accord), particular food (honeydew), etc.

Notice how Lebron Carter creates a sense of the atmosphere in this scene:

But it's no use, and suddenly Nick has lifted me by the collar of my shirt, and he's holding me two feet off the ground against the window. Looking down, I can see my Reeboks hovering above the beige bathroom tiles. Greg's snickers are filling the small room, echoing off the walls, accompanied by Nick's hoots, and the two of them together sound like some sort of drunken duet, their voices overpowering the sound of the dripping faucet near the door— my only hope for escape.

Lebron gives us a good sense of atmosphere. Readers sense the narrator's dire predicament because they can see him in the surroundings of the bathroom. The mention of the narrator being lifted two feet off the ground, his Reeboks no longer in contact with the beige bathroom tiles, the derisive sounds and dripping faucet, all lets readers imagine a complete atmosphere.

How do the following sentences also give a good sense of atmosphere?

- The metal doors of the train suddenly slid shut, leaving me stranded in the freezing night. The steel cars quickly gained speed, blending into one hurtling death machine. Then it was gone, and the platform was as eerie as outer space.—Miriam Hager
- *I hate Mr. Washington!* Ten-year-old Andrew Jackson thought as he trudged through the snow, his footsteps leaving small canyons of white in the snowy depths behind him. The cold Carolina winter winds made his teeth drum their special winter song.—Rikki Moskovits
- Finally, he found himself in a huge basement. It was mostly empty besides for a few piles of unopened UPS boxes. Pipes snaked their way across the peeling ceiling. All he could hear was an echo of a leaking pipe.—Sarala Blatt
- Not wanting to be that kind of kid, I cautiously tip-toe across the front lawn. Looking up from behind Mrs. Moore's geraniums, I could see the computer's reflection from the study window.—Mimi Friedman

Instruction: Please turn to places I underlined in your writing and make the atmosphere come alive. You may ask your peers to help you.

MODEL THE DIFFERENCE SIDE BY SIDE

When teaching the right and wrong way of doing something, it's a good idea to model examples side by side so that students can see the blatant difference. For instance, suppose I want to impress upon students the importance of using the active versus the passive voice to write clear and direct sentences. Here's how I'd present the information on a handout:

Handout

Regarding: Third draft short stories
Subject: Active versus passive voice
Task: Turn your passive sentences into active ones.

Choose the active versus the passive voice to write clear and direct sentences. How do you know the difference? In sentences using the passive voice, the subject is either missing from the sentence or found in the predicate part of the sentence. In sentences using the active voice, the subject performs the action expressed in the verb. For example:

Passive: Some puzzled looks were exchanged.
Active: Some guests exchanged puzzled looks.
Passive: A rope ladder was rolled up when the gym teacher walked into class.
Active: Max rolled up the rope ladder when the gym teacher walked into class.
Passive: The lecture was given by a tall professor.
Active: A tall professor gave the lecture.

Instruction: Check your short story for passive sentences and turn them into active ones.

Now students clearly see the difference between the active and passive voice and can look back at this handout if necessary to refresh their memories. If you think the class can benefit from more examples, pile them on the page. I'd rather students tell me, "We get it already!" than overhear them saying, "I still don't get it."

PROVIDE EXPLANATIONS FOR EXAMPLES

Sometimes recognizing and correcting a particular error is a bit more complicated for students. The dangling modifier, for instance, seems to mystify my students. For most, spotting the dangling modifier takes a bit of practice; correcting it, a bit of skill.

To help students conquer an error such as the dangling modifier, explain the error for each example and how to fix it. Once again, provide as many examples as the class needs to fully comprehend the concept. To demonstrate, here's a handout on correcting dangling modifiers.

Handout

Regarding: Grammar review
Subject: Dangling Modifiers
Task: Correct dangling modifiers in sentences.

Avoid dangling modifiers. The dangling modifier muddles the meaning of the sentence. What exactly is a dangling modifier? The dangling modifier is a word or a phrase that modifies a word not clearly stated in the sentence. You correct a dangling modifier by revising the sentence to include the missing word. For example:

Famished, the pizza was gone in five minutes.
Famished is a dangling modifier. Why? Because the *pizza* wasn't famished. What is the missing word? The missing word is *we*. Revision:
Famished, we devoured the pizza in five minutes.
Lazy and careless, Susie's work ethic is awful.
Lazy and careless is a dangling modifier. Why? because Susie's *work ethic* isn't lazy and careless. What is the missing word? The missing word is *Susie*. Revision:
Lazy and careless, Susie has an awful work ethic.
While driving on Argyle Road, an elm tree almost fell on Noah's car.
While driving on Argyle Road is a dangling modifier. Why? An *elm tree* wasn't driving on Argyle Road. What is the missing word? The missing word is *Noah*. Revision:
While Noah was driving on Argyle Road, an elm tree almost fell on his car.

Instruction: Correct the dangling modifiers on page 73 in your workbook. Be ready to explain why each sentence contains a dangling modifier.

Work on Correcting Mistakes Together

Checking for understanding is the key to effective teaching and learning. Type up incorrect sentences from students' papers (without their names) and run through the sentences to see if the class understands how to revise them. Don't allow for a chorus of answers. Call on students individually to try out the examples.

Handout

Regarding: Mystery papers
Subject: Review of grammar and language skills
Task: Revising mystery papers to correct fragments, clarify the subject, and remove redundant usage.

Be careful to write complete thoughts. What word(s) are missing from the following sentences?

- I was standing there alone, pitch black outside.
- I heard noises but was too busy focusing on my friend's tombstone.
- I unfolded from the rail.
- He slipped in letting the door ease.

Don't let characters' eyes, hands or other body parts act independent from their body. How would you revise these sentences?

- Her eyeballs stared at her parents.
- Bert's head charged forward bashing into Gary's.
- Amanda tried to resist, her hands attacking the assailant.
- Her toes gingerly tiptoed across the cold floor.

Don't use superfluous words. What's redundant in the following sentences?

- Jayden fled immediately after back to his hometown.
- The number was not familiar, one I had never seen.
- But then, I was left standing all alone in that impenetrable darkened room. There was no source of light in the room.
- Austin's stomach plummeted to a great depth.

Teach Life Skills

> "The most important outcome of education is to help students become independent of formal education."—Paul E. Gray

Teach skills that can be used universally and are not exclusive to any subject or stage of life. Don't let your teaching only serve the "here and now." After all, we want to provide students with the means to school themselves for the rest of their lives. Always ask yourself, "Am I preparing my students for success in life?"

The following lessons teach give students the tools they need for a lifetime.

Managing time. This is the typical case. Your students complain they have too much homework. You suspect they're wasting time doing what teenagers do, namely, talking on the phone, texting, hanging out, surfing the net. You are about to set these time wasters straight with a "when I was your age…" rant. But wait. Do yourself a favor.

Instead of admonishing kids to manage their time better, teach them this crucial life skill. To this end, students create a to-do list and put the items in order of priority. Then in pairs, students discuss the items on their list and chart reasonable blocks of time for tasks and breaks. At home, students attempt to follow their schedule, making sure not to procrastinate tasks or go overboard with leisure time. Before bed, next to the tasks in their charts, students write what they've accomplished and which obstacles interfered with their plan.

The next day, together with their teacher and peers, students discuss common obstacles and how to contend with them in the future. Discussions might involve how to deal with distractions: phone call interruptions, siblings or others who ask for urgent favors; or better incentives to keep oneself on track (such as using timers). Based on this counsel, students write new to-do lists and try once again to manage their time more wisely at home. This practice and review can go on as long as necessary. The teacher might work individually with students to fine-tune their schedules. The result? After a few trial practices, students manage their time better.

Budgeting for basics. This lesson is about letting a high school class figure out personal future budgets based on different variables—for example, whether they'll be living in a dorm, on their own, or with a roommate. Students research the cost of living and build a realistic weekly, monthly, and yearly budget for themselves. They estimate how much money they'll need for tuition and books, rent or a mortgage, for food and utilities, insurance, clothing, and personal expenditures. After itemizing their expenses on an Excel spreadsheet, they can easily calculate the weekly, monthly, and yearly expenditures. Then they decide how they will obtain the money. Frequently, they have to modify their expenses to match their budget. What a better way to prepare students for future life experiences than to have them work on financial management skills?

Making better food choices. If you're like me, you are not a health nut, urban naturalist, or modern day hippie. Yet, in face of overwhelming evidence in favor of healthy eating, you will agree it's imperative for educators to raise an awareness of healthier eating options. Talking about the detriment of constantly eating junk food, though, doesn't turn kids off Kool-Aid or potato chips. Neither does preaching about nutrition inspire kids to reach for the carrots. Show students how to make better health choices, and they might do just that.

How about having students bring in their favorite junk food for a lesson on its food value? You can invite a nutritionist to discuss unhealthy ingredients in their junk food and then present healthy alternatives. You can hand out ingredient labels of snacks such as taffies, chocolate bars, and pretzels and ask students to rank them in order of food quality. Next, you can show the class a video clip of an insightful registered dietician teaching how to decode ingredient labels. Then students can go back to the previous ingredient labels and discuss any misconceptions they've made. Based on what they learn about ingredients, students can now make healthier food choices before choosing snacks or different brands of snacks. For instance, knowing that white sugar is harmful to the body, they might choose one brand of tortilla chips over another if one of them contains fewer grams of sugar.

You might consider carrying the lesson even further. The class can throw a fruit and vegetable fest where students get to sample fruits and vegetables they never knew existed. A teacher I know organized an apple fest where students got to discover the difference between many varieties of apples such as Red Delicious, Cortland, Golden Delicious, Granny Smith, Gala, Fuji, and McIntosh. Students can come up with five of their favorite fruits and vegetables and discuss how to incorporate them into their daily diet. Students can bring in healthy recipes and combine them in a cookbook for the class. They can learn about healthier substitutes for certain ingredients and reinvent recipes to make them more nutritious. Any of these activities make students more liable to choose healthier foods in the future.

TAKE THE TRIP

Trips can be lessons in themselves. Teaching about machines? Why not take your class on a trip to an ice cream factory to see how ice cream is made? Students find it fascinating to see how the liquid ingredients in a huge tank mix with dry ingredients, travel to the pasteurizing section, blend in the blending machine, pump into freezing chambers, and pour into containers! What a process!

"Going green" with your class? Why not visit a large recycling plant to see how it takes apart gadgets like computers, cameras, and printers? Students marvel at the productivity!

Teaching about "the Fed"? If you aren't too far, visit the Federal Reserve Bank in Manhattan to learn about how money is made and the role the Fed plays in the U.S. economy. Descending eighty feet below street level to visit the gold vault, the tour gets to view billions of dollars of gold—seeing is believing!

Trips can also promise great fun! Mrs. Gitty Pultman, a colleague of mine, teaches her students about physics by taking them to the Coney Island Cyclone. Students watch (and then experience) how the law of energy conservation plays out over the complete circuit; potential energy is transformed into kinetic energy and back again as the coaster continues going up and down hills.

Trips can prove sobering, too. Another colleague brings her class to Green-Wood Cemetery, in Brooklyn (founded in 1838, it is a Revolutionary War historic site and a National Historic Landmark since 2006), which contains the remains of many famous people, from Civil War generals to baseball legends. Inspired after reading tombstones that suggest life stories, students write their own elegies of famous historical figures or of their own relatives or friends who have departed.

Education is useless when it leads us away from practicality and idealism. It is useless when it distances us from real life. Rote learning has nothing to offer students beyond confusion and futility. It insults students' intelligence, ignores their common sense, and damages their spirit and personality. We don't want to raise a generation of people that doggedly memorize information for a test and then know nothing at all.

Validating learning is everything. Immediately putting knowledge into practice, applying theory, and seeing results they can build on, all give children a worthwhile education. Our students deserve an education that does more than teach long division and the difference between types of rocks. We want students to think and act for themselves, and eventually to contribute something to society and even the world.

4

Choosing Less
to Produce More

"There is more to life than simply increasing its speed."—Mahatma Gandhi

Are We Getting Nowhere Fast?

As the world turns on a speeding axis, we gasp to keep up with its pace. No more strolling along a promenade, or reading *Jane Eyre* on a park bench, or playing Monopoly all Sunday afternoon. If we want to keep up, we need to speed up.

The world's need to accelerate its pace is not a new concept. In 1871, Lewis Carroll satirizes this racing folly in *Through the Looking Glass, and What Alice Found There* (chapter 2):

> Alice never could quite make out, in thinking it over afterwards, how it was that they began: all she remembers is, that they were running hand in hand, and the Queen went so fast that it was all she could do to keep up with her: and still the Queen kept crying "Faster! Faster!" but Alice felt she *could not* go faster, though she had not breath left to say so.
>
> The most curious part of the thing was, that the trees and the other things round them never changed their places at all: however fast they went, they never seemed to pass anything. "I wonder if all the things move along with us?" thought poor puzzled Alice. And the Queen seemed to guess her thoughts, for she cried, "Faster! Don't try to talk!"
>
> Not that Alice had any idea of doing *that*. She felt as if she would never be able to talk again, she was getting so much out of breath: and still the Queen cried "Faster! Faster!" and dragged her along. "Are we nearly there?" Alice managed to pant out at last.
>
> "Nearly there!" the Queen repeated. "Why, we passed it ten minutes ago! Faster!" And they ran on for a time in silence, with the wind whistling in Alice's ears, and almost blowing her hair off her head, she fancied.
>
> "Now! Now!" cried the Queen. "Faster! Faster!" And they went so fast that at last they seemed to skim through the air, hardly touching the ground with their feet, till suddenly, just as Alice was getting quite exhausted, they stopped, and she found herself sitting on the ground, breathless and giddy.
>
> The Queen propped her up against a tree, and said kindly, "You may rest a little now."
>
> Alice looked round her in great surprise. "Why, I do believe we've been under this tree the whole time! Everything's just as it was!"
>
> "Of course it is," said the Queen, "what would you have it?"
>
> "Well, in *our* country," said Alice, still panting a little, "you'd generally get to somewhere else—if you ran very fast for a long time, as we've been doing."
>
> "A slow sort of country!" said the Queen. "Now, *here*, you see, it takes all the running *you* can do, to keep in the same place. If you want to get somewhere else, you must run at least twice as fast as that!"

As Carroll implies, we don't get farther in life when we speed breathlessly through it. Yet, today more than ever, the race to "keep up" has infiltrated our lives. Like the Queen, we rush our students to cover ground, albeit intellectual ground rather than literal ground. And the problem with hurrying to cover material? It gets us nowhere fast!

An example of this inane race to cover material took me by surprise in what I had thought a progressive high school. Upon my request to observe an inspirational teacher, the principal sent me to a particular tenth-grade biology class. The students, so I've been told, were about to give dynamic Power Point presentations on the human body systems, namely, the cardiovascular, skeletal, digestive, and respiratory systems. They were to explain the function of their system and how the system works with the other systems. In addition, each group was to display a drawing of their system on a cardboard outline of the human body along with labels defining the parts.

Sounds impressive? Yes! Did I think profound learning would take place? Maybe if the entire class qualified for Mensa! Cramming the information of four major body systems into a 45-minute period sounded pretty incredible to me. Would the lesson work in reality? I would soon see.

In what seemed like a parody, I watched as each group stood awkwardly before the class and parroted the information on their slides. Students exhibited little comprehension of what they were saying, speaking in rushed robotic tones and mispronouncing words. This delivery of dry facts was repeated in the same painful vein as the groups read the labels on their cardboard drawings. With the teacher's continual admonishment about an upcoming quiz, a few audience members struggled to take down information. The rest sat, weary and subdued, tuning in for maybe ten seconds as each new group headed to the front of the room. Once again, my big question: Was anybody learning? Leaning over to one of the kids, I asked, "Do you understand anything they're saying up there?"

"Nope," he said.

"You?" I asked his sidekick.

"Huh?" she asked.

"Are you getting this stuff?"

"I wish."

"How do you pass the quiz?" I questioned her.

"We memorize the book," she said, listlessly.

My presence didn't arouse curiosity, either. I was just another irritating adult, coming from who cares where to ask them about their learning. I felt pity for these kids, cheated of their education and time. Having wasted enough time of my own, I caught the teacher's eye, mimed an apologetic, "I have to go now," and skedaddled out the door.

Upon further research, it seems this marathon method of teaching is rampant in many classrooms across the states. Pressed with heavy curriculums, teachers keep moving on to new material. But quick-paced lessons of any kind are ineffective. It takes time for people to internalize information. In Vicki Abeles' documentary video *Race to Nowhere* an educator says, "Our students are pressured to perform. They're not necessarily pressured to learn deeply and conceptually." I couldn't agree more.

Less Is More

So what's to be done? The way I see it, principals and educators have to think what makes more sense—hustling along and having the kids know five to ten percent of the material or slowing down and ensuring they know ninety to a hundred percent of it? Taking the time to teach well ultimately covers more of the curriculum and saves teacher and student needless frustration. In his 1855 poem, *Andrea del Sarto,* Robert Browning coined the phrase "Less is more." That 19th century proverbial phrase should strike with vehemence today, warning educators of the marathon folly. Less is more. Less is more. Let's make it our mantra.

Slowing down, however, isn't the sole key to breaking the marathon and beating the system. Merely slowing down can be as fruitless as racing if you don't employ proper techniques and create the proper atmosphere for teaching the subject. Here are various techniques and strategies you can implement in the classroom to strengthen learning while maintaining a comfortable, stress-free environment.

Techniques for Ultimate Learning

> "If a child can't learn the way we teach, maybe we should teach the way they learn."—Ignacio "Nacho" Estrada

LOSE THE LECTURE

Teachers often lecture to cover ground. Yet, plain lecturing is the worst tool to depend upon in the classroom. Listening to a lecture from anyone, even one's peers, doesn't brighten the dullness of the format. Typically, students remember 5% of what they hear spouted in a lecture. Whether the lecture comes from teacher, peer, park ranger, or celebrity, it usually falls on bored ears.

ACTIVELY INVOLVE THE CLASS

What happens though when the teacher actively involves the audience? Learning jumps to 50–90 percent! When the teacher immerses students in discussing, discovering, practicing, and performing, students learn quicker. These activities may take more physical time than lecturing, but students retain a whole lot more and have fun in the process.

Let's look back at the tenth-grade class listening to a whirlwind of dull lectures on the body systems. This class wasn't learning or retaining much, which was a shame. Learning the body systems is fascinating when done right. How does a savvy teacher approach the task? By purposefully enamoring the class with each body system.

To teach the cardiovascular system, for instance, the class can watch a short video on the path that blood takes throughout the body and discuss why the cardiovascular system is called the body's lifeline. They can draw a flowchart to illustrate the cardiac cycle. They can write a poem about the way the heart works. To make the cardiovascular experience real to them, students can look at capillaries under a microscope. They can learn how to examine an EKG. They can learn how to check their heart rate, take their own blood pressure, practice strength training and resistance training, and discuss the effect of exercise on the cardiovascular system.

Challenging the class's creativity, the teacher can have students put on a play for younger kids that acts out the jobs of the cardiovascular system and teaches about heart-healthy diets. To make the learning matter further, the teacher can encourage community advocacy by having students write a letter to the surgeon general suggesting he ban certain unhealthy TV commercials and proposing ways he can better influence food industries.

Thoroughly absorbed in understanding, experiencing, and synthesizing aspects of the cardiovascular system, students learn the material well. They can repeat it with great enthusiasm and will know it when they're adults. The classes take more time, but the time is well-spent. Ultimate learning happens when the entire class is engaged in discussing and doing.

PROVIDE BREAKS

Any lesson that requires students to memorize huge amounts of information is doomed to fail. Our students' brains aren't computers. People can only retain about seven pieces of information at a given time. We learn better with spaced practice, meaning learning a few chunks of information with breaks in between. In his book *Use Both Sides of Your Brain*, Tony Buzan demonstrates how short breaks during a one-hour learning session or study period keeps understanding and retention high. Stepping away from learning gives the mind time to process information. Without these breaks, retention proves low. Therefore, during a 40-minute period, I suggest giving students at least one break from imbibing material. During this break, students can stand up and stretch, do an exercise routine, look out the window, talk to a friend, or eat a snack.

STOP THE SENSELESS BUZZ

Upon his visit to bustling Manhattan in 1876, Samuel Clemens, more famously know as Mark Twain, remarked, "There is something about this ceaseless buzz, and hurry, and bustle, that keeps a stranger in a state of unwholesome excitement all the time, and makes him restless and uneasy, and saps from him all the capacity to enjoy anything or take a strong interest in any matter whatever—something which impels him to try to do everything, and yet permits him to do nothing."

Can you sense Clemens' disorientation? I imagine you can, and I'm sure you'll agree it's not a good feeling. Place a child in a Manhattan of activity in the classroom and you can bet he feels the same way.

True, we've come a long way from the traditional classroom atmosphere with the students sitting in straight rows clasping their hands before them. And yes, we want activities to supersede staid lecturing. But these days, I can't help lamenting the tumult that goes on in classrooms where students are frequently left to their own devices (often in disorganized groups) in the name of "creative expression." Worse are instances where the teacher believes the kids must constantly jump about or clamor a chorus to remain motivated in an activity. The excessive movement and noise disturbs the quality of learning. We need to keep activities under control and decaffeinate lessons when they call for senseless hyperactivity.

CHECKING THE MENTAL AND PHYSICAL ATMOSPHERE OF THE CLASSROOM: THE SCIENCE OF DECORATING A CLASSROOM

Decorating a classroom doesn't seem like a scientific process, yet it is. With too much stimulation in the physical atmosphere, jitteriness takes the place of learning. I remember visiting a fourth-grade classroom which attacked me with a cacophony of harsh color and design. A maze of neon posters, charts, and paper pyramids wallpapered the walls. Emblazoned printouts on the bulletin board admonished: "Don't Yell!" "Be Respectful!" "Think Big!" Hanging on the windows, opaque plastic curtains shouted lists of dates and equations in colorful markers. A clothesline strung across the center of the room waved a concoction of freshly painted forests. Cupboard shelves spilled forth with paint supplies, glue sticks papier-mache, and spider plants. In the midst of all this, the teacher was trying to involve the class in a discussion about the Articles of Confederation. The children couldn't sit still on their rainbow mats, their eyes darting back and forth from a confusing jumble of shape and color.

Therefore, I suggest using discretion when setting up your classroom. Don't overcrowd the atmosphere. Choose harmonious hues, easy fonts for posters, and a five-foot distance between posters so that the atmosphere can breathe. Don't let anything flap in people's faces or crowd the path in the classroom. Hang artwork on bulletin boards. Set up side tables to display projects. Keep cupboards neat by stacking items or placing them in bins. If possible, provide little alcoves where students can read or do their work in solitude.

Finally, in creating a mental and physical healthy atmosphere, why not consider letting the class help you? Children like to contribute directly to creating their environment. Students can hang up their work, family photos, personal drawings, and interesting articles. They can display their art or hobbies in showcases. Everyone expresses curiosity about classmates' personal contributions and when shared, the atmosphere becomes homey rather than "educational." Undoubtedly, more learning takes place in this environment than in one that forces kids to stare at myriad of facts and formulas.

Don't Ignore the Process

Much of teaching involves a process. Ignore the process and you'll botch up the result. For instance, let's say you ask novice Nellie to paint a room. You know the way the room will look depends on the type of paint she selects, how she dips the roller in the pan, the strokes she uses on the walls, how well she smooths over streaks and takes care of drippings—not to mention the careful attention to the moldings. But anxious for Nellie to paint the room quickly, you forget about the process and spew forth instructions and warnings expecting good results. What do you get? A bad paint job.

Likewise, when educators zoom through guidelines while teaching a skill (whether it's in math, science, art, language, or writing) they are in for a rude awakening when they receive poor quality work. Unfortunately, instead of analyzing where they went wrong, many teachers decide their class is lazy. Here's how it usually goes. Having little patience for the process, Mr. Davis rushes students through the steps of essay writing. Frustrated with poor results, Mr. Davis punishes the class by assigning additional essays, admonishing them to do a better job. What Mr. Davis doesn't realize is that he can't expect his students to write coherent essays if they don't comprehend the process. Better for Mr. Davis to slow down and work on writing one essay at a time, ensuring students understand the fundamentals such as choosing a topic, gathering information, writing the outline, and so forth. Once teachers break down the complexity, the task becomes doable and students don't repeat previous mistakes.

In some cases, ignoring a process may even cripple students in the long run. Whenever I am tempted to skip steps in a process, I am reminded of what almost happened to Maria Tallchief, the internationally renowned American ballerina. Her first ballet teacher had her dancing on pointe and performing without teaching the basics of ballet technique. A later teacher, shocked by this training, remarked that it was a miracle Maria hadn't permanently injured herself and insisted that she go back and learn the ABCs of dancing!

The lesson? Just this. There's no abracadabra to reaching a goal. No instructor can skip parts of a process without repercussions. Doing so may cripple children's abilities to do something right (possibly forever). Looking around my classroom, I see students holding their pens in odd grips because their first-grade teachers went straight to forming letters without demonstrating the correct way to hold a pencil. Try fixing that in the eleventh grade! Likewise, many students can't type without looking at the keyboard because they weren't trained at the get-go to look at the screen and not the keys. Other students never learned the times tables with the proper mnemonics and have difficulty doing the simplest calculations. Teachers must study the material and think of the process before attempting to teach a skill.

ACKNOWLEDGING THE MENTAL PROCESS: WALK STUDENTS THROUGH

Ever come across students who forget how to analyze problems? Basically, they need help reviewing the mental steps necessary in coming to correct conclusions. Yet, the teacher doesn't take the time to help with this review, often showing displeasure to the student who doesn't make snap connections and calling on another student instead to provide the correct answer. With just a bit of coaching, teachers can turn on the light for confused students by walking them through the material to the correct answer.

A real example from the classroom. During a grammar lesson Sima stiffened when I called on her to detect a hard-to-find subject in the sentence. Knowing that horrible feeling of not knowing the right answer, I decided to walk her through the process of finding the subject in the sentence.

First, I said, "Sima, if my teacher called on me and I couldn't find the subject right away, I'd take a good look at the sentence and ask myself which part of the sentence can't be the subject. (pause) I'd remind myself that the subject of the sentence will never be found in a prepositional phrase, so I'd mentally blot out the prepositional phrases from the sentence. (pause) Next, I'd ask myself who or what is doing the action in the sentence. (pause) I'd assume that the who or what is the subject of the sentence."

Before I could finish this last statement, Sima blurted out the correct answer. Students around her also smiled in satisfaction in coming to the answer themselves. Walking students through the mental process provides a good review and stresses the need for logic and patience in coming to conclusions.

CONCENTRATE ON PACE AND PRACTICE

I cannot stress enough the need for slowing down the pace and giving exercise work. What often seems like students' inability to learn is usually a mirror of fast-paced learning without the necessary practice. Pushing students to move along to the next rule (or concept, equation, law, or topic) triggers confusion when the current information isn't clear in their minds. Students need to spend time absorbing each concept and applying it. Many teachers, oblivious to the connection between pace and practice, don't see where they're going wrong.

For example, Mrs. G. complained to me that her fifth-grade class was stupid. "They just don't follow," she said. "I've been teaching the rules of commas the whole week, and they're not getting them." When I suggested she work with the kids at a slower pace, giving practice examples for each rule, she agreed to give it a try. Sure enough, the following week, Mrs. G. reported that the class grasped the rules. All they needed was an easier pace with more practice sessions.

GIVE STUDENTS AUTONOMY

The iconic William Glasser, in his book *The Quality School Teacher*, took the need for pace and practice even further, suggesting students learn mostly on their own. For instance, Glasser suggested students teach themselves math from textbooks, sitting in groups, and asking classmates for help when they need it. Before progressing to the next level of problems, students must show their mastery of the current level by solving new problems correctly while the teacher is watching. Students must be able to show and explain the process. Glasser asserted that this method of learning calls for one hundred percent accuracy and understanding.

A more modern version of Glasser's idea is the Khan Academy, created by Salman Khan in 2006. It offers a series of free interactive math curricula (also science, computer programming, history, art history, economics, and more) for students to master independently. The academy intentionally does away with one-size-fits-all classes. Without breathing down students' necks, the computer teacher on the site advances the students' education according to their progress, after they've taught themselves correctly and completed consecutive examples on a topic. The program sets challenges on par with the students' ability. When students get stuck on a problem, they can read a hint or watch a video and learn how to complete the task.

A tremendous bonus to this program is its tracking system. The teacher can see from a dashboard numerous data: which videos the students watched, when they paused them, which exercises they did, which examples they got wrong, how long they worked on them, and in which areas they faltered. In this way, teachers track students who are having a harder time and help those children tackle concepts that hinder them or set up a peer tutoring system. Similar to what transpired in Mrs. G's grammar class, the program shows that the kids who are slower at first, race along once they get a concept, catching up to the quick learners. Khan believes his program humanizes the classroom, freeing up time from ordinary lecturing for teachers to interact one hundred percent of class time with students.

If you think about it, an autodidactic approach makes sense, especially in subjects where students' strengths and talents vary. No one feels good when they can't keep up with the class. With the right textbooks, students can teach themselves any subject. The continual sense of accomplishment they feel after mastering a level engrosses them in the subject. What started out as "no man's land" turns into familiar ground which eventually feels steady and good and easy to build on. The advanced students also benefit from moving smoothly forward from topic to topic without the constraints of periods where they must sit through boring reviews or listen to peers asking the teacher questions irrelevant to their own learning.

Are you an adventurous teacher? Perhaps you might observe what happens when students study an instructive course independently or partly on their own. It works for my public speaking students who individually choose to learn particular speaking skills and implement them in their speeches. The personal feedback I offer prompts them to brush up on their weaker skills before delivering their next speech. Pleased with their progress, students feel they're headed to become distinguished toastmasters.

EXTEND WORK TIME

Any haste decreases the joy of learning. Think about it. If you want to enjoy your dinner, are you going to gulp it? When you're reading a good story, do you skim its pages? Of course not. When you want to enjoy something, you don't speed it up. You do the opposite—you slow it down! Letting kids lose themselves in a task offers them the time to learn what they can, at their own pace. Given this chance, students learn deeply, experimenting in their own fashion and coming up with marvelous results.

A real example from the classroom. Observing an art class for special education students, I couldn't imagine how they would settle down to paint. The teacher explained: "They come in here and they're haywire, but once they absorb themselves in the task, you'll see how they become intent on doing the job." Sure enough, when the bell rang at the end of the period, the kids protested, but when the teacher told them they may continue for another 40 minutes, they cheered and turned right back to their landscapes and turned out exceedingly creative work.

Why was that? Because losing oneself in a task is exceedingly pleasurable. When students get caught up in creation, they want to continue and see where it takes them. Having a time limit breaks their train of thought and pressures them to pass over opportunities. I think Willa Cather had it right when she wrote, "At any rate, that is happiness; to be dissolved into something complete and great" (*My Antonia*). We all crave the chance to forget the outside world and absorb ourselves in something meaningful.

How about setting aside a block of time every now and then for students to finish a task at their own pace. Imagine how they'll cherish that time and retain that experience. For instance, it might take a while for kids to work out a scientific experiment, or immerse themselves in a computer project, but once they have an idea and are working at it, why not let them continue for as long as possible: beyond the bell or bells? You might have to negotiate with other teachers to swap these chunks of time, but the rescheduling will prove worthwhile in the long run.

Don't make the mistake of thinking that if you're not always hurrying, you're already behind in teaching. To the contrary, when teachers retire their sense of urgency and recognize the learning process, they convey a sense of purpose. Students then know they're in class to focus and learn. Before you know it, students begin to catch on and develop good working habits.

Choose less to produce more. You won't regret it.

5

Promoting Discovery

"The art of teaching is the art of assisting discovery."—Mark Van Doren

"Obviously, it has to do with the strings," Robin says.

"Well, what about the strings?" Stacy inquires.

"They all look the same to me," Jerome says.

"Yeh, they're just a bunch of coils," Stacy remarks.

"But some are thicker and some are thinner," Robin points out.

"I see what you mean," Jerome says.

"They don't feel the same either," Robert says, plucking the strings.

"Look how these three are wound more times around the tuners than the others," Stacey remarks.

"You're right," Jerome notes. "Some strings are pulled tighter than others."

"Not so much tighter," Robert says, plucking at the guitar strings again.

"Maybe the sound changes by the way you strum the guitar," suggests Jerome.

"What do you mean by 'the way'?" Stacy asks.

"Maybe by how hard you strum them," Jerome responds.

"That would only affect the loudness," Robin says, "not the pitch."

And the group's conversation goes on. Mr. Leffler's music class is trying to determine which three factors affect the pitch of a string instrument. Each group is examining a basic six-string guitar with flat wound strings. They're plucking and strumming the strings, probing for answers, questioning each other's reasoning, and writing down assumptions.

Subsequent to this task, Mr. Leffler challenges his students to put their assumptions to the test by creating their own effective string instrument. Mr. Leffler provides rubber bands of various sizes and thicknesses and empty, large tissue boxes. Knowing they'll have to stretch the rubber bands to play them, groups stretch various bands over their tissue boxes and pluck at them to hear the different notes. Once they conclude that the bands stretched thinner and tighter create higher pitches, groups manipulate bands over their tissue boxes to create distinct sounds. A few groups stretch same-sized bands of various thicknesses and lengths over the tissue box. One group stretches various-sized bands of the same thickness over the tissue box. Still, another group stretches a combination of bands that vary in size and thickness over the tissue box.

Before long, all groups figure they can pick a tune more easily if they sequence the bands from the lowest sounding to the highest sounding. So that students can pick a tune better, Mr. Leffler hands out pencils that students slide under the bands on each end. To demonstrate the effectiveness of their instrument, group members proudly play a simple tune for the class. Finally, Mr. Leffler calls on students to describe the discoveries they made while designing their string instrument.

The key to promoting discovery is to have students take control of learning and come to their own conclusions. This experiment leads students to the conclusion that the length, thickness, and tension of the strings affect the pitch of a string instrument. Now that students get the basic idea of how a string instrument works, the guitar isn't just an instrument they're learning to play by rote. It's an instrument that makes sense in its design: Students understand how it's possible to pick tunes of their own. They're more eager to learn to play chords and scales. They're also way ahead when it comes to tuning the guitar strings.

Learning through discovery isn't just a smart way for students to learn, it's the natural way. In fact, discovering things is really your students' birthright. Think about it. After birth we're off on our own—to examine toys, to taste dirt, to try climbing a fence, to see if Mr. Tomskin, our dog, likes Jelly Bellies better than Kibbles—and we're allowed the pleasure of the discovery. But before long, we're thrown into an instruction environment where teachers and textbooks have already done the discovering for us, practically robbing us of the spectacular mental surge that comes along with *figuring out things on our own.*

The good news is that any lesson can be taught through discovery. How do you know you're promoting discovery in your classroom? Simply by conducting experiments or assigning tasks that require students to use the power of deduction to reach conclusions.

While we're on the topic of music, let's take a look at how Mr. Rivera conducts a guided discovery lesson on sound. Why don't you participate in this lesson and see how much you discover!

Mr. Rivera begins his lesson with a thought-provoking question: How is it possible to hear a conversation in the next room by pressing your ear to the wall when it's impossible to do so by standing right next to the wall?

While students are pondering this, Mr. Rivera places a ticking clock on his desk.

He gives the definition of sound. Sound is energy that moves through and vibrates molecules in the matter. Sound travels through gas (air), solid, or liquid. He asks students to stand quietly nearby and listen to the clock's ticking. Then, the class takes turns pressing their ear against the surface of the wooden desk to hear the clock ticking. "Which ticking sounds louder?" Mr. Rivera asks them. Next, the class holds a wooden stick against the clock and listens to the clock's ticking from the other end of the stick. What do they conclude? Is air or wood a better conductor of sound?

Mr. Rivera teaches the class the following: The tighter packed the molecules, the easier sound can travel through it. Density is a measure of how tightly molecules are in the matter. The denser the matter, the tighter the molecules are in the matter.

Mr. Rivera asks the class what can they conclude about the molecules in the desk and the stick versus the molecules in the air? Which matter is denser?

Next, Mr. Rivera sends students off to listen to the ticking of analog wristwatches through different materials in the classroom. Students hold the watches against textbooks, plastic binders, glass beakers, computers, locker doors and listen to the ticking from the other side.

They record their findings on a table:

How Ticking Sounds through Wood, Plastic, Glass, and Metal

Material:	wood	plastic	glass	metal
very loud				
loud				
soft				
very soft				

Now Mr. Rivera asks the class questions like, "Is plastic a better conductor of sound than wood? Is glass a better conductor of sound than wood? Is metal a better conductor of sound than glass? What did you figure about the molecules in the glass versus the molecules in wood? The molecules in metal versus the molecules in glass? Which material is the best conductor of sound? Which is the worst? Which material absorbs the most sound? The least? Which material is the densest? The least?"

Based on the information his students discovered so far, Mr. Rivera continues to encourage them to explore sound. He asks the following question, "Which solid matter is best to sound-proof a room?" Students form groups and are given the following: an alarm clock, a shoe box, and different types of "insulation" to experiment with, ranging from newspapers and thick cloth to small sandbags. Students test the solid matter among the materials to see which is best at dampening the sound of the alarm in the box.

Afterwards, groups are given new piles of "insulation" (each group receives different materials), i.e., egg cartons, bubble wrap, wood chips, and foam. Using their deductions from the previous experiment, students are asked to form a hypothesis about which new material will be best at dampening the sound of the alarm within the box. Mr. Rivera calls upon one member from each group to present and test his group's hypothesis in front of the class. Afterwards, students write scientific theories they've learned based on conclusions of their successful experiments. Then Mr. Rivera reviews these theories and critiques them if necessary.

Toward the end of class, Mr. Rivera's students recap what they discovered about sound, namely that:

- Sound travels faster through solids than through air. Mr. Rivera adds that sound waves travel about thirteen times faster in wood than air (and four times faster in water!).
- Sound travels at different speeds through different solids.
- The density of matter depends on how tightly packed the molecules are found in the matter.
- The denser the matter, the better the matter will conduct sound.
- The less dense the matter, the better the matter will absorb sound.

To check that students can apply this information about sound, Mr. Rivera asks them to write scientific answers to at least four questions on a worksheet.

Questions on Sound

- Why do you think a person who puts his ear to the ground can hear the hoof beat of horses miles away?
- Why do you hear your humming louder when you cover your ears with your hands?
- How come you can sometimes hear your own heart beating in your ears?
- Can you explain how a stethoscope works?

- How is it possible to create an effective mechanical telephone that carries sound without using a tube?
- Why do you suppose your voice sounds different to you on a recording?
- Why are bells made out of metal and not wood?
- What do you predict will happen if you place your phone in an empty glass and set its alarm to wake you in the morning? Will the alarm sound softer or louder? Why?
- How do earplugs block sound?
- Which do you think absorbs more sound in a room, heavy clothing or light clothing? Is it easier for a speaker to project his voice when the audience is wearing winter or summer clothing? Why?
- Why is there no sound in outer space? (Outer space is a vacuum. The molecules are too widely spaced to carry sound.)

As you see, many of these questions are designed to make the class notice how science is actually knowledge we depend on in daily life. Students can figure out answers by putting two and two together. Exclamations of "Oh, I know why!" or "This is so cool!" as students survey the questions testify to the impression the discovery lesson has made on the class. Throughout the lesson, students experience light-bulb moments that keep the discovery alive and pertinent. Even as they answer the worksheet questions, students are making new connections.

Before Mr. Rivera ends the lesson, he leaves the class to contemplate the following questions:

- How fast do you think sound travels through a liquid?
- Why do you think sound travels faster and farther on a rainy day?
- Do you think sounds travels faster on a foggy day than a clear day?
- Which do you suppose travels quicker, sound waves or light waves?
- Do you see a balloon burst before you hear it burst, or vice versa?

How long do you think Mr. Rivera's class will remember this lesson on sound? For a day? A week? A month? For the rest of their lives? It depends on the individual student, his participation, his reviewing, and his ability to build on information. Nevertheless, you can bet that learning through discovery is far more successful at embedding knowledge into students' minds than listening to a teacher's lecture or reading information in a book. Moreover, learning through discovery prompts students to explore the subject further through their own curiosity and experimentation.

Promote Discovery Across the Board

Whether you teach music, science, computers, English, art, history, or math, or whether you're addressing a class of 34 in an inner-city school or 12 students in a suburb of Santa Cruz, know that your students crave discovery lessons. Worried about the time frame? No need. While some discovery lessons can last a week, others can take ten minutes. Not sure you care for the grouping? Then assign independent discovery tasks. The following tasks promote discovery for diverse subjects, several calling for independent work. Notice how all these tasks call for deductive reasoning. With discovering the reward, students will embrace these tasks and implore you for more.

DISCOVERY TASKS FOR MULTIPLE SUBJECTS

- Use two search engines (such as Bing and Google) for the same research. Why might someone prefer one search engine over the other? Which search engine do you prefer? Why?
- Read two fictional stories by the same author. What do you notice about the author's writing style? What, if any skill, do you want to emulate?
- Write a paragraph about *Savage Carrot* by Ingrid Tomey without using the words is, are, am, was, were, be, being, or been. How often do you find yourself substituting these words? Which words do you use as substitutes? Do those words have something in common? Do you like the result of your paragraph? Why? Why do you think creative writers like to keep away from being verbs?
- Sketch this picture upside down. How did your drawing turn out? Were you surprised? What do you think interferes with your drawing as you sketch a picture right side up? How might an artist see the world differently than other people? Knowing this, how can you improve your drawing skills?
- Read two current events articles from different newspapers on the same topic. What do you discover about journalism? What do you discover about the particular news reporter? How has this discovery influenced your opinion about what you read?
- Working with a partner, design four model paper airplanes. Test the airplanes' flight. Which model flies farthest? Why? Record the distances of each model and graph your data. How do you suppose the design of an airplane affects its flight?
- What do our gestures say about us? Watch clips of three famous speakers giving speeches before an audience. Do their gestures matter? How so? Do you see gestures common among the three speakers? powerful gestures? confident gestures? charismatic gestures? What can you conclude about the gestures of highly effective speakers? Which gestures would you adopt?
- Get ready to toss a coin 20 times. How many times do you think you'll get heads? tails? Go ahead and try it. Tally the results. What did you discover? Now what if you tossed two coins 20 times? How often do you predict you will get two heads? Two tails? One of each? Go ahead and try it with a partner. Tally the results. Which result came up the most often? Why was this result more probable than others?
- Write a story about a spooky moment in your life while listening to a piece of absolute music such as Bach's *Art of the Fugue*. How did the music influence your writing? Next, try writing the same account while listening to program music such as Mussorgsky's *Night on Bald Mountain*. How was your writing different? Why? Now get together with your group and discuss your experiences. What did you discover about these two genres of music?
- Find the lyrics to your favorite song online. Print the song and circle any prepositional phrases you find. Read the song without the prepositional phrases. What did you discover?
- Do this experiment with a partner. Place a cylinder of clay on a flat surface. Balance a book on the clay for six seconds and record the book's weight and the clay's new height. Keep adding books on the clay, removing them, recording the books' total weight and the clay's height until the clay collapses. How did the clay behave with

each added book? What did you discover about the clay? Based on what you know about brittle and ductile materials, is the clay a brittle or ductile material? Do you think steel is a brittle or ductile material? How do you think bridges react to stress and strain?

- Sketch a scene to illustrate the meaning of each sentence on this worksheet. Do your images look amusing? What did you discover about these sentences? What if I tell you the sentences you sketched all contain misplaced modifiers? What do you think is the definition of a misplaced modifier? How would you go about correcting the misplaced modifiers in these sentences?
- Take out your favorite photograph and the description you wrote on it. Swap your photograph with your partner's. Write what you see and imagine what is happening in your partner's photograph. Take into account every detail. When you're finished, read your descriptions to each other. What do you think of your partner's description? Does your partner's description do your photograph justice? Is there anything your partner left out? Did your partner mention something important that enhances the meaning of your photograph? What did you discover about objective versus subjective writing? Will you revise your description? How?
- Your teacher asked you to make a new student feel at home in school. This means including him in every aspect of your day. Think of three ways flexibility on your part would help you carry out your mission. What changes might you make? How does thinking about these changes make you feel? What did you discover about your flexibility level? On a scale of 1–10 how would you measure your flexibility? How important is flexibility? What can you do on a daily basis to improve your flexibility?
- Go to the class's email. Check out the link to the video clip that's sent to your group about an event in WWII. During or after your viewing, write the key points of the video in complete sentences. Then write the upshot of the video (for example: American naval forces defeat the Japanese navy at the Battle of Norway on June 4–7, 1942). What did you discover about the event that you didn't learn in class? Share your responses with group members. What about the video brought this discovery to light? Has this discovery changed your viewpoint about something or someone during that period in history?

Discovery thrills us to the core. It helps us build on previous knowledge with playfulness instead of a sense of chore. Giving us new eyes, discovery propels us to embrace learning and celebrate life. When the class feels they're on the threshold of discovery, you don't see greater joy. And the best thing about discovery? We don't need to discover great worlds to appreciate that the universe has vast treasures to offer us. With each discovery, in the classroom, scientific or otherwise, students' awe grows and they can't help but share what they know with others.

Awaken students to discovery and they'll embark upon it for the rest of their lives.

6

Blossoming with Bloom

"I cannot teach anybody anything; I can only make them think."—Socrates

Can you answer these questions?

- What is sensational news?
- Why do people like sensational news?
- Would you want to be the subject of a sensational story? Why/why not?
- Why is sensational news so fleeting in its entertainment?
- Do you think something is wrong with enjoying sensational news? Why/why not? Can you make up a sensational story of your own? What would it sound like?

If you could answer these questions, you have demonstrated your ability to work your way up Bloom's Taxonomy.

What Is Bloom's Taxonomy?

Bloom's Taxonomy (or Bloom's Levels of Taxonomy), published in 1956, is a hierarchy that distinguishes between low level questioning and higher level questioning. The lower level questions test for knowledge, comprehension, and application of material. The higher level questions test for analysis, synthesis, and evaluation (critical thinking). Bloom created the taxonomy to show teachers how to build students' thinking skills.

Is Bloom's Taxonomy Relevant Today?

The relevance of this taxonomy is timeless. Direct and simple to understand, Bloom's Taxonomy revolutionized my method of questioning in the classroom. It trained me to gear my lessons toward higher level thinking. It taught me to think deeper when planning lessons and to expect deeper thinking from students too. A revision of this taxonomy was published in 2001 to adapt to newer understandings of learning. The concept of Bloom's Taxonomy basically remains the same but the levels read in verb form, a few of the levels are renamed, and the top two levels are reversed in order of complexity. The difference between the two taxonomies are presented in the following chart.

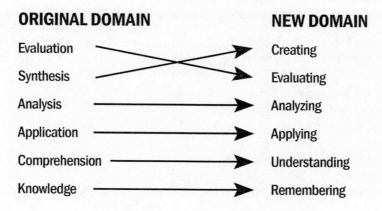

Original Domain/New Domain

Do Students Respond Well to the Taxonomy?

You better believe it! Not surprisingly, they gravitate to the higher level questions. In fact, studies revealed that asking higher level questions leads students to respond at greater length and at higher levels (M. Mahlios and D'Angelo, 1983). Accordingly, the higher you climb this hierarchy with your students, the more rewarding the experience!

Why the Staircase?

This staircase (hierarchy) for Bloom's Taxonomy indicates how each level of the taxonomy is a stepping stone to the next. Consequently, the thinking involved on each higher level of the taxonomy also includes the thought process of the lower level(s). Therefore, keep this in mind: Whenever you increase the rigor with Bloom's Taxonomy, you challenge students more than the average teacher.

Ready to check out Bloom's Taxonomy in its rising glory? Let's begin the climb!

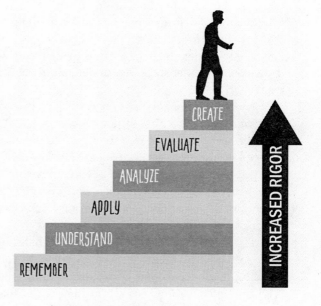

The hierarchy of Bloom's Taxonomy.

The Six Levels of Bloom's Taxonomy

Remembering

This level calls for memory retrieval. Either the student remembers (the fact, definition, rule, sequence, words, tune etc.) or doesn't.

Questions/instructions that call for remembering:

- Who wrote *David Copperfield*?
- What is the definition of irony?
- What's the rule in addition for carrying a number?
- Identify the five stages of sleep.
- Can you recite the poem "The Violet" by heart?
- What is the capital of Spain?
- What are signs of internal bleeding?
- How many feet are there in a yard?
- How long did the Renaissance Period last?
- What are the stages of photosynthesis?
- What is six times eight?
- Can you sing "This Land Is Your Land" by Woody Guthrie?
- How many syllables are there in the haiku form?
- How do you spell privilege?

To be sure, the knowledge level can't be skipped. The information has to be known. You can't build upon information that's not there. The knowledge level, however, typifies the lowest level of learning because it does not ensure comprehension. For example, Scott can memorize lines of a Shakespearean sonnet without knowing their meaning. Nancy might recite the rules of a fire drill without having an inkling of how to follow them. Miranda might define metamorphosis but not understand what happens during that stage. Many teachers fool themselves into believing that if a student can recite the words, she has discerned the meaning; if she can provide the answer, she comprehends the question; and if she can name the stage, she understands the function. Unfortunately, that's not always true.

That's why the aim for every educator is to persuade students to think beyond rote learning. What's startling, if not shocking, is that according to Bloom's studies, teachers' questions for the most part fell into the Remembering category. This means that learning stopped at this base level in most classrooms! Studies today show that not much has changed. Even after decades of research proving the benefits of higher order thinking, a more recent study (Tienken et al., 2009) which collected data from 98 certified teachers in 13 schools, exhibited that 76% of the questions asked in grades 3–12 fell into the lower order category.

The consequence, you can imagine, is that students become programmed to memorize information—providing the teacher with the "correct" answer but often without understanding it. Henry Adams, grandson of John Quincy Adams, had it right when he said, "Nothing in education is so astonishing as the amount of ignorance it accumulates in the form of facts." Over a hundred years later, Adams' words still prove true in schools across the nation.

What's even more disturbing is that often the information students process on this Remembering level is so misconstrued that students end up memorizing gibberish. Beverly Cleary brings this notion to a comical light in her book *Ramona the Pest* when her plucky character, Ramona, listens to her teacher singing "The Star Spangled Banner" and mistakes the phrase "by the dawn's early light" for "by the dawnzer lee light." Assuming that a dawnzer is a lamp, Ramona later shows off her new word to her big sister Beezus suggesting that Beezus turn on the dawnzer to help her read. What a blow it is for Ramona's sensitive ego when she finds out her mistake!

Ramona's mistake is classic. I remember how my sister got a taste of what it felt like to be in Ramona's shoes. Back in the day, my sisters and I enjoyed performing choirs for any audience who would listen. Our favorite song was "Small Piece of Heaven" by Abie Rotenberg. The chorus of the song speaks about the potential of the small piece of heaven in everyone's heart. Words in the chorus state, "It will sparkle and shine if we each do our part to reach out and touch it with love." Once, upon belting out the conclusion of the song for prestigious company, my younger sister, Sara, then no more than a baby, sang, "It will smarkle and shine if we each do our part to reach out and touch it with gloves!" Completely taken aback by the ensuing laughter, my sister was clearly unaware of her mix up. Obviously, she was mimicking what she thought were the correct words.

When it comes down to it, no child wants to memorize without knowing. We all seek to learn things the right way. We educators owe it to our students to test their understanding. And so we come to the next level of Bloom's Taxonomy.

UNDERSTANDING

The Understanding level ensures that the student masters the meaning of what he's taught. The student must describe, interpret, explain, or otherwise show his comprehension of the material.

Questions/instructions that call for understanding:

- What kind of person was Stalin?
- What happens in Act 1 of *Our Town*?
- Does this graph show a function? How do you know?
- Explain the process of digestion in your own words.
- How does the author interpret a balanced life?
- According to the data table, how many trades of IBM were made?
- Write the meaning of the lyric in simple prose.
- What is the song "Richard Cory" about?
- State the information given in the pie chart.
- What are the consequences of living in Gattaca as portrayed in the movie?
- What is the advantage of a Pilates workout?
- Sort the following elements into metal and non-metal categories.
- How would you interpret this political cartoon?
- According to this advertisement, what's the benefit of eating Cheerios?

Once students prove their comprehension, the teacher is in business. Students have acquired new learning. But once again, the teacher cannot sit back on her laurels. While this comprehension level is vital to achieve, it demonstrates the lowest level of understanding. In short, comprehending something doesn't guarantee that the student can employ the knowledge in new situations. Meaning, we cannot presume that if Ian can explain a function he can practice it, that if Mindy comprehends what she sees, she will recognize it in a new context, or that if Steve understands a concept, he can apply it to his life or perceive it elsewhere.

You know the common saying, "Knowledge is power" (Francis Bacon)? Well, knowledge is power only when students put it to use in some way. The teacher's complacency at this understanding level shortchanges her students. Testing our students' application of knowledge is paramount at this point of the taxonomy.

APPLYING

For a student to be proficient at this level, he must prove to his teacher that he can use the information. The application level checks the student's ability to put learned functions, concepts, theories, or methods into practice, to apply them to personal life, or recognize them elsewhere. The educator has to keep confirming his students' expertise on this application level or the knowledge loses its purpose.

Questions/instructions that call for applying:

- How would you demonstrate good interpersonal skills in this situation?
- Using litmus paper, test two solutions to determine whether they're acidic, basic, or neutral.
- Edit this video by splitting and cropping it.
- What two metaphors does Langston Hughes use in his poem "Dreams"?
- Is Mrs. Johnson's deal blackmail? Why or why not?
- According to the food pyramid, list the foods in your lunch in order of priority.
- Which type of law is Michael breaking if he throws trash onto the highway?
- Which character can you identify with most in *All My Sons*? How so?
- How would you have responded to the Whiskey Rebellion?
- Calculate how much money Jimmy would accumulate if he keeps $2,000 in the bank for 10 years at a 4.5 percent annual interest rate.
- Why would the chant, "Rain, rain go away…" be non-existent in the story, "All Summer in a Day"?
- Find ten vivid verbs in the article "Corruption: Now You See It, Now You Don't."
- Would you have supported the progressives had you lived during the Progressive Era? Why or why not?
- Based on what we learned about echoes, why do you think many movie theaters cover their walls with carpet or fabric?

Officially, at the Application level, the teacher has taught the material effectively. Letting students master application gives them ownership of their education. But what a shame to stop here! Want to really motivate your class? Get them to analyze. Everybody will want to try their hand at it!

ANALYZING

At the Analyzing level we come to a higher level of thinking which starts to give students credit for their magnificent brainpower! Analyzing facilitates a deeper understanding and naturally causes students to develop an intrigue in the subject matter. Why? Because as Richard Feynman, the Nobel laureate, put it, "Everything is interesting if you go into it deeply enough."

An expert at analyzing knows how to dissect information. He breaks down information into different forms. He detects disparities, forms categories, compares and contrasts, finds links, recognizes patterns and hidden meanings, distinguishes motives, and draws inferences. Creativity isn't important at this level, just pure logic.

Questions/instructions that call for analyzing:

- What instruction is missing in this gingerbread recipe?
- Can you create three distinct categories for these family photographs?
- What is an underlying theme of *Sarah, Plain and Tall?*
- What do you presume would happen to the economy if all farmers switched to growing organic crops?
- Which provides more stimulation for the skeletal system: biking or jogging? How do you know?
- What do the square, rectangle, parallelogram, and trapezoid have in common?
- After studying civilian life during wars in many countries, what can you conclude about a war's effect on civilians?
- What's the difference between being polite and being "two-faced"?
- How would you place the numbers 1–9 in the 3x3 grid so that none of the columns, rows, or diagonals share the same sum?
- According to our definition of creativity, are the Stone Age paintings depicted in *Painters of the Caves* by Patricia Lauber creative?
- How does the editorial fall short?
- What is bound to happen when you pour the Epsom salt into this mixture? How do you know?
- Identify an important motive Wilbur exhibits in *Charlotte's Web*.
- What evidence can you find to prove that some kinds of fungi are good for the environment?

Once students become good at analyzing, they realize that just because they don't see something at first, it doesn't mean it's not there. As a result, the world opens for them. They begin to analyze everything, from literature to advertisements. They take the information they see and make the most of it. But just because they can analyze doesn't mean they can form solid opinions—which brings us to the next level of Bloom's Taxonomy.

For the Evaluating level, permit me to remind you of your good old school days when you and your buddies got all riled up shouting opinions in Mr. Hamilton's class. You were bent on getting your point across because you had something to say! Perhaps the teacher kept trying to calm everyone down, with or without success. But one thing was for sure, you couldn't convince anyone of anything unless you had some kind of evidence to back up your opinion.

To ensure your students can take the information they've analyzed and make sound judgments, you want to test their evaluation skills. Exercising this level of the taxonomy, the student effectively learn how to criticize, debate ideas, size up situations, give solid opinions, judge what's best, weigh options, lend support, and help others come to decisions.

EVALUATING

This level tests the student's ability to make judgments based on specific criteria. A master at this level bases his evaluation not on bias but on objective thought, although he may point out the bias behind notions.

Questions/instructions that call for evaluating:

- What is *The Canterbury Tales'* most remarkable message? Please explain.
- What do you consider a justified punishment for someone who sprays graffiti on personal property? For someone who sprays graffiti on public property? Please explain.
- Evaluate President Reagan's speech in form of its message and delivery.
- Would you agree that one's personality is determined by birth order? Why or why not?
- Is Citizen Kane's behavior in this scene an example of good citizenship? Why or why not?
- Select the most effective solution for helping the homeless. Please explain your choice.
- Might there be a better title for *The Little Prince*? Please explain.
- What are the pros and cons of sitting in the front of the classroom?
- Did Sydney Carton make the right decision at the end of the story? Why or why not?
- What's worse—to flatter a person or intimidate him to get what you want? Please explain.
- Which is the most vital natural resource? Please explain.
- Francis Beaumont said, "You are no better than you should be." Do you agree with his belief? Why or why not?
- What is it that determines the age level or age appropriateness of a book?
- What is something you think Golding leaves unresolved, unexplored, unexplained, or unanswered in *Lord of the Flies*?

And now, we come to the highest order of thinking in Bloom's Taxonomy—my students' favorite, the Creating level. Logic would tell you this level is quite taxing on the brain, but because it provides the most freedom, it's also the most fun! If you have a great imagination, you naturally gravitate to this level in your teaching. The good news is that most students have great imaginations and love to respond to questions of this level when given the chance!

CREATING

Creating has been determined to be the highest level on the taxonomy because it requires abstract thought. What is the purpose of creating? Creating allows people to invent things, reinvent things, revolutionize systems or possibly the world. Students who think at this level hypothesize, compose, invent, design, and develop things. Several variations or outcomes are possible to questions on this level.

Questions/instructions that call for creating:

- If Abraham Lincoln applied for a position in this school, what job would you give him? Why?
- How would the world be different if it shared a universal time zone?
- Devise an experiment to show diffusion/osmosis in action.
- Make up a different ironic ending to "The Ransom of Red Chief."
- Compose a song that will help you remember the layers of the earth along with their properties.
- Put on a skit to show the influence of peer pressure in our daily lives.
- Design a board game that puts knowledge of multiplication to the test.

- Write an epilogue to *Lord of the Flies*.
- Design a fake web page advertising the play within the play of *Hamlet*.
- Write an interview between yourself and Plato.
- Create a mnemonic to remember the four types of chemical reactions.
- How would you create a print advertisement for Miracle Whip?
- Can you think of another test to see whether a person is right-brained or left-brained?
- Write a journal entry that might have been written by Paul Revere.

Using All Levels of Bloom's Taxonomy to Develop a Lesson

The following illustrates questions for three lessons covering all levels of Bloom's Taxonomy. Picture the staircase in your mind as the questions work their way from low order thinking to higher order thinking. Prepare questions for your lessons using all the levels so you can easily make your way up or down the taxonomy.

QUESTIONS FOR A LESSON ON THE PLEDGE OF ALLEGIANCE

Remembering: Recite the Pledge of Allegiance.

Understanding: What does it mean to pledge one's allegiance? What is the Pledge of Allegiance saying? Write the meaning of the Pledge of Allegiance in a short paragraph.

Applying: What does living in America mean to you? Do you feel allegiance to the United States of America? Do the words of the Pledge of Allegiance express your feelings toward America?

Analyzing: What does showing allegiance to our country do for us? What does it do for our country? What does our allegiance mean to the rest of the world?

Evaluating: Do you think it should be mandatory for public schools to recite the Pledge of Allegiance daily? Why or why not? Do you think it's a sign of disrespect toward our country if someone refuses to recite the Pledge of Allegiance? How about if someone refuses to stand while reciting the Pledge of Allegiance? Why or why not?

Creating: Write your own Pledge of Allegiance to the United States of America. Besides for pledging our allegiance, what are some ways we can portray our allegiance to the United States of America? If you had access to any resource, how would you show your allegiance to your country?

QUESTIONS FOR A LESSON ABOUT EXCLUSION

Remembering: What's the definition of exclude?

Understanding: What does it mean when someone feels excluded? What does it mean when a group excludes others? What does it mean when a group is exclusive?

Applying: Did you ever feel excluded? How so? Did you ever exclude others? How so?

Analyzing: Why do people exclude others? Do you think there's exclusion in this class? How so?

Evaluating: Do you think it's okay to exclude people who want to join your group? Why or why not? Do you think cliques should be broken? Why or why not?

Creating: How can we make people feel included instead of excluded? Are there any class rules we can establish to ensure that everyone feels included?

QUESTIONS ON NORMAN ROCKWELL'S OIL PAINTING "THE PROBLEM WE ALL LIVE WITH" (1964)

Remembering: What do you see in the painting?

Understanding: What's happening in this painting? What might be the story in the painting?

Applying: How did you react to the painting? Why? How would you have reacted if you were in Ruby Bridge's shoes?

Analyzing: What is "the problem we all live with" as depicted by Norman Rockwell in the painting? How does Norman Rockwell impact his theme?

Evaluating: Do you think "the problem we all live with" still exists today in some form? How so? Do you think it's a grave problem? Why or why not?

Creating: What scene might Norman Rockwell have painted today to depict a problem in our society? Please explain. Can you sketch or paint that scene? What suggestions do you have to solve the problem?

GAUGING YOUR STUDENTS' LEVEL DURING A LESSON

You might prepare many questions for each level so that you can spend more time on one level if necessary. While teaching, employ the taxonomy to gauge the level of student understanding. When students are foggy in their answer to a higher level question, ask a lower level question to see where students are missing information. The converse is true too. If students only have to give little thought to your questions on a particular level or seem bored by them, proceed to a higher level.

There are other questions an educator might have before exercising Bloom's Taxonomy.

IS THE TAXONOMY A GOOD GUIDE FOR SLOWER LEARNING CLASSES?

Should educators stick to lower level questions for the slower learners? You'd think so, right? Wrong! Educators mistakenly believe that the complexity of higher order thinking should be reserved for the fast learners. Bloom found, however, that the only stumbling block for slower learners is the time factor. Slower learners need more time to process and sort information. One of my students figured this out for herself: "I have difficulty internalizing information in a short span of time," she told me. "All I really need is time." Too bad she came to this realization in the twelfth grade, thinking all through the years that she was mentally inferior to her classmates.

Given sufficient time to register information or to complete a task, slower learners can successfully reach higher thinking levels of the taxonomy. In studies, Bloom discovered that once slower learners grasped each concept, they were able, in some cases, to outdo the faster learners in their achievement! As a matter of fact, Bloom believed that most human beings can learn any given task if they want to and if they're properly prepared for it.

IS THERE A DIFFERENCE BETWEEN A MORE DIFFICULT QUESTION AND A MORE COMPLEX ONE?

Yes. A question can be made more difficult on each level but not more complex. How so? A more difficult question includes more thinking on the same level while a more complex question means jumping to the next level of the taxonomy. Teachers often think they're deepening thinking skills by making questions more difficult instead of more complex.

The following table displays the difference between same level questions, more difficult questions on the same level, and more complex questions which jump to the next level. The difficult question includes two tasks on the level instead of one. Do more difficult questions serve a purpose? Certainly, but only if you want to see more effort or practice on a particular level. Use more complex questions when you think your students are ready to think on a higher level.

Difficult Versus Complex Questions for Bloom's Taxonomy

Bloom's Taxonomy	On the Same Level	More Difficult, on the Same Level	More Complex Level/Next Level
Remembering	List the causes of World War I.	List the causes and effects of World War I.	Explain the causes of World War I. **(Understanding)**
Understanding	How is Sadao courageous in "The Enemy"?	How are Sadao and Hana courageous characters in "The Enemy"?	Can you identify with one of these courageous characters? Why or why not? **(Applying)**
Applying	Name an action within the movie that demonstrates Newton's First Law of Motion.	Name an action in the movie that demonstrates Newton's First Law of Motion and Second Law of Motion.	Can you mention an action within this movie that contradicts the laws of physics? **(Analyzing)**
Analyzing	Analyze the artist's use of color and shadow to express mood.	Analyze the artist's use of color and shadow to express mood and depth.	Does the artist do a good job in using color and shadow? Explain. **(Evaluating)**
Evaluating	Is the electoral college system a fair way of electing the president? Why or why not?	Is the electoral college system more democratic than England's parliamentary system? Why or why not?	Can you think of a fairer system than the electoral college system for electing the president? **(Creating)**
Creating	Design a brochure for an Asian country including tourist attractions, and photographs.	Design a brochure for an Asian country including tourist attractions, photographs, and tips for tourists.	

Would You Like to Check the Level of Questioning Your Students Prefer?

Here's an idea: Prepare questions to a popular fairytale using all the levels of Bloom's Taxonomy, and ask students to circle the questions they like best. You can keep the questions together for each level or mix them. In any case, I guarantee most students will circle the higher-level questions!

The following displays questions for the fairy tale *Little Red Riding Hood* that run the gamut of the taxonomy. (You would, obviously, omit the titles of the categories when presenting the questions to your class.)

Remembering:
Why was Little Red Riding Hood going to visit Grandmother?
What did Mother warn Little Red Riding Hood not to do along the way?
What did Little Red Riding Hood promise her mother?

Understanding:
How does the wolf trick Grandmother?
How does the wolf trick Little Red Riding Hood?
How did the woodcutter's job come in handy for saving Little Red Riding Hood?

Applying:
How do you suppose Mother would have reacted if she learned that Little Red Riding Hood spoke to a stranger?
How would you have reacted if you were in Little Red Riding Hood's place when she learned of the wolf's intention?
Who might the wolf represent in real life today?

Analyzing:
When did Little Red Riding Hood realize she was in trouble? How do you know?
What inference can you make based on Little Red Riding Hood's ignorance of the wolf's identity at Grandma's house?
What's the turning point of the story? How do you know?

Evaluating:
How do you think her encounter with the wolf affected Little Red Riding Hood?
Do you think Little Red Riding Hood is an appropriate story to read to small children? Why or why not?
Why is this fairytale a favorite for so many children?

Creating:
Rewrite the story from the wolf's point of view letting the reader in on his motive and thought.
How would the story be different if it were set in the modern day?
Create a rap in which Little Red Riding Hood turns the tables on the wolf.

Want to See If Your Students Can Grasp the Distinction Between the Levels of the Hierarchy?

Ask students to study the categories above (with their titles) and to ascertain the difference between them. Then challenge students to model Bloom's Taxonomy using another fairytale of their choice (for example, *The Three Little Pigs, Cinderella, Goldilocks, Peter Rabbit*). My students go to town with this activity, sometimes writing sets of questions for three or four fairytales!

The core to building a solid education, Bloom's Taxonomy will never go out of style. The magic of the taxonomy sparks as soon as you use it in the classroom. All of a sudden, lessons become more intriguing, participation increases, creativity goes wild. A staple for all tests, the higher levels of thinking takes the doldrums out of test days. Throughout the year, I raise the learning in the class with the taxonomy, which never lets me down. Let your year blossom with Bloom's Taxonomy and you will wonder how you ever managed without it!

7

Giving Homework a Brain

"The worst thing a kid can say about homework is that it's too hard."—Henry Jenkins

"Is this your holiday homework?" asked Sarah. "Don't do it, Rose! And Eve will write you a note to say it's iniquitous to give eight-year-olds homework. You will, won't you, Eve?"

"I could never spell 'iniquitous,' Sarah darling!"

"Hot concrete," said Rose mournfully, prodding her porridge.

"Write this," ordered Saffron. "'The ancient Egyptians are all dead. Their days are very quiet.' Porridge is meant to look like hot concrete. Eat it up.... Read the next question!"...

"'What would you say if you bumped into Tutankhamen in the street?'"

"'Sorry!'" said Sarah at once. "Put that."

"We have to answer in proper sentences."

"'Sorry, but it was your fault! You were walking sideways!'" (Hilary McKay, *Indigo's Star*, 17–18).

Got Homework?

Students are behind on it, have to admit they didn't do it, or toil through it. Across the country, homework constitutes the worst part of every child's evening. So how do we get rid of the long sighs, the half-hearted attempts, the doldrums of doing homework? How do we give homework a good rep? By making it matter.

MAKE HOMEWORK MATTER

First, to get students to do their homework more enthusiastically, it must not represent an extension of the same work they've been doing in school. Homework assignments should involve critical thinking skills where students' responses will vary. Students are drawn to do this type of homework since it compels deeper thinking and creativity.

Understandably, sometimes teachers must strengthen the knowledge of concepts by giving homework that calls for repeating similar functions. In this case, always "throw in" challenge questions or verbal problems to invigorate the task. Instruct students to prepare explanations for problems that elicit uniform answers. In this way, students have no incentive to copy homework, and they do their homework for understanding. Additionally, the review in class becomes much more rewarding when students share explanations rather than simply supplying the correct answer.

62

GIVE "POWER-FULL" HOMEWORK ASSIGNMENTS

Not given much say in the grown-up world, students crave the power to influence agendas, even imaginary ones. Empower students with homework assignments that rely upon mature, high ranking or superhuman decision-making. Students will do these assignments with relish and astonish you with their creative resourcefulness.

Examples of "Power-full" Assignments:

- Following a tradition begun by President Ronald Reagan, every outgoing U.S. president writes a personal note to the incoming president, giving advice or encouragement. Let's begin Reagan's tradition earlier on in history. You are President Franklin Delano Roosevelt about to vacate his office. Write a message to your successor, Harry S. Truman. Be sure to take into account Roosevelt's accomplishments and the challenges facing America at the time.

- For homework, you will receive a copy of a student's ungraded economics test. Pretend you are the teacher. Determine how many points each part of the test should be worth before grading the paper. Review and grade the test fairly. You may give partial credit. Please write specific praise for three correct answers. Comment on why you're taking off credit for at least two incorrect answers. Finally, put the student's score on the paper.

- Research castles during the Middle Ages and write a 400-word report on castles and life in the castle. Then write a 300-word report about which four current-day amenities you'd implement in castle life that would make life more pleasurable but wouldn't detract from the charm of the era.

- You've just been hired to protect the citizens of the United States against identity theft. Design a fraud prevention program that will go into effect immediately for the entire country.

- You are a judge chosen to award the story of the year. Give a top literary prize to one of the stories we've read this year. Write an essay discussing three reasons for your selection.

- You are the defense attorney for Madame Defarge. How will you defend her? Write an opening statement for her trial that will sway the most stoic jury in favor of her acquittal.

- Please examine the mayor's preliminary budget for next fiscal year for New York City. What would you do differently in the mayor's shoes in budget spending? Which of the following departments would you give more money to? Less money? To the Education Department? Police Department? Fire Department? Public Safety Department? Parks and Recreation Department? Why? On a spreadsheet, design a budget that divides $84.67 billion among these departments, and write a 500-word essay justifying your reasoning.

- The faculty asked you to design report cards. What kind of evaluation system will you implement? How will your system better affect education in this school? Provide a sample of your report card and a brief essay explaining the rationale of its content.

- You desperately want to join Shay's Rebellion. Please write a resumé (including a cover letter) that describes why you qualify as a Shaysite and what distinguishes you from the other insurgents applying for admittance.

- Create a tutorial using Microsoft Office PowerPoint on congruence, proof, and constructions. Include action buttons, three images, and one video clip.
- You have the influence to alter one program in this school. Which program do you choose? How will you alter it? Write your response in a respectful proposal to the Dean's Office. Try to get at least 20 signatures from peers who favor your proposal.
- If you were given unlimited funds to better the world, how would you spend it? Please explain your logic in a 350–500-word essay.
- If you could cure one disease in this world, what would it be? Why? Include explanations of the urgent nature of the disease and how it affects the body.
- As a city planner, you are hired to redesign your neighborhood. Draw a map of your current neighborhood and a blueprint of your new improved neighborhood using any of the map-making computer programs we explored in class.
- You have the authority to make one rule for all parents in the world. What is your rule? How will your rule benefit all children? Please write your response in formal letter style to an organization, existing or imaginary, that can implement your rule. For example, Child Services or the HEEB: Help Eradicate Embarrassment Bureau.
- You are the world's most influential talk show host. Record yourself on video opening your talk show with a slanted monologue on a current newsworthy topic.
- Fashion a new coin that represents a political, economic, or cultural symbol(s) for one of the states joining the Union prior to 1812. Use your drawing ability to design symbols for both sides of the coin. Cut out and paste both sides of your coin on colored paper and write an appropriate caption below each drawing.
- Watch the video clip on Discovery Education titled "Man vs. Wild S01E07 African Savannah" and write a critique of the video, taking into consideration its interest level and clarity of information. Mention at least two praiseworthy aspects of the video and two areas that need improvement.
- Read the text of the speech "I Have a Dream" by Martin Luther King, Jr. Highlight one paragraph that contains one of MLK's dreams still not fully realized in our society. Think of one strategy that would help our society attain this dream. Be prepared to present your strategy before the class. You may prepare a notecard.
- Create a resumé for a character in literature, person in history, or present-day personality, taking into account his or her abilities and character traits. Follow standard resumé guidelines.
- Write your obituary. Invent a whole future life for yourself, recounting an adventurous, glamourous, highly vigorous, noble, or heroic lifestyle. After you put the final pat on your obituary, think of what you discovered about your goals. Are they practical or idealistic? Did you awaken a passion for doing something worthwhile?
- Create a chemistry audience game with a partner over the weekend that includes at least 15 questions and answers. Please cover concepts about molecules and compounds, chemical composition, chemical reactions, and stoichiometry. Your game can model an audience game you know, but it may not merely test memorized knowledge. On paper, please write a paragraph or two about your game's instructions. Once your game is graded, revised, and approved, it will enter a lot. We will draw three games from the lot and play it as a review for the chemistry test.

LET STUDENTS SEE HOW HOMEWORK
COUNTS IN A LITERAL SENSE

Students should be aware of how each assignment affects their grade. Show students a grading system you will apply at the end of the term that takes into account their homework assignments. Does this put too much value on grades? I don't think so. While we want our students to learn for the sake of learning, it's tough for students to apply themselves after a long school day. Students will complete a homework assignment with greater volition when they see the tangible credit they are building for themselves. In addition, conveying to students that their homework will make up an integral part of their grade takes the emphasis off test results, which are many times a poor reflection of a student's effort.

FIND A WAY TO CHECK HOMEWORK

So you give students practice for homework (in math, chemistry, grammar, computers, French, etc.). At the beginning of class, review the homework or collect it and grade it. Be unpredictable with your checking method. Review the homework one day and collect it the rest of the week. Review it for three days and collect it the next two. Alternatively, you can review the homework and collect it from one row only, or from students wearing pockets on their shirts, or from the students sitting in the back.

ALWAYS GRADE WRITING ASSIGNMENTS

Any writing homework which includes more than 20 minutes of labor deserves your personal feedback. Grade the assignments and return them quickly, preferably within the week so that the students are still interested in seeing the results. Set aside time to review the results with a discussion and display of accomplishments and errors. When homework assignments are systematically reviewed or graded, students appreciate their relevance.

GIVE EVERYONE THE OPTION
OF HANDING IN WRITTEN WORK

Whenever you don't collect a short assignment because you plan to discuss it in class (for example, you asked for a brief paragraph describing a character's motive), give students the option of handing it in anyway. Some students, proud of their work, feel cheated when the teacher doesn't grade their papers.

SHOWCASE STUDENTS' WORK

You don't have to display every essay on the bulletin board, but try to showcase samples of students' work. Homework acquires a new dimension when students can anticipate seeing what their peers accomplished or wrote. Here's a selection of extended analogies eleventh graders wrote for a homework assignment which I compiled in a class booklet of quotable quotes.

Quotable Quotes (Grade 11):

"Friendship is like money. It needs to be earned."—Bassie Hirsch

"Praying is like fishing. You drop a line and wait."—Goldie Wolf

"A secret is like a present. We tend to dress it up in ribbons and bows to make it more interesting."—Aliza Erlbaum

"Fashion is like the weather forecast. It changes each season."—Felipe Bourdon

"Happiness is like the waves of the ocean. It ebbs and flows."—Jesse Ventura

"Feeling gratitude and not expressing it is like a letter without a stamp. It has a destination but will never reach it."—Yehudis Shuter

"The human body is like a car. At a certain point it breaks down and can no longer be fixed."—Miriam Hershkowitz

"Life is like a roller coaster. It has ups and downs and comes to an end."—Suri Samel

"The difference between soil and dirt is like the difference between a call and a text. One is more beneficial than the other."—Avigail Rubin

"Daring ideas are like balloons. Someone may pop them but they might also reach the sky."—Elisheva Shaliyehsabou

"A person is like a vehicle. Both need a boost at times."—Sarala Jacobson

"A good friendship is like a hard-boiled egg. It starts out delicate but grows strong."—Devory Charach

TURN HOMEWORK INTO EXTRA CREDIT!

You can give students a true appreciation for learning by presenting many homework assignments as extra credit projects. Extra credit assignments should involve higher order thinking, preferably creative thinking. Students tackle extra credit assignments with alacrity because they're not forced to do them. Usually, I give students a week to turn in extra credit for smaller projects and a semester's length for larger ones. Students relish working at their own pace, not having to meet a looming deadline.

What is more, students never lose out when doing extra credit assignments. If they do not like the result, they do not submit the work—if they do submit work, they can't lose points. Furthermore, when the teacher gives partial credit, any sincere attempt becomes worthwhile. Therefore, homework becomes fun when it's extra credit.

Give extra credit assignments all students can achieve on their individual level—not assignments that call for exceptional skills (like genius puzzles). The following assignments cater to middle and high school students. For each assignment, I display the worksheet (note the shortened version) along with model examples of students' work. Note: Model examples do not mean the best. They mean examples that adequately match the criteria.

Extra Credit Worksheet 1

Do Clichés Dull Your Style?

Do clichés dull your style? Yes, they do. A cliché is an expression so often borrowed that it lacks freshness and originality: Tommy ran *as fast as lightning* to the bus stop. *Heaving a sigh of relief*, he *hopped onto* the bus just *in the nick of time*. As you see, only amateur writers use clichés. For each pair of sentences below, notice how the "amateur writer" uses a cliché but the great author uses a scintillating substitute:

The sail was as *old as the hills.*

"The sail was patched with flour sacks and furled, it looked like the flag of permanent defeat."—Ernest Hemingway, *The Old Man and the Sea*

It snowed almost every day until the whole world seemed to be *blanketed with snow.*

"Outside everything looked different; the apple tree was a crooked ghost, the bushes were fat scoops of ice cream, and the bird feeder wore a white hat."—Jean Van Leeuwen

The wind howled through the canyon.

"The throat of the canyon was hoarse with wind."—Glendon Swarthout, *Bless the Beasts and the Children*

They act *like animals.*

"A surging, seething, murmuring crowd of beings are human only in name..."—Baroness Orczy, *The Scarlet Pimpernel*

Our mouths dropped open in surprise.

"We were all as surprised as a hen who hatches a turkey egg."—John D. Fitzgerald, *The Return of the Great Brain*

"Don't look like *it's the end of the world.*"

"No dying cow looks."—Frank B. Gilbreth and Ernestine Gilbreth Carey, *Cheaper by the Dozen*

Instructions: Please write at least one sentence that contains a cliché and a corresponding sentence that substitutes the cliché with fresh sensory detail. (You may hand in as many examples as you like.)

Students' Model Examples of Cliché Substitutes:

The child moved *as slow as a snail.*
The child took sleepy steps.—Michal Mahpari

My mind was blank.
My mind was as empty as a pig's trough after dinner.—Sara Feinstein

I was *huffing and puffing.*
My breath came in gasps, the sound like cloth ripping.—Matthew Packert

He was moving *as slow as molasses.*
He was moving as slow as a walrus on land.—Deborah Glick

They stood *as straight as a pin.*
They stood as straight as raw spaghetti.—Jared Demaske

The town was *blanketed with snow.*
The frosty bristles of pine trees poked out like pipe cleaners, and the houses had on giant white cloaks.—Sara Malka Goldstein

She was *as fat as a pig.*
She was as fat as a mouse in a cheese factory.—Estie Klein

She was shaking *like a leaf.*
She was shaking like a wind chime.—Esther Bresler

The room was *as light as day.*
The room was full of all sorts of bright lamps.—Chaya Glazer

Extra Credit Worksheet 2

Are You Flamboyant, Colorful, or Loud?

Bertrand Russell introduced a novel vocabulary game on BBC radio in 1948 which he called "conjugating irregular verbs." Basically, it demonstrated the human tendency to make ourselves sound more charitable than our peers. Russell jokingly gave the following example:

I am firm.
You are obstinate.
He is a pig-headed fool.

Soon the game caught on and *New Statesmen* magazine offered prizes for the best entries of "irregular verbs." The idea is to use a euphemism for the "I" statement, the next best choice for the "You" statement, and the worst choice for the "He" or "She" statement.

I challenge you to play the game of "conjugating irregular verbs." Let's see how fast you get the hang of it. Remember not to play the modest role. All I know is that I'm colorful, you're flamboyant, and she's loud. Get it? Submit three entries of your own mimicking Russell's vocabulary game.

Students' Model Entries for "Russell's Vocabulary Game":

I'm just being honest.
You're too blunt.
She doesn't know when to stop.
                        —Miriam Rabinovich

I'm a side splitting comedian.
You could use a better punch line.
She's downright corny.
                        —Shira Hirth

I like to keep to myself.
You don't have many friends.
He's socially awkward.
                        —Nechama Listhaus

I keep necessary mementoes.
You never throw anything out, my dear.
He is a hoarder.
                        —Sarah Schwebel

I am thorough.
You're a perfectionist.
He has OCD.
                        —Chaya Neiman

I do what I can to help our economy.
You buy a lot of unnecessary things.
She's a shopaholic.
                        —Ariella Ghatan

My surroundings reflect my
varied interests and hobbies.
You should tidy up your room
every once in a while.
She's a slob.
                        —Lonna Gordon

I am a firm believer that the study
of quantum physics is an excellent
stimulant for mental growth.
You are very studious.
He's a geek.
                        —Yael Greenfield

I lead people towards success.
You delegate what needs to be done.
She's a dictator.
                        —Yael Rabinowich

I'm generous.
You splurge.
He squanders his money.
                        —Malka Stern

I look before I leap.
You take your time.
She's a procrastinator.
                        —Anthony Bruno

Extra Credit Worksheet 3

Copying a Poet

Throughout the year, we've learned a lot about poetry by analyzing a poem's form and content. Now you have a chance to write poems copying poets' style and skill. Please follow the instructions for assignment 1 and 2.

Assignment 1 for Copying a Poet:

Write a poem that presents two contrasting statements as Elizabeth Coatsworth does in "Swift Things Are Beautiful" (https://allpoetry.com/Swift-Things-are-Beautiful). Give vivid examples in your stanzas to depict the truth of your statements. Copy the style of Coatsworth's poem as best as you can: Keep to the same rhyme scheme and make sure the fourth line in each stanza extends the meaning of the third. The skeleton form of Coatsworth's poem will help keep you on track. Try to keep *some* of the articles, conjunctions, and prepositions of the skeleton intact when you write your poem.

Skeleton form of "Swift Things Are Beautiful":

Stanza 1:

_____ _____ are _____:
_____ and _____,
And _____ that _____
_____ and _____,
_____ and _____,
_____ in the _____,
The _____ _____ _____
The _____ _____ _____.

Stanza 2:

And _____ _____ are _____:
The _____ of _____,
The _____ of the _____
That _____ _____ to _____,
The _____ that _____,
The _____ _____,
And the _____ that _____ _____
In the _____ of _____.

Students' Model Examples

"Old Things Are Beautiful" by Susan Barre

Old things are beautiful:
Wistful and gray
Parchment that tells
Tales of yesterday,
Tradition and customs,
Ink and the quill,
The emperors of dynasty,
The French fluff and frill.

And new things are beautiful:
The morning song of the bird,
The newborn that wails
As he enters the world,
Shirt sleeves that rustle,
Smooth fountain pens,
And the hesitant beginnings
As we become friends.

"Noise Is Deafening" By Charles Augustin

Noise is deafening:
Rapids and rivers
The honking and beeping,
Of impatient drivers,
Loudspeakers and radios,
Motorcycles whizzing by,
The banging of doors,
And the child's loud cry.

And silence is deafening:
The house that stands bare,

The empty, clean classroom
At the end of the year,
The love that is suppressed,
The cemetery at night,
And the tears that fall unchecked
At a burial site.

Assignment 2 for Copying a Poet:

Write a poem mimicking Anne Sexton's poem "The Fury of Overshoes" (http://www.americanpoems.com/poets/annesexton/8023), where an object brings back a flood of reminiscences for the speaker. Please write your poem in free verse and keep to the style of Sexton's lines.

Student's Model Example:

"The Fury of a Typewriter" by Russi Soffer

It sits all alone
in the back of the closet.
Faded beige, all stained
with dust and grime.
Remember the high-pitched *ping*
of the inky
typewriter
or the clicks of the rotary
phone
or winding your watch
and the cry of
that piercing whistle
when it was time for your
herbal tea?
Remember, grandson
when an apple was a fruit
and blackberries were something
you ate in jam?
Now the world isn't
mine,
It belongs to
the young people.
With no GPS
I sit lost
driving round and round
as cars pass me by
at night.
They made me give up
my vinyl records
and camera
and my know-how.
Oh, typewriter,
don't you
remember me,
pushing your keys up and down
by the lamp at night?
Oh, tomorrow,
stop and slow down.

I'm so confused.
Where is my future
when will I get there,
typing and texting
all day
each day
and thinking
nothing of it?

HOW DO STUDENTS USE THEIR EXTRA CREDIT?

Like me, you might allow students to use their extra credit toward any test or essay. The way I look at it, if the student earned the extra credit points, she learned something extra and deserves a higher grade on the report card for it. Who cares if the boost in the grade reflects effort instead of a test average? What about teachers who worry that students will collect twenty points by the end of the semester to erase a poor grade? Once again, who cares? If weak test takers can earn better grades by doing extra credit, good for them! Ironically in my experience those who accumulate a large number of points rarely need them. These students do extra credit for the discovery of where it will take them, not for the sake of raising their grades.

In fact, accustomed to expressing themselves creatively in their homework and extra credit work, many students begin dabbling with their own writing ideas and submit extra writing without expecting points in return. I'll come in one day and find a composition or poem on my desk a student wrote over the weekend just for the heck of it.

Take the following poem a student wrote in protest of Henry Abbey's poem "What Do We Plant When We Plant the Tree." After we discussed Abbey's poem in class, something about the poem didn't sit right with my student, Adina. Mimicking Abbey's style, Adina expressed her objection in poetic form just because she wanted to share her viewpoint in a creative, fun way. Entering the classroom, Adina whipped the poem out of her notebook and silently handed it to me. I present Adina's poem here alongside Henry Abbey's for comparison.

"What Do We Plant When We Plant the Tree"
by Henry Abbey (1842–1911)

What do we plant when we plant the tree?
We plant the ship, which will cross the sea.
We plant the mast to carry the sails;
We plant the planks to withstand the gales—
The keel, the keelson, and the beam and knee;
We plant the ship when we plant the tree.

What do we plant when we plant the tree?
We plant the houses for you and me.
We plant the rafters, the shingles, the floors.
We plant the studding, the lath, the doors,
The beams, and siding, all parts that be;
We plant the house when we plant the tree.

What do we plant when we plant the tree?
A thousand things that we daily see;
We plant the spire that out-towers the crag,

We plant the staff for our country's flag,
We plant the shade, from the hot sun free;
We plant all these when we plant the tree.

With apologies to Henry Abbey:
"What Do We Plant When We Plant the Tree?"
by Adina Reichman

What do we plant when we plant the tree?
We plant a treasure for all to see,
We plant the branches to climb on and swing
We plant the blossoms that tell us of spring,
The apples, the acorns, the trees that will be
We plant all these when we plant a tree.

What do we plant when we plant a tree?
We plant sweet air for you and me,
We plant the halo of leaves turned gold
We plant the secrets its hollow will hold,
The piles of leaves we jump in, carefree
We plant a friend when we plant a tree.

What do we plant when we plant a tree?
We plant a gift for eternity,
We plant a soldier to stand through all weather
We plant the friends who will play there together,
We plant a future our children will see
We don't plant a tree for the wood it'll be...

One Last Word About Homework

If you're an advocate of homework, please don't give much of it. No studies have proven that loading on the homework increases learning, a sense of responsibility, or test scores. Yet the volume of homework students receive today keeps escalating, intruding upon family time and plaguing students over weekends and even holidays.

And if homework isn't appealing, you might as well omit it. Once students dread doing homework, they've lost their drive for learning. We educators have to think about quality versus quantity. That means teachers have to cut out all busy work: the burdensome pages of the same type of practice (are 30 math problems a night really necessary?) and the time-consuming projects which require assistance from a parent, sibling, or some distant knowledgeable relative ("Give your cousin Albert a call. He's a physicist. Maybe he can help you.").

Children should take homework home only when they feel it will be beneficial—a compelling writing task, an experiment or interview they're excited to carry out, a survey they're eager to complete, a poster they can't wait to design, an extra credit assignment that challenges them. We want a student's attitude toward homework to be the same as their attitude toward a favorite hobby. Let students love their homework. Let it empower them. Give homework a brain and some intrigue for the learner. Make it matter!

8

Employing Visual Aids

"Well-designed visuals do more than provide information; they bring order to the conversation."—Dale Ludwig

Ever come across someone who has memorized sports statistics or astrology signs? Someone who can recall a gazillion dates in history or phone numbers of virtual strangers? Do you stare at these people in wonder? I certainly do. To retain information, I need to see a visual image, and I'm not alone. Approximately 65% of the population are visual learners. In fact, the brain processes visual information 60,000 times faster than textual information. That's why the visual image is the tool of any good teacher. Since our students are primarily visual people, seeing is not only believing, but a huge part (90%) of their understanding.

A visual impression, therefore, makes an indelible imprint on the mind.

Bring in Visual Aids

Visual aids provide material images for the class when mental images might not be enough. When should educators use visual aids? Whenever they naturally fit into the lesson.

The thing to remember is that visual aids let students grasp abstract ideas more effectively. For instance, saying that the United States ranks the highest in obesity compared to 27 other overweight countries, doesn't impress students as much as seeing a bar graph that shows the United States' obesity rate in comparison to the other countries'. Likewise, telling students they're guzzling loads of sugar doesn't have the same effect as showing them, with the aid of sugar cubes, how much sugar is in their favorite beverages.

Lessons in math, science, and ethics especially, call for visual aids. Understanding ratios in word examples, for instance, can be confusing, while working with marbles makes the concept more concrete. Likewise, using a 3D knot from a 3D printer can help explain a complicated concept like knot theory. Similarly, large Slinkies prove great hands-on tools for students to create and see transverse and longitudinal waves. Demonstrations with simple materials such as popsicle sticks can teach lasting morals to children. Give students one popsicle stick to break in half. They'll find it easy. Give them two, it's harder. They keep trying to break an increasing number of popsicle sticks. When holding a bundle, try all they might, the popsicle sticks remain intact. What a lesson to embed about the strength of unity. Visual aids cannot be overrated.

Therefore, before teaching a lesson, it does us well to think what we might exhibit or produce to crystallize the main points of our lessons. While graphs, math manipulatives, and other visual aids might avail themselves to you within the school's supply closet, you might have to search a bit harder to find other items in stores, institutions, or online services. For instance, if an article speaks about gunny sacks used to transport potatoes or grains, the teacher might get a hold of a gunny sack from a grocery proprietor so the class can see its texture and durability. Likewise, to acquaint students with some effects of vision impairment, the teacher might pick up a card from a blind foundation (such as Lighthouse) that let students compare the effect of macular degeneration, cataracts, glaucoma, diabetic retinopathy, and total blindness by holding sections of the card to one's eye. Similarly, for the purpose of comparing different kinds of thermometers, the teacher might buy samples of a mercury, electronic, and liquid crystal thermometer for the class to look at and handle.

All these exhibits heighten students' interest in the lesson and their understanding of it. You will see your students perk up when you turn on the overhead projector to show them an x-ray of the spine or take "Harry" the skeleton model out of a bag. They will remember your visual aid and its connection to your subject. Only be careful not to bring in farfetched objects that distract the focus of the lesson. Like a colleague of mine once stated, "You don't bring in an elephant to teach the color gray!"

Now let's take a closer look at the benefits of specific visual aids.

PROFESSIONAL HAND-DRAWN ILLUSTRATIONS

Give someone a sheet with a text and illustration and the eye automatically goes to the illustration. While all illustrations, digital or traditional, absorb students' interest, I'm most taken with hand-drawn illustrations. Hand-drawn illustrations present the depth that digital drawings can't offer. No digital media carries the story or the character of illustrations done with pencil, charcoal, pastel or other simple materials. Therefore, when you want to vivify an old historical period, impart a scientific concept, or teach technological information, you might turn to expert illustrators who use the traditional media.

For example, when I taught American history to seventh grade, I made use of *Colonial Living,* where Edwin Tunis sets the stage of pioneer life in North America during the Colonial Period of 1564–1770. Tunis describes the industries, society, culture, and growth of coastal settlements. His beautiful hand-drawn detailed illustrations underscores his descriptive text as he depicts the construction of homes: a New England seventeenth-century house, the frame cottage of a small tobacco planter, the "Big House" of a large plantation. Other drawings detail operations such as the spinning of yarn and its weaving and dyeing, the interior mechanism of a windmill, and the workings of a sawmill. Tunis also illustrates accurate products of craftsmen, ranging from the cozy trundle bed and New Netherland alcove bed to the birch broom, Ladder-back chair, and a variety of men's wigs. Enlivening the Colonial Era became easy with collages I'd create for students with these illustrations.

By doing a bit of exploring, you can find illustrations that highlight important factors in other early eras. To give students a glimpse into consumer habits, social norms, and advertising methods of the late nineteenth century, for instance, I present the 1897 Sears Roebuck & Co. Catalogue with its elaborate illustrations. Aside from amusing themselves with the up-and-coming products sold in those days (Dr. Rose's $8.00 Obesity Cure that "will reduce corpulency in a safe and agreeable manner."; $3.75 Ladies' Bicycle Suits consisting of cap, jacket, skirt, leggings, and bloomers; Dr. Warner's $1.25 Abdominal Corset made with extension steels and elastic gores), students love to compare more familiar items with ones they buy currently, from shoes to jewelry, fountain pens, and bicycles. Who'd think the Ladies' and Gents' fine semi-precious stone and diamond rings would sport designs similar to the ones today?

For a writing project, students compare and contrast the 1897 Sears Roebuck & Co. Catalog with either the Montgomery Ward & Co. Catalogue of 1895, or Bloomingdale's Illustrated 1886 Catalog, or Sears' current virtual catalogues. The authenticity of the hand-drawn illustrations makes the project intriguing. Along with the wording of advertisements, students take into account the layout, the design and quality of products, even the style of customer reviews! For a history fair, students sew late nineteenth-century clothing and model them. For visual and textual exhibits, they make model replicas of soaps, tonics, hats, books, and eyeglasses. They write up orders from the old catalogues:

$0.79 Arsenic Complexion Wafers
$1.75 Brass Tubular Lantern
$0.25 Men's Summer Shirt
$0.06 Ladies' Scalloped Swiss Handkerchief
$5.25 Flat top, Heavy Duck Cover Trunk
$4.35 Iver Johnson Hammerless Automatic Revolver

In addition, students use the inflation calculator online to adjust a given amount of money for inflation, according to the Consumer Price Index. To viewers' amusement, they write a side-by-side account of items' prices and how much they would cost today (if they were available in equal demand). For instance, a $4.35 Automatic Revolver in 1897 would cost $123.48 in 2018.

All this immersion leads us to conversation in the classroom where I ask the following questions: From a sociological standpoint, has our society progressed? What would you buy from this catalogue? How have needs and desires changed? What has been the impact of government over the last century until today (for example, drugs and pharmaceutical regulations)? If you lived in the late 1800s and still got your current allowance from your parents, would you feel rich? Would you agree to live in the late 1800s if you could afford whatever you wanted? Which products of that time are probably more in demand today? Why? Do you think we get more or less for our money today? To what consideration do you attribute this claim?

Turning aside from history, many hand-drawn illustrations found in books impart scientific concepts. By far the most informative, David Macaulay's books illuminate difficult concepts through straightforward drawings. Teaching about levers? You will find an enlarged clear illustration in David Macaulay's *The New Way Things Work* of a nail clipper that delineates how the device is a neat combination of two levers working together to produce a powerful cutting action. To strengthen the concept of centrifugal force, you might flip to Macaulay's illustration describing the workings of a seat belt. Or maybe you can drop the structured science lesson and let students pore over the hundreds of other illustrations in the book that show the intricacies and workings of machines such as the airplane, photocopier, smoke detector, burglar alarm, and microchip. It is impossible while exploring each machine not to pick up on the scientific principles behind them.

Especially wonderful are Macaulay's technological illustrations in *Underground,* which divulge hidden places. Are your students curious about what's going on beneath the surface of city streets and sidewalks? What's under fire hydrants, manhole covers, and sewer drains? Macaulay's *Underground* takes you down into the modern network of systems below a city cross street. Macaulay reveals the walls and columns that support buildings, bridges and towers. He depicts life-supporting systems: the function and interaction of water lines, sewer and electrical systems, steam and gas distribution systems, and telephone cables. Along with vivid illustrations of these utilities, Macaulay also shows the construction of tunnels for subway systems. Emerging from these scenes below, no city kid or country visitor will ever take the technology underground for granted!

SIMPLE BOARD ILLUSTRATIONS

I'm a big advocate of board illustrations because they can easily express ideas difficult to convey in words. For example, to explain how a literary character feels stuck in a rut, I draw a stick figure character standing in a deep underground rut, resembling a grave, which I mark as 20 feet deep. Then I ask my class to explain the complexity of the character's problem.

Noting that the character has no ladder and no one available to help her out of the rut, a student says, "She has no way to get out of the rut on her own." Score a point for her.

Another says, "She feels very lonely down there."

"She is in the dark and can't reach the light."

The answers keep coming: "The effort it would take to climb out is too much for her."

"She doesn't know if anyone is nearby to help her."

Now had I just verbally told the class that the character is stuck in a rut and asked them to describe the complexity of her problem, they would have probably said, "She doesn't know what to do." But seeing my illustration, they come to the conclusion that she sees no way out because she has no tools and no way of getting them. Hence, when a good Samaritan shows up in the story, the class predicts that the Samaritan will play a vital role in helping the character climb out of her rut. The rut becomes something they see in their minds; it's not just an abstract psychological state. And at the end of the story, when the character emerges from the rut (somewhat muddied from the experience), they feel the character's delight in rejoining a world of illumination, freedom, and expansive opportunity.

PROFESSIONAL DIAGRAMS

Use professional diagrams, if possible, to elucidate any abstract concept big or small. Try not to rely on your own diagrams. No matter how wonderful your artistic ability and precision, unless you're as good an artist as David Macaulay, depend on professional diagrams for your lessons. For instance, you can easily obtain helpful online diagrams for the following important topics:

- The concept of symmetry
- Positive and negative reinforcement
- The communication process
- The adolescent brain and addiction

- The pH scale
- Maslow's hierarchy of needs
- The rock cycle
- The nitrogen cycle
- Plato's "Allegory of the Cave"
- The computer memory hierarchy
- Shigley's model of the design process
- Energy flows and material cycles
- The accounting cycle
- The cycle of abuse
- Homeostasis and temperature control
- Description of the innate immune system
- The wheel of retailing
- Examples of hardware in a computer
- Relationships between organisms and the environment

EDUCATIONAL CARTOONS

In a clever cartoon, two atom comrades are in a battle together. One says, "I'm hit! I'm hit! I lost an electron!" The other atom asks, "Are you sure?" to which the injured one replies, "I'm positive!"

Whether illustrated with pun or satire in mind, educational cartoons give lessons a lift with their humor. Spice up any lesson with a cartoon or two to jumpstart a discussion, to use as part of a review, a question on a test or extra credit assignment.

No matter the topic, you can find the perfect cartoons, whether you're teaching about chemistry, immigration policies, economic recovery, the swine flu, student loans or presidential debates.

Believe it or not, there are cartoonists out there who you'd think were working for you to make your teaching a success. Take American cartoonist and mathematician Larry Gonick. His books of cartoons, *The Cartoon History of the Universe*, span world history from prehistory to 2008. Any teacher of world history, American history, or current events can find a plethora of cartoons to choose from in his books. Like Gonick, many other cartoonists depict the historical cause and effect and the motivations behind discoveries, inventions, wars, explorations, achievements and errors. Their cartoons empower themes.

And then there are other cartoonists more playful than satirical, like Keaton Staos, whose educational cartoons evoke a plain old good-natured laugh. Your students will welcome those too! (For example, check out http://www.math-problem-solving.com/images/funny-math-cartoon2.jpg.) I like to place these cartoons on the bottom of worksheets and tests just to lighten the mood.

MOBILE DEVICES

In the olden days (about ten years ago), when I couldn't answer a student's question on the spot ("What do geckos eat?" "Who invented flip-flops?" "Why do people become bald?"), I'd look it up later and get back to the student. Today I say, "I don't know; why don't you look it up and get back to me about that?" Laptops, iPads, and other mobile devices are great hands-on tools that give the class instant access to educational information. Steering students toward them to find out answers, do research, and design projects fosters autodidactic learning. In addition, these tools compel students to leave their comfort zone and take on a participatory role. What's more, while working on projects, students can zoom in and manipulate images. They can insert Smart charts and photographs and produce much more polished work. More delightfully, the collaborative nature of these devices allow students to showcase their learning and share findings with peers, instructors, and the outside world. At home, students can find assignments online and email their teachers questions which the latter can respond to before class the next day. Teachers can suggest particular apps for advanced students to deepen their learning and for those who need additional practice in a subject. In the long run, navigating programs lends students the familiarity with equipment they will come across outside school in the marketplace.

THE SMARTBOARD

Born into a technological world with multimedia at their fingertips, today's children find the Smartboard intriguing. Watching the teacher use the Smartboard, children quickly learn computer skills. Kids love the kinesthetic manipulation: coming to the board to type information via the keyboard or to use the touch screen, to control applications, move/drag objects, play games, or explore a topic on their own.

Catering to a variety of learning styles, but mainly visual learning, the Smartboard proves an indispensable tool that has changed the standard of teaching in classrooms. With the built in gallery tools, teachers can pull up documents, graphs, pictures, diagrams, political cartoons, or photographs and even write all over them—labeling or defining parts. A teacher can embed video clips and sound files into presentations and call upon them to illustrate a point with a touch on the board. Anticipating questions, she can prepare links to websites and click on them when needed.

Teaching concepts in certain subjects reportedly takes a quarter of the time with the Smartboard. A simple algebra equation, $X + 9 = 13$, for instance, takes the children four times longer to calculate than when using circles on the Smartboard to substitute the numbers. A teacher can separate easily confused topics by using distinctly separate visuals. To differentiate between the events of World Wars I and II, for example a history teacher can dramatize the lessons with two very different animations and visuals. A high school physics teacher can teach a concept in physics such as negative velocity and negative distance in one day with the Smartboard and electronic measurement software, whereas without Smartboard tools it would take her a week.

Editing homework papers with the class has never been easier. The teacher can write notations directly on the work, circle or underline text and manipulate sentences and paragraphs. She can color-code items for comparing and contrasting and highlight key topics. Using Dual Page View, a teacher can display two pages at once for example, showing different paragraphs written about the same topic, or comparing the same paragraph before and after it's edited.

The Smartboard enriches practice activities. Colleagues report that the visual aids and interactive games enhance their students' retention "to a ridiculous extent." Math activities with animated features capture students' interest as they work with interactive protractors, dice, spinners, and other tools. With an interactive response system such as Senteo, students can give the teacher quick remote feedback as to whether they understand the lesson. The program can test students' knowledge with multiple choice, true or false, or numeric responses. Feedback to the teacher through a bar graph or pie chart can provide a statistical response.

THE PHOTOGRAPH

We can't deny that photographs prove special for reminiscing and safekeeping. They capture Kate's attempt at baking chocolate mousse, little Robbie watching the tractor cut grass, and Granddad yelling at the races. We look at photographs and relive moments. We want our descendants to take out our albums and mull over them. Yet other types of photographs carry great meaning because they educate us about the world. As indisputable evidence, they alter our perceptions. These photographs astound, inform, persuade, and inspire. Struck by their enduring impressions, students quickly learn new concepts from them. Soon the teacher finds that the power of photographs has no limit. Let's further analyze different genres of photographs and their influence.

Nothing brings the poignancy of a moment to life better than a documentary photograph. I'll never forget walking into a colleague's classroom one day to see a photograph on her desk of a vulture hovering near a starving child in Sudan. That picture still haunts me today. Similar photographs of current poverty—a woman drawing water from a hand-dug well in Niger, two children living in a garbage dump in Honduras—shock students to harsh realities and arouse in them a desire to contribute to the betterment of the world.

Other compelling photographs, old and new, define moments of injustice, defiance, and heroism. Who isn't moved by a photograph of small children working in a textile factory in Tennessee in 1910, or of a bold youth stopping a column of tanks during the revolt in Beijing's Tiananmen Square, or of firefighters at Ground Zero working in the rescue effort after September 11? Photographs like these inspire discussion about human rights and American values, swaying the class's opinion more effectively than textbook information.

Many documentary photographs not only chronicle significant historical events but also convey much about the subjects' motives. For instance, take the well-known photograph of Eisenhower at the D-Day Invasion in June 1944. This photograph shows General Eisenhower speaking to a group of paratroopers who will be dropped into enemy territory in Normandy. In 24 hours, these soldiers know they will most likely be dead. Using this photograph, the teacher can broach thought-provoking questions such as: What does the determination on General Eisenhower's face tell us about him? Do you think he feels justified in sending these men on a suicide mission? What does the quiet resolve on the faces of the men tell us about their beliefs? Why are they willing to trade their lives for freedom? Are these paratroopers heroes? Why or why not?

Vintage photographs also do a fabulous job at portraying time periods. What gives students a clearer picture of life on the American frontier than photographs of homesteaders and sod houses, women sewing at a quilting bee, cowboys branding cattle, a stagecoach brimming with passengers, and men working at mills and mines? What lends students a better notion of how people traveled during a time period, let's say the early 1900s, than vintage photographs of a horse-drawn carriage taking children to a storytelling festival in Wright Park in Tacoma, Washington, a man driving a Model T Ford on a snowy Detroit street, or a Broadway trolley carrying a mass of passengers in New York City?

Incidentally, students also get a kick out of comparing the dress and lifestyle of yesteryear with theirs. So when discussing the 1950s in America, for example, the teacher might show photographs of the typical American teenage girl in her poodle skirt, knee-length shirtwaist dress, or pedal pushers, the stereotypical housewife with her bouffant hairstyle, blouse and full skirt and pillbox hat, the teenage boy in his flannel dark suit or the man in his cardigan. The teacher might show authentic family portraits, or even portraits of TV families (*Father Knows Best, Make Room for Daddy, Leave It to Beaver, The Adventures of Ozzie and Harriet*). Comparing the fifties' mode of dress and lifestyle with that of the modern day, students note a glaring difference. To project the lifestyle during the fifties, the teacher might display photos of Mom at home baking and Dad, the breadwinner, at work. The teacher might exhibit photos of families at drive-in theaters, or eating dinner together at home, celebrating holidays, or playing board games like Monopoly.

To pique students' interest further in comparing the American past to contemporary times, the teacher might ask her class, "How has the American family changed from the fifties to today? What are some good changes? Some bad ones?" Along with photographs of families during the fifties, sixties, seventies and so on, the teacher might show poll results that raise thought-provoking questions. For example, according to polling company AIPO, a surge of people from 1955–1960 claimed they were very happy. Measuring happiness across the decades, another study placed the fifties as "peak smiling time," with optimism falling rapidly from that time to the moaning present. The profound questions: Do you think dress and lifestyle attributed to the happiness in the fifties? Might dress and lifestyle attribute to the obvious discontent in families today?

Now onto nature photographs. Boasting unusual sights of the world, nature photographs transport students beyond the ignorant present to a realm of wonderment. Why not spellbind students with a photograph of a plague of locusts swarming the skies in Ethiopia or of a herd of wildebeest thundering across the savanna in Kenya. Let your class "ooh" and "aah" over aerial photographs of a crater in Northern Arizona, a comet shooting across the Southern Hemisphere, a rainforest in Washington state, the Everglades in Southern Florida. Let them shiver upon seeing photographs of blue holes, ice circles, and swirling tornadoes. You need only to show students these photographs for them to appreciate the grandeur of the world.

On the other hand, let them see the tiniest microscopic organisms we take for granted or don't even know exist: The cute faces of maggots or the soft-faced eyelash mites that live in our eyelashes eating cell sheddings and keeping follicles unclogged. The traffic jam of microscopic creatures in one drop of seawater. If this doesn't get the class wondering about the intricacy of our living world (and enthusiastic about lab class!) nothing will.

Undoubtedly, many genres of photographs clarify concepts. For example, a teacher can talk about the dangers of global warming, but showing a photograph of Greenland's ice cap fissured by meltwater can portray the magnitude of the problem. Likewise, the peril of elephant poachers in the ivory trade hits home when students see a photograph of elephants' tusks seized in an illegal Cameroon ivory market. Furthermore, many photographic images play a significant role in verifying what we're told or what we already know. We're all told, for instance, that no two snowflakes look exactly alike, but there's nothing like seeing the distinction for oneself. Bentley's *Snowflakes in Photographs* portrays microphotographs of seventy-two flawless hexagons, all with individual intricacies. What better way to impress students with the miracles in their midst than to show them Bentley's snowflakes on the first snowy day of the year?

Equally astounding are photographs that don't fit into a specific category. While many provoke life lessons, others arrest us merely with their incongruities or startling information. You can exhibit these photographs whenever they come in handy—a snowfall in the Sahara Desert (February 18, 1979) as a springboard to a lesson on weather changes, a photograph of uncommon heroes such as the musicians who kept playing on the sinking *Titanic* within a lesson on altruism. Occasionally as a reminder of our good fortune, you might whip out a photograph showing someone experiencing a joy we take for granted, for example, five-year-old Harold Whittles' amazed reaction to hearing sound for the very first time after a doctor places a hearing aid in his ear. Furthermore, for students to appreciate modern inventions, you can display a contrast to our modern technology—for example, a photo of the first room-sized U.S.–built ENIAC computer weighing 30 tons (1946). What a disparity to the thin, nearly weightless laptops we carry around today!

Also striking for their shocking effects, graphic photographs prove useful to deter students from unhealthy lifestyles. For example, everyone knows that smoking is harmful, but showing students photographs of cancerous mouth and throat diseases brings home the dangers of smoking more forcefully than package warnings or statistics. Along the same vein, photographs of skin cancers caused by ultraviolet radiation warn students against sunbathing or using tanning beds. Graphic photographs can even put people on a better diet. Hand students a photograph of a heart, lungs, and abdominal cavity surrounded by fat and they'll think twice about reaching for the third Big Mac; give them a photograph of cirrhosis (chronic liver disease) and they'll ask themselves in the future if bingeing on alcohol is worth it.

Lastly, cultural photographs teach about the diverse cultures that blend together in American society. Here's what I always find astonishing. Our youth dine upon Mexico's tacos and burritos, Japan's sushi, French bread and Italian pasta, and think these foods originate from the corner Take Out. Worse, many students have no idea how cultures worldwide have contributed to America. Showing photos or slides of these cultures thriving or existing within the United States—for example, Mexican folk art, the Piñata tradition, Japanese landscaping (in *The Japanese Gardens of North America*), Asian martial arts classes, French design (of architecture, furniture, and clothing) and Italian sculpting (the Lincoln Memorial, the lion statues outside the New York Public Library)—all display how our melting pot boasts a fine weave of global culture.

Still other cultural photographs can teach us how to live more simply and creatively. Mindless acquisitions, the many dizzying devices and toys that bleep, zap, and blip about us, rob our children of living in the moment. To show how it's possible to live simply and creatively, show your class photographs of people worldwide who by choice or necessity engage in olden day practices—an Amish man pressing apple cider in Lancaster, Pennsylvania; a farm woman spinning wool into yarn in Romania; a man twisting syrup to make candy in a market in Old Delhi. Inspired by these photographs, students realize the joy of making something with one's own two hands. In turn, students take up creative hobbies, like bread baking, canning, and candle dipping. Artists as well pop up in the classroom, as students try their hand at embroidering pillows, sewing vogue bags, and weaving place-mats.

Further inspired by photographs of African children and their handmade toys—a boy from Uganda playing with a plastic bottle car, a boy from Malawi holding a soccer ball made from plastic bags and rubber bands—students discover they too can create something useful from practically nothing! Recycling becomes popular as students turn raggedy t-shirts into pillows, old shoes into planters, bubble wrap into rain jackets. They make bottle cap mosaics, candy wrapper wallets, braided twine bracelets, CD sun catchers, tin can musical instruments, and sock puppets! Soon they figure they can use materials such as cardboard from cereal boxes to duplicate games like checkers, chess, Battleship, and Othello!

So what do photographs achieve? Photographs teach students not just to look at the world around them but to look into it. When you frequent lessons with photographs, you're telling students to take a minute to reflect, to ponder, and respond to the world. Despite the numerous distractions around us, everyone willingly takes the time to look at a photograph. The savvy teacher seizes every chance to utilize photographs in lessons.

All visuals, whether employed for a huge chunk of the lesson or for a few minutes, lend your class something tangible to commit to their memories. Long after I've taught a class, I meet a student in the street who tells me, "You once showed us a magnified bar code and explained how it's read by an optical scanner. I just explained how it's done to my son." Or someone will say, "I remember the model of the skin you brought in that showed the three layers of skin and its hair, blood vessels, sweat pores, and sweat glands. I learned that sweating is a blessing." Or "I still remember that photograph of the four children for sale [Chicago, 1948]. I will never take for granted my happy upbringing." These remarks attest to the power of visual aids.

Which visual aids will you bring into class today?

9

Maximizing
Children's Books

"A children's story that can only be enjoyed by children is not a good children's story in the slightest."—C.S. Lewis

Maximizing Children's Nonfiction

Children's nonfiction contains just as much value for adults as for children. They present the most simple and direct way of explaining a subject matter, yet we turn instead to the hard stuff. For example, if you want to learn about the brain and its functions, you may naturally decide, since you're an adult, to look up the information in an encyclopedia, science book, or website. But these resources tend to present complex ideas and intimidating diagrams. How many times were you determined to decipher material only to find that it confounded you? Learning fundamentals through children's nonfiction gives the educator not only a more amenable approach, but a solid starting ground. Once you have acquired the knowledge offered by these books, you can build upon it and graduate to more complex reading without feeling overwhelmed by the material.

While we're on the subject, might I also suggest the benefit of reading nonfiction children books for their own sake? A veteran to this idea, I borrow a bunch of nonfictional children's books from the public library every week on any topic that draws me—related or unrelated to my teaching material. Topics range from famous duels in history to spooky old houses, to wine-making, to Mr. Ferris's wheel. Because children's books are so congenial and light, I savor reading them at my leisure. As a result, I keep myself equipped with enlightening information which helps me in multiple ways. To begin with, my mind and spirit are on a constant *high* with the joy that comes along with acquiring knowledge.

Furthermore, you'd be surprised how information from these books comes in handy during a lesson. For example, when discussing how people take things for granted, I refer to the children's biography I read on Noah Webster which talks about young Noah savoring a few chocolate-covered raisins he received as a holiday gift and putting the rest in his pocket for later. My students, while pitying the boy, get the idea of how much we take for granted in our lives even in the candy department!

In addition, the new-found knowledge affords me the opportunity to reinvigorate old lessons or spice up current ones. For instance, by following the instructions provided in *The Body Book* by Donald M. Silver and Patricia J. Wynne, I could easily make a hands-on model of the inner ear for my class. In preparation to a lesson about bridges, *The Time for Kids Big Book of How* supplied me with excellent instructions for building and testing the strength of a spaghetti bridge. To put a zing into a lesson on the eight phases of the moon, I taught my class how to create a lunar flipbook adapting ideas from *Making "Movies" Without a Camera: Inexpensive Fun with Flip Books and Other Animation Gadgets* by Lafe Locke.

Now let's discuss bringing children's books directly into the classroom. Introduce nonfiction children's books (and some young adult ones too) and watch how your students' knowledge, know-how, and retention, will fly off the charts! Truly indispensable, nonfiction children's books always find their place in school, whether as springboards of discussions, main parts of lessons, appendages to lessons, or as independent reading. They present vistas of information for all subject matter and cater to individual needs and personalities. How can non-fiction children's books work as a tool in your classroom? Let's begin to count the ways.

Here are specific ways nonfiction children's books can work for you:

- Is bravery the theme of the week? Delight students with *Henry's Freedom Box: A True Story from the Underground Railroad* by Ellen Levine—a narrative about an intrepid fugitive slave who shipped himself to freedom by freight mail!
- Want students to understand difficult concepts such as the enormity of big numbers— what size tank do you need for a million goldfish?—or on a somber note, the enormity of the Holocaust? Whip out *How Much Is a Million?* by David M. Schwartz, which explains quantities in terms children can understand.
- Do you have reluctant readers in your class? Try prying them from a book like *Spies* by Clive Gifford, which uncovers the world of espionage: secret agents and spy rings, hidden cameras and electronic bugs, secret codes, disguises and more!
- Want kids to practice presentation skills? Let them read and follow the steps in a book like *Cool Card Tricks* by Steve Charney.
- Are Hard-to-Please Pam and Whiny Winston complaining they can't find a cool science experiment? They will clamor over Janet VanCleave's *202 Oozing, Bubbling, Dripping, and Bouncing Experiments.*
- Teaching about wildlife? Consider bringing in *It's Moving Day!* by Pamela Hickman, which surveys the many woodland animals occupying an underground burrow throughout the seasons.
- Want to show the extent of someone's tenacity or perseverance? How about introducing *Thank You, Sarah* by Laurie Halse Anderson, which discusses Sarah Hale's 38-year unwavering attempt (and triumph!) to secure Thanksgiving as a national holiday!
- Exploring natural resources with your class? Blow their minds with Mark Kurlansky's book *The Story of Salt,* which displays facts about salt and its vital role in history. (Who'd have thought salt was the object of wars and revolutions?)

Philosophical books and advice/how-to books for young adults often serve a dual purpose in the classroom. As a good read, they imbibe students with information and also inspire divergent thinking. For instance, impressed by serendipitous moments and lessons in John A. Jenson's book *Lost and Found,* students take a new look at what seemed like lost opportunities in their lives and realize the lessons in them. On another creative note, after reading the book *Transparent Tape: Over 350 Super, Simple and Surprising Uses You've Prob-*

ably Never Thought of by Vicki Lansky, students have no problem writing their own book modeling Lansky's, enumerating the many uses of a different helpful device, for example: *Over 20 Amazing, Convenient, Practical Uses of a Rubber Band,* or *Over 30 Astounding Uses of a Paper Napkin.*

Having a hectic week? Don't have the time to find good books for your class? Take advantage of reading book titles in the library's nonfiction young adult section. Titles alone can spur ideas for assignment and discussion. Try this: Scan book titles on library shelves to see which ones grab you. Then brainstorm how those titles can facilitate lessons. For instance, the title *When I Was Your Age,* a collection of pivotal stories about growing up, edited by Amy Ehrlich, inspired me to have my students write advice stories to younger children based on their own childhood experiences. Along the same track, Mark Sanborn's book *You Don't Need a Title to Be a Leader: How Anyone, Anywhere, Can Make a Positive Difference* was the impetus I needed for a class discussion on just that: practical ways people anywhere, anytime can make a difference! As a favorite occasional activity, my class predicts the contents of books by their titles and then checks them out to see the extent to which their predictions were correct.

An ever-rising concern is the lack of students' basic literacy skills. Building knowledge helps builds literacy—and how does one do that? With nonfiction books for all school ages. Widen students' knowledge with all genres of nonfiction. Here are the basic ten categories and some topics covered and examples of books you can find in each category.

Ten Categories for Nonfiction

000—General Information

Topics: encyclopedias, almanacs, fact books, unexplained mysteries, newspapers, guides to children's literature

Books: *Stuff That Scares Your Pants Off! The Science Scoop on More than 30 Terrifying Phenomena!* by Glenn Murphy; *Oh, Yuck! The Encyclopedia of Everything Nasty* by Joy Massoff

100—Philosophy

Topics: psychology, perception, emotion, logic, ethics, peer pressure

Books: *What's So Funny? Making Sense of Humor* by Donna Jackson; *Think for Yourself: A Kid's Guide to Solving Life's Dilemmas and Other Sticky Problems* by Cynthia MacGregor

200—Religion

Topics: concepts of God, Bible stories, Greek myths, books about different religions

Books: *The Bible and African Americans: A Brief History* by Vincent L. Wimbush; *Beyond a Reasonable Doubt: Convincing Evidence of Truths of Judaism* by Shmuel Waldman

300—Social Sciences

Topics: government, civil rights, economics, law, social and environmental problems, jobs and money, customs, holidays, folklore

Books: *Media Madness: An Insider's Guide to Media:* by Dominic Ali; *See How They Run: Campaign Dreams, Election Schemes, and the Race to the White House* by Susan E. Goodman

400—Languages

Topics: English, German, French, Italian, Spanish, Greek, etc.; dictionaries, sign language

Books: *Grammar Snobs Are Great Big Meanies: A Guide to Language for Fun and Spite* by June Casagrande; *Write (Or Is That "Right"?) Every Time: Cool Ways to Improve Your English* by Lottie Stride

500—Natural Science

Topics: how things work, math, physics, electricity, lightning, chemistry, rocks, weather, oceans, rivers, dinosaurs, cells, plants, wild animals, the universe, grasslands, bedbugs, dust mites

Books: *Overcoming Math Anxiety* by Sheila Tobias; *Elephants Can Paint Too!* by Katya Arnold

600—Technology and Applied Sciences

Topics: inventions, health and medicine, farm animals and pets, submarines, firefighters, food, nutrition, cookbooks

Books: *Good-bye Tonsils* by Juliana Lee Hatkoff and Craig Hatkoff; *Noodlemania! 50 Playful Pasta Recipes* by Melissa Barlow

700—Arts and Recreation

Topics: art galleries and museums, landscape art, architecture, sculpture, painting, crafts, photography, music, games, magic, sports, comic strips, drawing books, fashion design, photography, Olympics, combat sports

Books: *Look What I Did with a Shell* by Morteza E. Sohi; *Something Under the Bed Is Drooling: A Calvin and Hobbes Collection* by Bill Watterson

800—Literature

Topics: plays, poems, essays, speeches, letters, satire and humor, joke books

Books: *A Kick in the Head: An Everyday Guide to Poetic Forms* selected by Paul B. Janeczko; *The Nuttiest, Wackiest, Funniest, Skits Ever* by Stanley Snickelfoose

900—History and Geography

Topics: map skills, travel books, discovery, exploration, flags, ancient civilizations, World War I and World War II, countries, United States history, revolutions

Books: *The Travel Book: A Journey Through Every Country in the World* by Lonely Planet Kids; *Sky Sailors: True Stories of the Balloon Era* by David L. Bristow

Biography and Autobiography

Topics: artists, authors, explorers, musicians, leaders, presidents, inventors, scientists, mathematicians, entertainers and other noteworthy individuals

Books: *Catherine the Great: Portrait of a Woman* by Robert K. Massie; *Pretending to Be Normal: Living with Asperger's Syndrome* by Liane Holliday Willey

Recognizing the Value of Children's Storybooks

"There are some themes, some subjects, too large for adult fiction; they can only be dealt with adequately in a children's book."—Philip Pullman

As you can imagine, the list of nonfiction is extensive. But what about children's and young adult fiction? Does it take second place? Not at all. Equally valuable, children's fiction educates readers with its profundity, poignancy, beauty, or wit. How does children's fiction work in the classroom?

Use children's fiction to teach complex concepts. Children's fictional picture books offer a treasury of material for lessons. Lower level stories (or simple plots) prove useful for explaining higher level concepts. Books like *A Bargain for Francis* by Russell Hoban and *Leonardo, The Terrible Monster* by Mo Willems impart integral lessons in decision making. An all-time favorite like *Clifford the Small Red Puppy* demonstrates Norman Bridwell's genius in removing a character from its stereotype. It's a prime book choice for a discussion about bias and stereotyping. The whole Norman Bridwell's Clifford series, in fact, comes in handy for teaching children life lessons such as kindness, responsibility, and the power of love.

Profound in their insight, many fiction books portray skills of emotional intelligence. For instance, Molly Lou in *Stand Tall Molly Lou Melon* by Patty Lovell arrests readers with her resilience in looking past her buck teeth and frog voice to celebrate her uniqueness. Similarly, other books contain spunky characters who teach principles of self-mastery. For example, the books *When Sophie Gets Angry ... Really, Really Angry* by Molly Bang and *My Mouth Is a Volcano* by Julia Cook, display the characters' ability to manage their feelings and behave appropriately in a social setting.

Children's books can also prevent unnecessary drama in the classroom. For instance, perhaps you notice people in your class exaggerating stories, telling fibs, or bold-faced lies? *Ruthie and the (Not So) Teeny Tiny Lie* by Laura Rankin gently makes a huge impact demonstrating that a lie is a lie. Seeing all the emotions that Ruthie goes through living with a lie and the relief she feels when she comes clean, teaches children it's better to stick to the truth. You can also nip a more disturbing problem in the bud with the right books. Let's say, for instance, you spot a few pushovers in your class, or you identify potential bullies. Erin Frankels and Paula Heapys' book series *Weird, Dare,* and *Tough* respectively teach the bullying victim, the bystander to bullying, and the bully herself how to face their challenges.

Serious or playful, written in prose or verse, many picture books supply invaluable writing tools for junior high and high school students. For instance, *Sometimes I'm Afraid: A Book about Fear* by Michaelen Mundy lets aspiring authors revisit the world from the small child's perspective so that they can fashion credible child characters of their own. Books such as *Peter's Chair* by Ezra Jack Keats renders a clear lesson on plot development and conflict resolution. Helpful for promising poets, *"I Can't," Said the Ant* by Polly Cameron portrays a good example of personification and consistent rhyme scheme. In addition, a bedtime classic like Margaret Wise Brown's *Good Night Moon* exhibits the skills necessary for matching verse with atmosphere and mood.

Storybooks sharpen students' critical thinking. You might challenge students to mimic writing styles. For instance, a colleague of mine and his tenth graders mimic Mother Goose rhymes to devise clever parodies of themselves. As its name suggests, *Deductive Detective* by Brian Rock gives readers a page-by-page exercise in deductive reasoning. Critiquing literature becomes irresistible for students once they get hooked onto a whimsical author like Dr. Seuss who, beginning in 1939 with *The King's Stilts,* wove symbolism and satire (and irony) into his imaginative plots. Students of all ages love responding to Seuss, discussing his political and social critiques. Given the chance, students also revel in altering parts of imaginative storylines. For instance, Mac Barnett's *Extra Yarn* delights my students with Annabelle's magical ability to sew colorful sweaters for her cold, drab town with her endless supply of yarn. But displeased with the archduke for stealing the box of yarn and laying a curse on Annabelle, my students manipulate the plot and design a conflict less menacing to young children.

This is certain: children's books (and those written for young adults) of all genres invigorate teacher and student. Expand your knowledge with children's books and employ them in lessons. Bring them in to tempt your students. Whether drawn to factual subjects, realistic or magical plots, animal or human characters, students broaden their knowledge and literacy by reading children's books. Let your students read children's books to learn about new subjects, people, places, and events outside their experience. Watch your students build upon intellect, hone communications skills and write with alacrity. Observe how they latch onto a subject with zeal and won't let it go until they've exhausted every corner of it. See how even the most imaginative plots inspire students to work out real problems. Catch your students doing some deep thinking while intrigued by characters' predicaments. Observe how your students exclaim with delight while reading poignantly beautiful sentences. Without doubt, the impact of children's books is transforming. I'm hardly surprised when students disclose that a particular children's or young adult book inspired them to reinvent themselves, explore exciting futures, or grab the world by its ears!

10

Implementing Recordings and Video Clips

"I have a very limited knowledge of recording, but the miracle of being able to capture sounds on magnetic tape and the miracle of electricity, and these little magnetic particles, is amazing to me."—Jeff Mangum, cofounder of the Elephant 6 Recording Company

Reeling in the Audio and Sound Recordings

In teacher training programs, you'll always hear about the benefit of visual aids but not so much about audio or sound recordings. Audio aids and sound recordings, though, run the gamut of intellectual and emotional conquest. They add immeasurable wealth to the learning experience.

How can audio and sound recordings enhance lessons? Let's count five ways.

1. Understandably, the act of listening itself justifies audio and sound recordings. Without visual distractions, a digital recording compels students to concentrate on what they're hearing. In a world of constant visual teasers on TV and video games, audio aids increase the attention span and bring back the focus.

2. Audio recordings can enhance the learning value of practically any new material. For example, students can learn much about reciting by listening to poets recite their poems. What a thrill to follow along with Robert Frost as he surveys "The Road Not Taken" in his gravelly voice! What a pleasure to be drawn into Anne Sexton's nostalgic recitation of "The Fury of Overshoes," or to listen to Shel Silverstein chanting a conglomeration of jocular poems. Following the poet's recitation, the teacher can discuss voice and impact—why the poet chose a particular tone or emphasis and how students can modulate their voice for better impact when reciting poetry or narrating works of literature.

3. Furthermore, audio recordings are a great tool for learning a new language. To improve pronunciation, students can follow a recording and mark stressed and unstressed words on a written text. Then students can practice reading the written text aloud before listening again to the recording for the words they've mispronounced. Additionally, students can listen to foreign language recordings to improve their listening comprehension of the language they're studying. Listening to spontaneous conversation in another language familiarizes students with the jargon.

4. More wonderful still, special speeches of yesteryear available only on audio inspire

students with their messages, direct or indirect. For instance, President FDR's "fireside chat" on the Dust Bowl crisis lends children great respect for a president's leadership. Ray Bradbury's narrated introduction to his book *The Martian Chronicles* weaves a realm of magical possibility in the minds of his listeners as he forecasts potential life on Mars. An exclusive audio interview with Rose Berman (a friend of mine) on her hundredth birthday, gives students pointers for life based on Rose's reminiscences of the twentieth century and vast experience in the world.

5. Mini lessons in form of podcasts draw students' attention to all subject matters. Podcasts, one of the fastest growing forms of new media, are digital audio recordings that sound like radio shows. When you play podcasts, a sense of calm settles over the classroom as students listen with avid interest. That's why you might sporadically play 1–15 minute podcasts on topics pertinent to your lessons. Popular podcasts run the gamut of subjects from math, grammar, writing, current events, games and hobbies, health, society and culture, science and medicine, etc. They take students on high adventure. For instance, in a podcast on *The Moth*, a journalist traces her precarious escape from rebel soldiers after her truck broke down on one of the most dangerous roads in Africa!

You can choose from millions of podcasts! To narrow the range, check out podcastdirectory.com. or other directories. Select podcasts for their format and style as well as content. You don't want to jade your class with the same monologue, interview, or storytelling styles. The following podcast series exhibit vastly different production styles: *Math Mutation, Grammar Girl, Authors on Tour—Live!, CNN news Podcasts, 60 Seconds Health, 60 Seconds Science, More or Less, Stuff You Missed in History Class, Stuff to Blow Your Mind, Radiolab, This American Life, ESL, Smart People Podcast, NASA Science Casts, Practical Money Skills.*

PODCASTS

Here are a few podcast programs my students appreciated:

- Emulsifiers in Food Linked to Obesity in Mice
- Kids Who Exercise Don't Sweat Tests
- Better Sidewalks Could Bring Improved Public Health
- Smart-Phone App Catches Depression Onset
- Defying Odds
- Ball Really Looks Bigger to Better Hitters
- Your Brain Can Taste without Your Tongue
- Haiku Winners
- Great Story Ideas More or Less
- When Companies Track Your Life
- The Most Profitable Product in History
- How Blackbeard Worked
- How the Great Wall of China Works
- Objects of Love
- But Mom! The Science of Whining
- The Mathematics of Happiness
- The Science of Cute

Once accustomed to different styles of podcasts, students can create podcasts of their own to tell stories, conduct interviews, makes short radio broadcasts of current events, or hold debates. Challenging students to come up with alluring titles adds to the fun of the project!

MUSIC

How can music recordings enhance lessons? Let's count seven ways.

1. Musical surprises in class boost sentiment and thought. I've always thought that if a picture is worth a thousand words, music is worth a thousand feelings. Passionate music like Pachelbel's *Canon* can stir the muse for writing. Using crescendos of music to introduce students' presentations raises anticipation. Classical pieces relax the class during independent work.

2. Studying music enhances listening skills. The good thing about music is that everyone loves listening to it. During the year, you can broaden students' music horizons by exposing them to different pieces of music. Among my class's favorite medleys are Paul de Senneville's and Olivier Toussaint's *Ballade pour Adeline* and Amilcare Ponchielli's *Springtime in Moscow*. With a smorgasbord of music available to them, students develop an appreciation for composers such as Tchaikovsky, Chopin, Beethoven, and Handel. Listening to medleys improves listening skills as students learn to differentiate between instruments and acquire tastes for particular instruments or types of music. Over time you can even test students' ears for music with a music challenge. For example, can students differentiate between real music and computer artificial music? First play a real recording of Chopin, then a virtual one created by David Cope using an algorithm. Can students detect the imposter?

3. Music can take students on an imaginative educational journey. To help students actively learn information, try this: Take students on an imaginative educational journey while playing reflective music. Good music picks for this journey are ones in a slow tempo such as *Velvet Dreams* by Daniel Kobialka. Have students close their eyes (or not) and relax as you verbally lead them through an educational process for instance, how a computer works. You can have students imagine the CPU as a brain that controls all the other parts of the computer as the brain controls the human body. They can imagine the motherboard as the skin and skeleton of the computer, holding every part together and making sure all parts work well together. In their minds, they can next picture the RAM as the "hands" of the computer, the power supply as the heart, and so on. In their relaxed state, students can visualize the computer and body analogy better and retain the knowledge. You might choose music that directly relates to a process for an added effect. For instance, if you're talking about erosion, you can play *Ocean Suite—In the Flow* by Steven Halpern for the ocean sounds in the background.

You can take students through a review journey while playing reflective music in the background. The review can come immediately after students learn new information or after you have finished a chapter or unit. You present the review information in bits or chunks on the Smartboard or projector as you see fit. The music serves to create a calm but highly focused atmosphere where students are not talking but merely looking and absorbing information. Students can jot down any questions they have during the review to discuss afterwards.

4. With a little ingenuity, the educator can integrate music with assignments to heighten

the quality of a learning experience. Several assignments I give in high school call for a musical component. For instance, provided with a variety of music, students select a piece appropriate to a passage from their favorite story. Students play their "soundtrack" softly in the background as they narrate the passage. This musical "sneak peek" into stories tantalizes the audience and warms them towards all genres of literature.

For another innovative assignment, students write their own stories to pieces of music. Painstakingly, students match the pace and mood of their writing to a melody. The musicians among the class match their stories to their own tunes. Like true composers, these students fiddle around composing songs with lyrics long after this assignment and use the class as a critical soundboard.

5. Recordings can play an inherent role in speeches and presentations. For instance, in public speaking classes, my class brings in music recordings and recorded performances that hold memories for them. They play part of the recording, and discuss their relationship with the material. We call it "play and tell"—an audio version of "show and tell." In a nostalgic vein, a twelfth-grade student once played her favorite rendition from her father's album "The Flatbush Waltz" and spoke about the memory of waltzing with her father to that music in her living room when she was a little girl. Another student played parts of the class's forgotten fourth-grade concert and the class reminisced about the chorus and narration, chortling as they recognize the melodramatic voices of their younger selves. Before we knew it, the class launched into a discussion about the validity of childhood memories, the purpose of school performances, and the function of melodrama in professional theater.

6. Reflective of societal values, political issues, and moral messages, songs lend an ethical appeal to lessons. "The Cat's in the Cradle" by Harry Chapin evinces the consequence of exchanging family time for business. The anti-war song "One Tin Soldier," written by Dennis Lambert and Brian Potter, raises the question about whether greed creates wars. Often, we hold songs up to scrutiny. For example, does John Lennon's song "Imagine" (1971) really conjure an ideal world? And then to the contrary, we listen to songs for an uplifting experience. "My Favorite Things" sung by Julie Andrew in *The Sound of Music* gives students a happy place to visit when times are difficult.

7. Teaching educational songs in the classroom prove worthwhile investments since they stick to the brain. "The Fundamental Algebra Song" by Tim Pacific teaches the rules for multiplying negative and positive numbers. "The Composters" by Stan Slaughter celebrates the bugs that decompose leaves. "Patriotic Medley" by Judy Leonard pays tribute to the authors of "America" and "America the Beautiful" while simultaneously teaching lyrics of the songs. Longer catchy songs such as "Hey Momma, When Do You Use a Comma?" by Kathleen Wiley will have your students remembering comma rules for the rest of their lives! For teachers who want to stimulate art appreciation, songs like "Vincent van Gogh: His Biography" by Sharon Luanne Rivera definitely endears students to an artist and his work. An abundance of songs that cover all subjects are within clicks away. You can find songs on video about regions of the U.S., linear equations, cellular respiration—you name it. Watching these videos, students won't be able to stay in their seats!

Here are a few warnings regarding music playing in the classroom.

• Don't have music constantly playing in the background. You want music to catch students' attention when you play it and not get students used to hearing it.

• Don't have music playing for any long period. Silence is golden in the classroom. Use silence as the backdrop and build on it with learning activities. More important than music is thought, collaboration, and discussion. Don't let music to take over this natural setting.

• Never allow students to play music for presentations without first receiving your approval. While you might encourage students to play songs from different eras of history or music from various countries, inform students that you accept no culture in the classroom that produces music with references, subtle or explicit, to drugs, hate, stereotyping, name-calling, or violence.

Implementing Video Clips

"The very first video experience I had was in high school. They brought a black-and-white closed-circuit surveillance camera into the classroom. I will never forget, as a kid, looking at that image."—Bill Viola, contemporary video artist

When it comes to spicing up a lecture, exhibiting the vitality of real-life scenes, exploring tough concepts, or inspiring the class to learn from others, video clips are the way to go. The sporadic showing of clips during lessons, let's say a ten-minute clip three times a week, proves a remarkable educational resource in the classroom, sparking attention and springing lessons to life. What to do about longer video clips? Implement them into your lesson as a treat when you feel the clip worthwhile of the time. Alternatively, you may assign longer clips for homework viewing and reserve the discussion or problem solving associated with the video for class.

Do kids like video clips? "Well, duh!" to that question. The perfect medium for visual and auditory learning, video clips rank high in popularity across the globe. Watching the different animations and listening to narrators or sound effects warm students toward the learning content. Better still, studies show that watching video clips engage both hemispheres of the brain. Definitely a strong reason to incorporate multimedia teaching in your lessons.

How do you start selecting video clips while preparing lessons? By asking yourself the following eight questions.

1. CAN I TEACH THIS LESSON FROM A DIFFERENT ANGLE OR VIEWPOINT?

Spectacular educational videos present material from unique viewpoints. Want to grip the class with factual information in a science elementary class? Join Ms. Fizzle's class on *The Magic School Bus*—to the Earth's core, or through the human digestive track, or into a world of non-friction! Narrated films on video also unfold real adventures that stick to the class's brain. For instance, watching even snippets of *Lewis and Clark—The Journey of the Corps of Discovery* by Ken Burns transports body and soul along the perilous journey of the American West though diary readings, sweeping vistas, and soundtrack. What is more, narrated films furnish more interesting backgrounds and tutorials to so-called boring topics. Play a video introduction to the Anglo Saxons for a lesson on Beowulf, a mini clip on how to play the G Major scale for piano playing, a three-minute demonstration on read-ing financial statements in a business class, and you'll keep the focus instead of losing the class with a lecture.

2. WHAT CONCEPT CAN I TEACH MORE EASILY WITH VIDEO CLIPS?

Perfect for mini lessons, video clips can teach difficult concepts in minutes. The reason for the viewer's instant learning is plain. Our minds like to see abstract concepts in concrete ways. Mrs. Toplan, an eighth-grade American history teacher, tells me it used to take her half a period to explain the concept of "trench warfare," but now with a clip of the Battle of Belgium, the kids pick up on the strategy in five minutes. Another colleague employs Dr. Brene Brown's brilliant RSA Short on empathy, a film which uses animal characters, visual analogies, and witty dialogue to clearly show the difference between sympathy and empathy. Viewing this short film cements the idea of empathy in her class's mind in less than three minutes. I know myself that I can give example upon example on writing accu-rate, visual comparisons, but when I play a video clip that demonstrates (with ink and water) how "strands of hair lifting and swirling" look very much like "ink spilled in water," students say, "Oh! Now I see!" and become so much more conscientious about exacting visual metaphor.

What other video clips come in handy to teach complicated concepts? Teachers may substitute demonstrative clips for scientific concepts in textbooks. That's why in teaching a tough biological concept like cell division, an instructor might show a video clip of the chromosomes' movement during cell division—how the chromosomes structurally organize in the mitotic spindle. No other method of explaining the process beats students seeing the dynamic process online under a microscope. In addition, even clips from movies can solidify non-visual concepts, for instance, *Castaway* (2000) acquaints students with literary devices such as motif and symbolism and the concept of living *in* the moment versus *for* the moment. *Fly Away Home* (1996) teaches about grieving, and *Robot and Frank* (2012) questions robot ethics, liability, and deception.

3. WHICH PLACES OR ANIMALS DO I WANT TO ACQUAINT MY STUDENTS WITH?

The answer: Ones they will probably never see in real life. Video clips from YouTube, the History Channel, Discovery Channel, and other media give students front seats to awe-some sights. Use these sources to give students a virtual tour of the largest submarine in the U.S. history, the USS *Pennsylvania*; a close up of the world's largest reptile, the saltwater crocodile, coming onto shore for a bite of fish; a first-hand account of the Mars lander Pathfinder bouncing to a stop on Mars (1997); an aerial view of thousands of caribou migrat-ing across the tundra. For a glimpse into the magnitude of natural disasters, let students witness the volcanic eruption of Mount St. Helens (in Washington state on May 18, 1980), a sandstorm sweeping across central Iraq, a Louisiana sinkhole swallowing trees as it grows to 25 acres (August 3, 2012). With these clips, students can virtually experience world won-ders while remaining stationary in the classroom.

4. Which Live Scenes from History Will Impact My Students Most?

Certainly with digital media, students get to witness history in the making—events that change the course of history. Look at your curriculum and find clips that speak to you. Some of my favorite video picks teach human perseverance and serve as great lessons on cause and effect: the Gandhi Salt March (1930), the moon landing (1969), Operation Entebbe (1976), the fall of the Berlin Wall (1989), Inside Darfur (2011).

5. What Person Would I Love to Invite into Class but Is Inaccessible in the Flesh?

Write these people down, and then go ahead and bring them in! Have JFK spur young patriots to action in your classroom with his admonition, "Ask not what your country can do for you, ask what you can do for your country." Let Martin Luther King, Jr., reach across time to promote racial unity within your class via his famous "I Have a Dream" speech at the Lincoln Memorial. Grant students the opportunity to hear Maya Angelou speak about how love liberates and doesn't bind.

You can use video clips to teach otherwise dull lessons through masters of their field: what better way to teach the relevance of the Constitution for example, than showing segments of the video "Our Constitution: A Conversation" where kids discuss the Constitution with Supreme Court Justices Sandra Day O'Connor and Stephen Breyer? What greater way to help students choose writing genres than playing clips of best-selling authors like Michal Chabon and Zadie Smith discussing why one prefers writing fiction and the other nonfiction?

Just as important, other valiant guests on video can empower students to take on life's obstacles: amazing people who've triumphed over the odds—among them, Kiera Brinkley, quadruple amputee dancer, performing at Polaris Dance Theater, and conjoined twins Abby and Brittany Hensel, who speak about their lives unpunctuated by solitude. I'll bring in any clip that teaches human grit—even famous people giving award speeches or commencement speeches. The triumph of a principled celebrity has great impact. Take J.K. Rowling, who rose from rock bottom using her wits to forge a life for herself. Students listen avidly to Rowling's eloquent speech at a Harvard graduation about the benefits of failure and the importance of imagination.

Were you ever impressed to hear about a good Samaritan who performed heroic acts never meaning to seek fame? A civilian who jumped to a sudden urgent calling for the sake of doing good? With videos we have the opportunity to bring into the limelight those who never meant to seek it. How heartening for the class to see live footage of a teen in a Walmart saving a baby's life by doing CPR, or people on the cashier line at Mattson's Family Market in Burlington, New Jersey, paying for a woman's groceries when the woman realizes she's short of cash, or passengers at a Perth Australia Railway station tilting a train to free a man whose foot got stuck between the train and platform. Witnessing this altruistic behavior restores faith in humanity and motivates students to give their best to the world.

As a hobby, I often like to bring in a video of a spectacular someone who made history after remaining unsung for years. Sir Nicholas Winton is a model example: a man who at age 29 single-handedly organized the rescue of 669 Czechoslovakian children from the Nazis on the brink of World War II by arranging for their safe transport to British foster homes.

What I found most incredible about this man aside from his humanitarian sacrifice is his humbleness in keeping this undertaking completely to himself. Winton's exploits first came to light almost half a century later, in 1988, after Winton's wife found a detailed scrapbook of his exploits in their attic. In a surprise tribute to Winton, which I show to my students, the BBC television program *That's Life* invites Winton to be a member of the audience for a show taping. The host, Esther Rantzen, describes Winton's achievements and asks whether anybody in the audience owes his or her life to Nicholas Winton. In a most moving scene, an entire segment of the audience stands up in revered silence while the surprised Winton rises himself and looks back from the front row at his now grown "children." None of my students have a dry eye after viewing this clip.

6. Which Online Experiments Should I Reserve for the Classroom? How Should I Present Them?

The answer is easy: Exhibit the ones that are either impossible, too time consuming, or impractical to reproduce. Here are a few top choices I inject in lessons. I present each to the class with an eye-opening question that arouses conjecture.

Will all objects fall on the moon at the same rate? In July 1971, Apollo astronaut Dave Scott drops a hammer and feather on the moon to prove that Galileo was correct: without air resistance, objects will fall at the same rate regardless of mass. What's more convincing to the class than seeing the real thing in a physics lesson?

Is racism a fact of life? The Barbie Doll Test (2006), which models Kenneth and Mamie Clark's doll test (conducted in the 1940s that shut down the "separate but equal" education for African American children) presents to children three identically featured Barbie dolls that differ only in skin and hair color. One doll is white, one Latina, and one black. In response to a series of questions, children point to the one they think is the best, prettiest, nicest, and bad. The majority of white and African American children show a preference toward the white Barbie and distaste toward Barbies of other colors. This experiment is a good springboard for discussion on whether or not racism will ever end and stands as evidence that racism still affects our children.

Can we learn a lesson about capitalism from rats? In "An Experimentally Produced 'Social Problem' in Rats" by O.H. Mower, three rats in separate cages learn that if they press a bar, a pellet of food will appear. Transferred to three different cages, this time with the bar on the opposite side of the pellet dispenser, the rats must work to get their food (press the bar, run across the cage to get the food). When the three rats are placed together in the same cage with the bar opposite the food dispenser, the rat that presses the bar cannot get to the food because the other rats devour it. On the second day, the rats all hover around the food disposal, none wanting to leave it to press the bar. Ravenous, by the third day, the rats try to chew the food slot open. On the fourth day, the hardest working rat realizes that if he presses the bar numerous times, enough pellets will drop for all, ensuring he will have some leftover food by the time he crosses to the other side of the cage! After a while, the other two rats don't bother pressing the bar at all, eating off the labor of the hardworking rat. Aside from the mind-blowing experience of seeing how even a rat can solve a problem, what a perfect demonstration for a lesson on capitalism!

What happens when people are told they are beautiful? A Turkish traveling photographer who goes by the name Rotasiz Seyyah took photographs around the world of women before and after he told them they're beautiful. A video slide of these photographs ("You Are So Beautiful") portrays the women's glowing or shy reactions to the compliment. While students have subsequently carried out Seyyah's social experiment in their schools, among girls and boys (with similar photographed reactions), what touches students in Seyyah's video is that the majority of the women are elderly and wrinkled, standing in obviously impoverished areas. The lesson to Seyyah's video is open to the class's interpretation. Several students remark upon the universal desire to feel beautiful or the fact that people recognize that beauty doesn't have one face. Others wonder how a person's behavior is influenced when they feel beautiful. Still others question whether feeling beautiful has anything to do with one's economic or social status. The thought-provoking conversations the video elicits attest to the value of its viewing.

Is texting and driving really as dangerous as they say? Relevant to my teenage students' stage of development, I especially like to show the class clips of experiments that portray recklessness. During a lesson on perceived success, for instance, I found a trial experiment that demonstrates what happens when confident drivers text behind the wheel. In January 2014, AT&T put teens to the test, on an obstacle course of cones at the Texas Motor Speedway, asking drivers to text while driving without knocking down any cones. The video showcases the distracted drivers' astonished reactions when they can't help but smash cones. The discovery? Drivers delude themselves into thinking they can text and drive safely. As the video confirms, driving while *intexticated* can cost lives. This clip makes an indelible impression on my students.

What's more, this trial experiment is a perfect preliminary to the 2015 AAA video analysis which reviews actual dash cam videos of New Jersey teenagers texting while driving and getting into crashes. Had I not shown the driving test before this video, students would have rationalized that the teenagers in the AAA video got into crashes because they were looking down too long or speeding on a highway. But the driving test proved the danger of texting while looking down fleetingly and driving at a slow pace. Now students are forced to conclude that texting while driving in any fashion, on a slow or fast road, can prove fatal.

7. Which Educational Information Will Students Research Just for the Fun of It?

To promote video research in education, you can do a bit of advertising with video clips. What do I mean? Just this: Pitch educational clips as if you were trying to sell them. Then play those clips and speak about them. The interest the clips evoke on the topic or related topics will set students off on independent clip sprees to further quench their intellectual curiosity.

Here's the way to advertise educational clips (during or outside lessons) using statements and questions.

- Ironwood trees are among the strongest in the forest. Could you believe there are people today who live in tree tops? Would you like to see these tree top dwellers, a Korowai tribe of Papua New Guinea, building a new house 114 feet high in an ironwood tree, using stone age tools?
- Did anyone here ever eat Honeycomb cereal? Do you know what a real honeycomb looks like? Do you know that bees store honey in honeycombs? Would you like to see how beekeepers remove honey from honeycombs?
- Do you think animals feel emotion? Which animals? Ana Julia Torres, a Colombian animal advocate, rescued an African lion and nursed it back to health. Do you want to see the lion's emotional response to her visit in its sanctuary?
- Did you ever read about Native Americans dances? I found the earliest video footage of Native American Sioux's ethnic drumming and dancing in war paint and costume in 1894. Anyone want to see it?
- Did you ever go skating on the frozen lake in Central Park, New York? Do you know people have been skating there for over a century? Would you like to see what the skaters looked like in the year 1900?
- Now that we identified many distinctive styles of jazz, anyone want to see people in the 1920s dancing the Charleston to ragtime jazz?

After the viewing, students automatically start shooting forth questions. Why do the Korowai want to live in treetops? Why in a jungle? How do they survive in this environment? Don't they want to modernize? Why don't we go there and show them the technology today and what they're missing? How do bees make the honeycombs? Why do they need them? How do people take away the honeycombs without getting stung? Why wasn't Torres afraid of the lion? Do lions really feel gratitude like people? How did this lion reach through the bars and hug the woman without crushing her?

Often I decide to trigger a particular discussion. For instance, in regard to the latter few clips mentioned above, I might ask these questions:

- How do you think these Native Americans were recorded in 1894? Do you think they were aware of the filmmaker? Who do you think filmed them? Why might the idea of filming their dance appeal to the Native Americans?
- What similarities do you see in the skaters' behavior on the lake in Central Park of 1900 with skaters of today? What strikes you noteworthy about these skaters?
- Do you think the Charleston could have a comeback today? Why or why not? What about the dance appeals to you? What doesn't? Do you think the Charleston is right for ragtime jazz? Can you think of different steps for the style of the music?

Once educational clips pique students' interest, they need no urging to pursue related video clips. Normally, students' research reveals their personal interests. For instance, amused with viewing first time footage, a group of students started checking up "first ever" videos themselves. But what do they look for? An aspiring pilot in the class finds the first plane flight October 23, 1906, by Santos Dumont. An avid horse rider discovers the oldest footage of the world's greatest steeplechase, the Grand National in 1911 at Aintree near Liverpool in England. A Yankees fan tracks down the first color footage of the World Series at Yankee Stadium in 1939 where the Yankees beat the Reds 2–1.

Not unexpectedly, another group of students, inspired by Torres and the lion video, is drawn to video clips portraying animals' intellect and emotional capacity. They show me a clip of a mischievous monkey messing with two tigers, reaching down from branches to pull on the tigers' ears and tails, and swinging away in the nick of time. They find a clip that depicts how elephants problem-solve to save a baby elephant from drowning. They show me a reunion between Damian Aspinall and a gorilla he raised and released five years earlier into a preserve in West Africa. In stirring scenes, the gorilla draws Aspinall close, introduces Aspinall to his gorilla family, and doesn't want to let Aspinall go!

8. What Advice Do My Students Need? Who's the Best Expert to Give It to Them?

Surely students have teachers and mentors to consult when necessary, but never before have our children had the opportunity to reach out and click to get immediate advice. Superb tutorials range from Excel training, to portrait drawing, to ways of attracting butterflies to one's backyard. I steer students to reputable tutorials whenever I'm stumped. The immense knowledge they derive from experts in these tutorial clips makes students increasingly independent. Getting immediate advice also outpaces the time and effort it takes to track down somebody who has the information. Therefore, tutorial clips save their viewers valuable time.

Common to our public speaking classes, famous motivational speakers impart wise advice (and unknowingly lend themselves as subjects of study for speech evaluations!). Exemplary for their charm, highly recommended are videos from people like Allan Pease, who discusses how to become a people magnet; Les Brown, who shows how to get unstuck; and Jack Canfield, who demonstrates how to swiftly reach one's goals. Thrilled to be let in on revelations, my class adores these distinctive clips and "collect" them to show family members. And then there's always that all-time favorite motivational speaker that rocks your students' world. For my class, it is Rick Lavoie. In his "When the Chips Are Down" speech he gives an analogy between self-esteem and poker chips to paint a clear picture of why some kids don't have self-esteem and how we can give it back to them. Check it out!

True to their motto "Ideas Worth Sharing," TED Talks are a fountain of extraordinary academic, idealistic, and practical information. Unashamedly addicted, I can't get enough of these talks. I do believe that one day, not so far in the future, perhaps in flip classrooms, our children can inspire themselves solely with TED Talks to choose worthwhile careers and pastimes, and expedite world improvement. Aside from having eye-opening "some-things" for everyone (for example, the math behind basketball's wildest moves, or a love poem for lonely prime numbers), a vast number of TED clips offer creative approaches to thinking about problems and solutions. What's great about browsing TED Talks is that most have transcripts. You can skim the talk before viewing it to see whether the information appeals to you. Then if you're interested in the clip, you can watch it, and go back to the transcript to mark off the parts you want to highlight in your lesson or snip from the clip.

As an added bonus, TED programs give you the option to design lessons around TED Talks (ideas worth sharing), TED-Ed Talks (lessons worth sharing) TED-Talk Lessons (lessons created using TED Talks) and Ted-Ed Selects (educational clips chosen from

YouTube). On the website you can filter your search by choosing the subject, content, grade level and clip length.

In a survey at the end of the year, I ask students to check off the video clips they found most memorable. The following TED TALKS were winners, striking a particular chord with my students.

- "The Surprising Science of Happiness"—Dan Gilbert, Harvard psychologist, explains how our "psychological immune system" allows us (if we let it) to feel happy even when things don't go our way.
- "The Power of Introverts"—In a society that praises extroverts, Susan Cain asserts that introverts bring extraordinary talent and abilities to the world and should have society's support and encouragement.
- "Lead Like the Great Conductors"—Using video snippets of six leading conductors, Italy Talgam illuminates different styles of leadership.
- "How I Stopped the Taliban from Shutting Down My School"—Sakena Yacoobi speaks about her courage in building schools in Afghanistan to educate men and woman despite threats from the Taliban.
- "Every Kid Needs a Champion"—Urging educators to believe in students and prod them to do their personal best, Rita F. Pierson proves from experience the difference it makes.
- "What I Learned from 100 Days of Rejection"—In a quest to desensitize himself from rejection, Jia Jang purposely pursued rejection and shares the gift behind receiving it.

So now you can choose video clips carefully for their impact. Continually search for clips to refresh your lessons. Stick to the eight question guide above and you'll have your students psyched for your video presentations. And this is just about all you need to know about video clips—except for one last thing. The final success of your video presentation depends upon taking the following factors into consideration. Please review them for supreme video viewing.

What to Bear in Mind
When Teaching with Video Clips

Gauge the suitability of the video clip, comparing its content with the intellectual and emotional level of your class. You don't want to show videos above or below the class's heads. Be sure to edit out parts of the video that contain insensitive or otherwise inappropriate material. For instance, in the video of the Korowai people building a house and in Rotasiz Seyyah's slides, "You Are So Beautiful," I clip images of scantily dressed women.

- Check the video's source for its credibility. You don't want to show videos that aren't authentic or accurate. If something about the video make you question its integrity, check it out more thoroughly or skip it.
- Make sure students understand why they're viewing the clip, but don't ruin surprises. For example, you wouldn't say, "Wait until you see who comes out from behind the curtain!" if the video's shocker is a person's sudden appearance.
- Refrain from giving your appraisal of the clip before the viewing. The class knows you chose the clip for a reason. Let them come to their own conclusions about its content.

• Make sure to link only the part of the video clip you need. Having the class wait while you find the place in the clip distracts students from the purpose and ruins the mood.

• Stop the clip to highlight a point, if you must—but not in the middle of a concept or emotional part. That ruins the pleasure of the viewing.

• Prepare a handout of specific discussion questions for longer clips that say what students should look out for, but don't give away any part of the clip within your questions. For an illustration, here's the discussion sheet I distribute for Les Brown's speech "Getting Unstuck."

- How does Les Brown use dialogue to enliven his speech? Do you think he's skilled in acting?
- Why does Les Brown use humor when speaking about a harrowing experience?
- Do you believe in Les Brown's message? Does the message pertain to you? How so?
- What type of gestures does Les Brown use when he's appealing to the audience? How do his gestures change shortly after that? Why?
- How does Les Brown move about on stage? What effect is he trying to achieve?
- What kind of energy is apparent in Les Brown's tone? Does he have good rhythm?
- Has this speech inspired you? Can you come up with a concrete goal that will get you unstuck? Would you like to share it with us?

Well-chosen recordings and video clips, educational or uplifting (or both), clearly increase understanding, and raise enquiry and discussion in the classroom that complement learning. The other day, I overheard a student telling friends, "We can't miss Mrs. Kantor's class. She's showing a documentary," and in concurrence the group relinquished their permission to stay out of class to prepare for an extracurricular activity. I can't imagine these students had inside knowledge of the documentary's content. At the same time, they felt compelled to attend class because they knew this teacher only brought in videos that held real meaning for them.

11

Getting Down
to the Actual Lesson Plan

"Give me six hours to chop down a tree, and I will spend the first four sharpening the axe."—Abraham Lincoln

Taking a Lesson from Hasbro

In 2001 Hasbro knew what they were doing as they set out to test their new video game, Pox. Market researchers entered video arcades, skate parks, and playgrounds throughout Chicago to ask boys age 8–13 the following question: "Who's the coolest kid you know?" Once they got the kid's name, they put the same question to him: "Who's the coolest kid you know?" Onward they climbed the hierarchy of cool kids, until they reached the kid who simply answered "Me" to the coolest kid question.

Rounding up all the coolest kids, researchers paid them $30 to play a prototype of the Pox video game. Watching these Alpha Pups from behind a one-way mirror playing the game, the market researchers and Hasbro executives could determine the game's future success. In fact, the enthusiasm with which these kids reacted to the game (ex. "This is better than Pokémon!") gave these Hasbro representatives the positive feedback they needed to send the kids home from the training session with 10 Pox Units for their friends. And of course, Hasbro made great sales from then on.

The moral I derived from Hasbro's venture is to find the right people—the best experts—to lend their expertise for whatever project I'm working on.

With this in mind, I adapted Hasbro's experiment for my own purpose. On a professional quest as a teacher, I headed into public schools and private schools and (with principals' permission) asked kids two questions: "Who's your favorite teacher?" and "Who's the best teacher you know?" When it was possible, I found those teachers and asked them what made them successful. Then I turned to their reading sources and mentors for guidance. By pursuing the hierarchy of excellent teachers, I acquired fabulous new ideas and approaches for lesson planning.

Asking a Variety of Experts

School teachers aren't the only experts one can consult for assistance in teaching. Proficient in various topics pertinent to our curriculums, many other professionals and workers out there can help us: principals, doctors, lawyers, parents, scientists, librarians, computer programmers, statesmen, insurance brokers, store owners, and repairmen. Educators can gain so much from interviewing these experts. Their knowledge lends great substance and credibility to subject material. And the wonderful truth is that you don't feel you're bothering these experts. Most experts relish speaking about their field of interest.

My eye doctor, for one, doesn't mind my inquisitiveness. Before teaching about eye care, I had loads of questions for the good doc. What causes a strain on the eyes? Can eyesight naturally get better? Do sunglasses really deflect ultraviolet rays? What are the ramifications of sleeping with contact lenses? Why do some people feel dizzy walking down stairs while wearing glasses? Why are people's eyes red at times when they wake in the morning? How do Visine eye drops make the redness go away? Are re-wetting drops safe for dry eyes? Throughout the bombardment of questions, the doctor responded with animation.

Sometimes acquiring a background knowledge requires educators to do a bit more investigative research. For instance, recognizing that knowledge of the judicial system is essential for understanding Reginald Rose's play *Twelve Angry Men,* I thought it best to acquaint myself with the criminal court system. To this end, I went down to the criminal courts in Kings County, Brooklyn, and interviewed judges, defense attorneys, and prosecutors, as well as sat in during trials. These interviews and courtroom experiences prepared me to discuss with my class the judicial procedure from the time a suspect is arrested to the time he is acquitted or sentenced. This research would allow me to speak confidently about jury selection and terms like misdemeanor, felony, booking, grand jury, indictment, testimony, and reasonable doubt. As an added bonus, I could regale students with amusing anecdotes of my courtroom experiences.

Like my eye doctor, these courtroom experts had no problem indulging me for my students' sake. Other experts solicited for different information complied with equal good humor. However, it's understandable that sometimes tracking down experts might not speak to your mood or practical schedule. In that case, you can just as profitably turn to online experts and gain significant information.

For instance, podcasts galore offer educators experts' strategies, insight, and recommendations easily transferable to lesson plans. At *Meet the Author USA*, for example, you might mimic the strategies authors employ to bring storytelling to life. As a matter of fact, you can check podcasts on very specific topics, for example, Roman history, and choose from abundant podcasts on that content. Teaching *Animal Farm* by George Orwell? Type "podcasts on *Animal Farm*" into a browser and you'll find helpful book club discussions that address topics such as "Does George Orwell's classic *Animal Farm* have resonance today?" Browse podcasts quickly by fast forwarding recordings and listening in on spots. Find the podcasts that speak to you. Remember, you want to find the best experts for your lesson plans. Not every expert will cater to your class's particular needs.

Gathering Your Resources

First, a note for the novice teacher. (Experienced teachers may read this too.) Don't feel daunted by the task.

Overwhelmed with curriculum preparation? Our 34th president, Dwight D. Eisenhower, had the right idea when he said, "The older I get, the more wisdom I find in the ancient rule of taking first things first—a process which often reduces the most complex human problems to manageable proportions." Keeping Eisenhower's words in mind, work through lessons one step at a time and you'll do marvelously. For now, take a deep breath and when you're ready, let's begin the process.

The Step-by-Step Process

Before planning your lessons, familiarize yourself with the year's curriculum. Get an overview of the curriculum's breakdown into units and lessons. Become acquainted with the textbooks and workbooks the school provides for you and your students. Even if you're responsible to teach the books' content, don't feel subjected to follow the exact format. Dull, outdated, or confusing books are the number one suppressors of learning. If the books appeal to you, fine, if not, record the pages you might consider using and find better books or rich supplementary material.

Next, read widely on topics, collaborate with colleagues, do research, and check out the children's books on specific topics. Virtually investigate places or sites pertinent to your topic (for example, the Great Wall of China), send away for samples of things (for example, free issues of scholastic magazines). Buy items within your means or the school's budget (for example, an ant colony). Gather materials—objects, photographs, articles, activities, videos, experiments, ideas for discussions, etc. It's okay if you don't have a planned order. Just work on collecting at this point.

Note: As you hunt for material, you might chance upon good material for potential later use. Grab it and set it aside in a different file. Just this week, I stumbled upon the following:

1. A personality survey that tests character strength.
2. A study pointing out that the more time people spend on Facebook, the more likely they'll get depressed.
3. Passages of Iris Murdoch's last novels that show her mental decline ascribable to Alzheimer's disease.
4. A video that displays children's choice to help a homeless man over buying ice cream.

I put all this material away in a miscellaneous file. In two weeks or so, I will reassess my stash, put some of it to direct use and allow the rest to resume its hibernation until future evaluation.

Okay, you found a collection of materials and have some good ideas of how to orchestrate your lesson. What follows? Getting down to the brass tacks—creating the format of the lesson plan. How do you do that? The following guide will help you arrange your lessons.

The Lesson Plan: From the Beginning to the End
of the Whole Business

> The White Rabbit put on his spectacles. "Where shall I begin, please your Majesty?" he asked.

"Begin at the beginning," the King said very gravely, "and go on until you come to the end: then stop."—Lewis Carroll, *Alice's Adventures in Wonderland*

Like most forms of communication, a lesson plan cannot be called complete unless it has some kind of beginning, middle, and end. The following guide lends a practical model for the lesson plan. It involves five components: the objective, opening motivation, presentation, reinforcement, and wrap up.

STEP 1. FORM YOUR OBJECTIVE

The objective is your goal. It states what your students will know by the end of the lesson. The word "will" is always part of the objective. Forming your objective helps you keep sight of your goal.

Examples of objectives:

- Students will analyze the difference between a "bed to bed" narrative and a story that focuses on the moment.
- Students will determine if they have good listening skills.
- Students will understand the concept of creative problem solving.
- The class will understand how cartoonists use literary allusions for humor.
- Students will understand the phases of the moon and why the moon appears to change shape as it orbits earth.

To specify how you will accomplish your objective, think of the main learning activity you'll be using in your lesson. Then include it in your objective. For example:

- In preparation to writing successful personal narratives, students will analyze the difference between a "bed to bed" narrative and a story that focuses on the moment.
- Listening to simple instruction, students will draw a stuffed creature and find out how well their drawings complement their listening skills.
- By trying to peel an orange without getting their hands sticky, students will understand the concept of creative problem-solving and apply it to life circumstances.
- By analyzing how cartoonists use literary allusions for humor, students will learn techniques to create cartoons of their own.
- By studying a still diagram of the moon's phases and a 3D animated diagram of earth-sun-moon rotation, students will understand the phases of the moon and why the moon appears to change shape as it orbits earth.

Now that you have your objective, you need to see if it's a practical one. Take a closer look at your objective and ask yourself the following questions: How valuable is this information? What do I want my students to come away knowing? Which skills will students learn for life? How well do I know this information? Do I need to brush up on my knowledge, do more research, check sources? Is the objective age appropriate? Does the content match students' maturity level? Is the objective realistic, or am I biting off more than the class can chew? Or to the contrary—is the objective too simple? Might the class know this information already? Might I need to alter the objective to make it more challenging?

When you're satisfied with your objective, you have the basis for your lesson. Now you're going to begin with a specific plan to execute your lesson.

"A goal without a plan is just a wish," said the wise Antoine de Saint-Exupery. With this sentiment in mind, let's look at the opening motivation.

STEP 2. ESTABLISH THE OPENING MOTIVATION

The opening motivation is any springboard that draws students' focus to the lesson. Why is the opening motivation necessary? When your students come into class, they have a million things on their minds, from what happened in gym class to the rough encounter on the playground. The opening motivation shuts off these whirling reflections and engages everyone in the moment.

Are opening motivations the only stimulants important to the lesson? Opening motivations are wonderful springboards, but they can't exist as the sole stimulus of your lesson. You don't want students to perk up for the beginning of class and tune out thereafter. That's why it's imperative to sprinkle motivations throughout the lesson.

The following table displays motivations you can use for the opening motivation or wherever they may fit within the lesson (the motivations last anywhere between seconds to fifteen minutes). The first column of this chart offers the learning agent and the second column, the springboard in form of inquiry or instruction. Note that earlier in this book, I mentioned the advantage behind using many of these learning agents.

Motivations

The Learning Agent	The Springboard Inquiry or Instruction
Incentive statement	"Who's ready to create a slide show of photographs with music? Come over here and we'll begin."
Model sample	"Can you find the puns in these Hallmark greeting cards?"
Prediction question	"Can you guess which of these objects will float or sink in the basin of water?" (What did you discover about the objects' density?)
Brief experiment	"Does your culture affect your perception? Take a look at this sketch and tell me what you see above the woman's head."
Peer activity	"Turn to your neighbor and discuss what you think might have happened to the people of Roanoke Island."
Short discovery activity	"Experiment mixing paint colors with your peers. Which set of colors do you think most appropriate to paint the eye of a wave? Why?"
Follow-up activity	"Based on your homework reading, can you provide appropriate captions for these illustrations of Colonial Williamsburg?"
Opinion poll	Do you agree or disagree with the following statement: "Beautiful people get farther in life."
Short survey	"When was the last time you wrote someone a letter by hand?" a) this week; b) within the past month; c) within the year; d) years ago
Video clip	"After you watch this clip, I'd like you to define 'play therapy.'"
Podcast	Listen to this podcast episode: *Arguments over the Establishment Clause* to answer the following question: "Do you agree with the separation of church and state?" Why?
Hypothetical storytelling	"Let's say you were in Benedict Arnold's shoes. Would you become a traitor to your country?"
Personal storytelling	"When I was a kid, someone tried to mug me in Sunset Park. At that moment, I could feel my adrenaline taking over my senses..."
Recording	"As you listen to this Spanish recording, can you guess where the conversation takes place?"

The Learning Agent	The Springboard Inquiry or Instruction
Teacher demonstration	"Here are two ways to 'fake a pass' in football. How can people 'fake a pass' in real life?"
Teacher oral instruction	"Follow these instructions to find your dominant eye."
Student demonstration	"Anita is going to show us how to find hidden files in Windows."
Excerpt	"After reading this excerpt, do you think a flawless memory is a blessing or a curse?"
Cartoon	"How is the cartoon poking fun of the women's suffrage movement?"
Photograph	"Who do you think created postcards of the Bisbee deportation of 1917? Who bought them? Why?"
Riddle	"Which digit is the least frequent between the numbers 1 and 1000?"
Song	"How would you improve upon this adverb song?"
Short task	"Write down one tactic Norton Juster uses in this excerpt of *The Phantom Tollbooth* to create suspense."
Fact statement	"Did you know that the tread marks of the astronauts on the moon will remain there forever?"
Application based question	"How can you tell the difference between opinions and facts in this editorial?"
Analyzing question	"How are these paintings by Picasso alike? How are they different?"
Thought-provoking question/ problem-solving question	What's an example of a gift you can give someone that doesn't cost money? What can you do if you don't have money to buy someone a gift but want to give one?
Challenge question	"How would you measure the absorbency of a paper towel?"

Here's the complication. Sometimes teachers think they have the perfect motivation and it falls flat. Why is that? Because they didn't examine its purpose closely. What should you keep in mind while planning motivations?

How effective is my motivation? Does the motivation tie in well with the lesson? Is the motivation a good attention grabber? Am I varying motivations from lesson to lesson so that no one type becomes predictable? Does the motivation invigorate the intellect? Will the class be eager for what is coming next? Is the motivation too overwhelming? Will the motivation overstimulate the class? Might it overshadow the lesson?

After your motivations pass this scrutiny, you're ready to work on the presentation.

STEP 3. IMPLEMENT THE PRESENTATION

The presentation introduces the new material; it's the focal point of the lesson. Two things you should note about the presentation.

1. The information in the presentation must meet the goal of your objective.
2. The presentation carries out the learning activity mentioned in your objective.

What tools might the teacher use during the presentation?

Common presentation tools might include visual aids, reading material, charts, diagrams, illustrations, video footage, handouts, demonstrations, activities, and experiments. Within the presentation, the teacher may also plug in additional motivations she prepared from the table above.

What is the teacher doing during the presentation?

During the presentation, the teacher might involve herself with any or a combination of the following: relating, explaining, showing, demonstrating, experimenting, inquiring, listening, responding, discussing, instructing, organizing, supervising, assisting.

What are students doing during the presentation?

During the presentation, the class might be doing any of the following: listening, observing, watching, inquiring, discussing, pondering, analyzing, evaluating, writing, hypothesizing, experimenting, solving problems, making inferences, researching, creating, debating.

How do you ensure you have a quality presentation? By asking yourself the following questions.

What's unique about my presentation? Am I using material that invigorates the intellect? What are the "hot spots" of my lesson? Are there magical moments? Elements of discovery? Does my presentation include an engrossing activity? And most importantly, does the presentation set me afire with the anticipation of sharing it?

Will my students comprehend this presentation? Does it stick to the objective? Is it organized? Does it have a flowing sequence? Am I keeping to a logical process? Do I guide the process well? Does the presentation go off on unnecessary tangents? Have I clarified each concept well?

Is the activity fair for all? Did I remove all competition or potential rivalry? Do all students have the ability to succeed? Does the activity include everyone's participation? If the activity calls for one group at a time, will observers be sufficiently occupied? Do I have enough space for the activity? Are safety precautions necessary? Will the activity be too tiring for some people? Will there be too much noise?

Do I have clear instructions for the activity? Are there too many instructions? Are the instructions easy enough to follow? How much time will the activity take? Does the activity involve too much repetition? How will students know when I need their attention?

How effective are handouts and visual material? Did I print enough handouts? Are the illustrations, photographs, and images distinct and sharp? Can I simplify complicated wording? Is the format and font pleasing to the eye? Can everyone see the Smartboard or whiteboard well? How long should I leave the material on the screen for viewing? Will I be showing an object to the class? Will people have to crane their necks to see it? Is an object I intend to pass about the room too heavy or too delicate? Will everyone get a fair chance to handle it?

What kinds of questions will I ask to promote participation in my class? Can they be worded better for clarity? Do I have too many questions? Do they all begin the same way? Do they spark curiosity? Do they call for high order thinking? Varied responses? Am I sufficiently prepared to answer my own questions? How will I check for my students' understanding?

When you have your presentation down-pat, you're well on your way to completing a successful lesson. What's next?

STEP 4. CARRY OUT THE REINFORCEMENT

The reinforcement is a review activity that tightens the nuts and bolts of your lesson. It ensures that the students have learned the material well enough to utilize it in their lives. Reinforcements may involve discussions, roleplaying, experiments, songs, review games, peer or group activities.

An important note about reinforcements: While the reinforcement directly relates to the presentation, it needs to do something more than reiterate information. It needs to reinforce previous learning with something absorbing. How do you ascertain if your reinforcement meets this criteria? By painstakingly running through these questions:

How crucial is the reinforcement to the objective? Does the reinforcement strengthen previous learning? Does it exercise critical thinking? Does it aid retention or is it merely busy work?

What's unique about my reinforcement? Is the reinforcement an exciting new experience students never had before? Is it a popular activity students won't mind doing again? Is it an overused game students are sick of playing? Will the activity appeal to the majority of students? Does it automatically give me feedback? Does it adequately measure students' ability and progress?

Does my reinforcement play fair? Does it allow everyone to test their ability in a fun way? Is the activity too intense for the class following the presentation? Does the reinforcement pit people against each other? Does it discourage rather than teach? Does it allow students a fair chance for everyone to contribute? Do I provide sufficient time for the activity? Can I stop the activity without disappointing too many people? Will students walk away from the activity energized and content? Will I spoil the activity if I tell the class to finish it at home or for homework? If necessary, can I continue the activity the next day?

Do I have clear instructions for the activity? Will students automatically catch onto instructions because they see the correlation between the reinforcement and their previous learning? How will students receive the necessary materials? Will they know what to do if they need more materials? Will they understand safety precautions? Will they understand boundaries? Will they know how and when to give me their attention?

You're just about finished with your lesson plan. How do you conclude? With the final step, the wrap-up.

Step 5. Wrap It Up

The wrap-up summarizes the lesson, but always leaves room for further exploration. During the wrap-up, students might read their work aloud, evaluate good work, share or work out final thoughts and opinions. Students might muse about the lesson, wonder about something, write down new questions they have. They might put on skits, set up fairs, or display work. They might receive enrichment exercises, homework, extra credit, or related topics for reading.

Educators don't think much about wrap-ups, which is a shame since a good wrap-up leaves students with deep reflections and a positive attitude about future learning. To create this desired impact for your lesson, check your wrap up with these questions:

Does the wrap-up conclude the lesson satisfactorily? Do students know what they can do with the information? Does the wrap-up inspire my students to explore the topic further on their own? Does it work students' brain cells, or unleash their creative spirit?

Congratulations! You've completed your lesson plan. You have your objective, opening motivation, presentation, reinforcement, and wrap up in place. Your lesson plan looks good!

Are you ready to bound into the classroom? Not just yet. Before you execute the lesson, take the time to ask yourself some questions for the final analysis.

What might go wrong during this lesson? Although seemingly pessimistic, this question is vital for your lesson's success. You'll see soon enough how the educator is often faced with sudden predicaments: The whole box of test tubes just broke. Five computers are down. No one wants to be the weird stargazer in the roleplay. Preparing for what may go awry gives you the foresight to order extra test tubes, think of ways to pair students during computer time, and prepare alternative roleplay exercises. Having a contingency plan lets you smooth over glitches during your lesson. It gives you confidence in carrying out your lesson. It allows you the peace of mind in knowing you can adapt a lesson without too much trouble.

So go ahead and imagine the worst. George Bernard Shaw said, "Both optimists and pessimists contribute to society. The optimist invents the aeroplane, the pessimist the parachute." As educators, we've got to exercise a combination of both traits—the optimist's ability to create and the pessimist's resourcefulness to save the day!

How Does My Lesson Sound?

Listen to the way your lesson sounds: Give a brand-new lesson a trial run. Ask a friend to indulge you by being your sounding board. If a child is available who is relatively the same age as the kids in your class, all the better. As you teach your "pupil" the material, listen to your sentences. Do you have an easy flowing style? Have you broken down concepts into manageable steps? Are your explanations free of fog? Ask your "pupil" to give you feedback. Ask your "pupil" which part of the lesson he got off the bat and which confused him. Be receptive to suggestions. Smooth awkward sentence structure. Think of different angles from which you can present information. Revise for clarity. Give better examples and analogies.

When you don't have a "pupil" to help you, play both teacher and pupil roles yourself. The object is to be a very patient teacher and a very niggling pupil. As you explain a concept to your "pupil" imagine him asking you questions. Let's say, for example, you're discussing the difference between similes and metaphors. You might imagine the "pupil" asking, "Why would someone use a metaphor instead of a simile?" or "Can an author compare something without using similes and metaphors?" Of course, you might not get these questions in class, but anticipating them will help you crystallize every step of your lesson.

Also effective, when practicing your lesson, imagine your "pupil" asking you the journalist's 5-W questions: Who? What? When? Where? Why/How? For instance, "Who wrote the Declaration of Independence? What does it declare? When was document written? Where? Why was it necessary? How did it influence the United States? How did it impact other nations?" Implementing these questions in your lesson assures that you're a step ahead of the class.

As the year progresses, the imagery in these ghost rehearsals will become vivid as your familiarity with real students gives you the power to predict their reactions and responses. Once you have established a relationship with your students, you can better cater to their individual needs. While you plan your lessons, practice playing alternate roles. First, as usual, be the teacher. Picture yourself playing out every aspect of the lesson. Then sit in particular students' desks and scrutinize yourself from each student's viewpoint. Ask yourself, if I were John S./Lance W./Jasmine R. would I like this lesson? Would it make sense to me? Would I think the teacher could do something better?

Later, after you have your lesson down pat, review it one more time before you enter class. The closer to class time the better. Then you can walk into class confident, with your ideas fresh in your mind.

Congratulations! Now you know how to plan your lesson. Take the time now to write an outline. Then proceed to the next chapter!

12

Seeing the Lesson
Plan Unfold

"The best teacher is not the one who knows most but the one who is most capable of reducing knowledge to that simple compound of the obvious and wonderful."—H.L. Mencken

Did you ever get inspired by ideas for lesson plans in books but wonder what they actually look like in practice? In this chapter, you'll get to see lessons unfold from start to finish, displaying the components of the five-step guide covered in the previous chapter: the objective, opening motivation, presentation, reinforcement, and wrap-up. Next, you will examine lessons that exhibit variations of the guide.

Lessons That Follow the Five-Step Guide

LESSON: WRITING

Topic: Personal narrative. **Title:** Using the write shortcut! **Grade:** 6–12. **Time Frame:** 45 minutes to 1 hour

Objective: In preparation to writing successful personal narratives, students will analyze the text of two children's books: *Bigmama's* by Donald Crews and *Shortcut* by Donald Crews to determine the difference between a "bed to bed" narrative and a story that focuses on the moment.

Opening motivation: Musing question: What makes a story interesting? Mr. Murphy writes the class' responses on the board.

Presentation: Mr. Murphy instructs the class to read the text of two children's books, *Bigmama's* by Donald Crews and *Shortcut* by Donald Crews. Students are to think about the difference between the author's narration of the stories.

Following the reading, Mr. Murphy asks these questions:

Which events did Crews focus on in *Bigmama's*? How does the story give the reader a "bed to bed" narrative in the story? Was *Bigmama's* more or less interesting than *Shortcut*? Can you define the term "bed to bed" narrative?

Which event did the story focus on in *Shortcut*? What tools does Crews use to focus on the moment? Which of these tools match the ones we wrote on the board? How did Crews avoid giving a "bed to bed" narrative in *Shortcut*?

Sharing a personal story, Mr. Murphy recounts what he once did at a school masquerade when an audacious student grabbed at his mask, attempting to reveal Mr. Murphy's identity. Mr. Murphy discusses the point at which he would begin the story in the personal narrative and where he would end it to avoid a "bed to bed" narrative and maintain the reader's interest.

Reinforcement: Mr. Murphy tells the class to think of their own personal narrative and how they'd write it. On a worksheet, the class jots down the answers to these questions: What's an interesting event that happened in your life? How will you avoid the "bed to bed" narrative in your writing? Where will you start telling your story? What moments will you highlight? Why? Where will you end your story? How will you make sure you don't go off on a tangent?

How will students know if they're on the right track? Mr. Murphy asks the class to share their personal narrative with a friend and ask which part sounds most exciting. Then they share their worksheet responses for feedback. Once students establish they have their ideas down pat, they prepare a rough outline for their personal narrative that focuses on one moment.

Wrap-up: Students touch up their outlines at home and bring it in the next day for further instruction.

LESSON: COMMUNICATION

Topic: Listening skills. **Title:** Do you hear what I say? **Grade:** 5–12. **Time Frame:** 1 hour

Objective: Listening to simple instruction, students will draw a stuffed creature and find out how well their drawings complement their listening skills.

Opening motivation: Mrs. Lee has a zany looking stuffed creature hidden in a bag. (She named hers Poochie.) Mrs. Lee asks the class this riddle: "How is it possible to imagine what Poochie looks like without removing him from the bag?" The answer: By listening to a description of him! Mrs. Lee invites the class to test their listening skills with the following experiment.

Presentation: Mrs. Lee gives students step-by-step oral instructions of how to draw Poochie on paper. This is done using pencils, so that students can erase when necessary to perfect their drawings. Afterwards, Mrs. Lee asks the class to tape their drawings to the board. (Students may omit their names.) The teacher removes Poochie from the bag and props the creature against the board for all to see. Students note which drawings resemble Poochie and which don't.

Next, Mrs. Lee exhibits the original drawing instructions on the Smartboard. Reviewing the instructions one by one, the class pauses to survey the drawings and determine which ones don't adhere to the instruction. During this process, Mrs. Lee keeps removing the incorrect drawings from the board until only the correct ones remain. Usually very few drawings, if any, remain on the board. Stunned by the numerous mistakes they've made in following simple instructions, students resolve to listen better in the future.

Reinforcement: Students test their listening comprehension a second time by attempting to draw another creature (this time "Dino") following Mrs. Lee's careful instruction. Afterwards, Mrs. Lee carries out the same review activity done with Poochie to see how well the class's new drawings match the teacher's instructions. Inevitably, a greater number of papers pass the scrutiny of the review.

Wrap-up: Students discuss why their listening skills improved the second time around. They share tips that have helped them listen or concentrate better.

LESSON: COGNITION AND MEMORY

Topic: Creative problem-solving. **Title:** How creative are you? **Grade:** 5–12. **Time Frame:** 1.5 hours

Objective: By trying to peel an orange without getting their hands sticky, students will understand the concept of creative problem-solving and apply it to life circumstances.

Opening motivation: Students bring in an orange from home. Gathering the class in the home economics kitchen (or around a covered table in the classroom), Mr. Rosario poses a creative problem-solving question: Imagine you have many household items at your convenience besides disposable gloves. How can you peel an orange without getting your hands sticky?

In groups, students think of non-sticky ideas and experiment peeling their oranges using kitchen supplies such as their fingers, plastic knives (sharper knives for older children), napkins, paper towels, and plastic bags. For a greater challenge, students need to make sure the peels can serve as a container or dish for the orange once the orange is peeled. Mr. Rosario provides extra oranges if needed.

Volunteers demonstrate how they were successful in peeling their orange without getting their hands sticky. The class decides which idea seems most practical.

Depending on the class's success, Mr. Rosario may or may not play two short video clips that demonstrate two different ways to peel the orange without getting sticky, one with fingers and one with a knife. (The videos are Orange Peel Trick at https://youtu.be/s0ZorQ6-qlg and How to Peel an Orange the Easy Way at https://youtu.be/FaR3ofRxjSo.)

Presentation: Back in the classroom, Mr. Rosario defines creative problem solving and discloses the three main techniques that encourages creative problem solving: mental state shift, problem refraining, and multiple idea facilitation. The class discusses which creative problem-solving techniques they naturally used in peeling the orange. Mr. Rosario asks them if they discovered anything about their thinking in relation to problem solving. To practice creative problem-solving for life situations, Mr. Rosario presents four separate creative problem-solving questions to different groups in the class:

- How can you find a good-paying job this summer without having prior experience?
- You don't want to go shopping with a pushy friend. How do you decline without making this friend mad?
- You have just gotten into a fight with your best friend and you're not on speaking terms. How do you get back to having an even better friendship than before?
- To raise five thousand dollars (for the school trip) you need to sell something of student value that you can get at low cost. What will you sell? Why do you think you'll make a profit?

Reinforcement: The teacher challenges students to come up with a problem in their present life and to write out a plan of action for solving it using the creative problem solving techniques they've learned.

Wrap-up: Mr. Rosario asks the class to act upon solving their problem with the creative problem-solving techniques. They will share their progress with classmates the following week.

LESSON: LITERARY ALLUSIONS

Topic: Creating cartoons with literary allusions. **Title:** How do cartoonists use literary allusions to make cartoons funny? **Grade:** 9–12. **Time Frame:** 45 minutes to 1 hour

Objective: By analyzing how cartoonists use literary allusions for humor, students will learn techniques to create cartoons of their own.

Opening motivation: Ms. Dimitri opens the lesson with a thought-provoking question and incentive statement:

Thought-provoking question: "What do you think makes a cartoon funny?"

Incentive statement: "By the end of this lesson you will know how to create a funny cartoon!"

Presentation: Ms. Dimitri hands out a booklet containing model samples of cartoons with allusions to specific fairytales and classics (for example, *Pinocchio, King Midas and the Gold Touch, For Whom the Bell Tolls, The Raven,* etc.). Ms. Dimitri asks the class if they recognize the literary references. Next, Ms. Dimitri defines literary allusions and students analyze tactics the cartoonists used to convey their literary allusions with humor. For example, in one cartoon, the witch from *Hansel and Gretel* says to the Old Woman Who Lived in a Shoe, "Sooooo … I couldn't help noticing that you have so many children you don't know what to do.…" Students realize the cartoonist's strategy in joining characters from two different fairytales to suggest a mutually beneficial proposition.

Here are several other tactics cartoonists use in the booklet:

- Using something prominent about a fairytale character to work against him (or for him). In the cartoon, Pinocchio failed his DWI test because he can't touch the tip of his nose.
- Incorporating a character who finds problem with a fairytale character's supernatural abilities. In the cartoon, King Midas's accountant urges King Midas to stop touching things because the former can't keep up with the figures.
- Using a well-known literary title or phrase as a pun. In the cartoon, a girl reading a book titled *The Cat in the Hat* looks like she's contemplating dressing up her cat, and a cat on the bed is thinking, "Don't get any ideas…"
- Using a familiar pun on literary words to create a whole new circumstance. The cartoonist shows a baby raven in a high chair saying. "More! More!" to its mother feeding him and the caption reads "The Raven Before He Got Old and Cynical."

Reinforcement: On the Smartboard, Ms. Dimitri brings up new cartoons containing different literary allusions and students apply their previous knowledge to mark off the humorous tactics the cartoonist uses for each one.

Wrap-up: For homework, students create a literary cartoon applying one of the strategies they've learned from the cartoon booklet or one of their own. If they wish, they may borrow graphics, pictures, clipart images, drawings, photographs, or magazine pictures to help illustrate their cartoons. They can work on scanning their cartoon, adjusting it and adding the caption with Photoshop.

LESSON: ASTRONOMY

Topic: The eight phases of the moon. **Title:** Does the moon change shape? **Grade:** 5–9. **Time Frame:** 2–3 hours

Objective: By studying a still diagram of the moon's phases and a 3D animated diagram of earth-sun-moon rotation, students will understand the phases of the moon and why the moon appears to change shape as it orbits earth.

Opening motivation: The previous day, Mr. McBride sent students on an assignment to find the moon in the sky, sketch it, and record the approximate time they saw it. Now, in a follow-up activity, students circle the image on the Mr. McBride's handout that best resembles the one in their sketch.

Presentation: Next, Mr. McBride hands out a diagram of the moon's eight phases during a month, along with a description of each phase and the time the moon rises and sets during each phase. Using this information, Mr. McBride asks the class to name the phase of the moon in their sketch: The New Moon, Waxing Crescent, First Quarter, Waxing Gibbous, Full Moon, Waning Gibbous, Last Quarter, or Waning Crescent. Mr. McBride explains the terms waxing and waning and gives a simple explanation for determining whether the moon is waxing or waning.

Then Mr. McBride says, "What if I told you the moon doesn't change shape during the eight phases? Can you explain why the moon appears to change?"

After listening and responding to the class's conjecture, Mr. McBride shows a 3D animation of an earth-sun-moon diagram that depicts the earth spinning on its axis, the moon orbiting the earth and the sun shining on both earth and moon. The class is able to see three things: first, that the sun always illuminates half the moon not visible from earth. Second, that as the moon orbits earth, different amounts of that light reflect on the part of the moon visible to us on earth. Third, that each moon phase is named after the illuminated area of the moon.

The class can make the following deduction about why the moon appears to change shape: The sunlight seems to move across the surface of the moon from right to left. What looks like the moon changing shape is really just a trick of light!

Reinforcement: Students make a lunar flip book of the moon's phases by drawing a picture of each phase on the corners of the pages. Students write a children's storybook in the flip book that corresponds with the passage of a month's time. Some moon drawings may repeat themselves on consecutive pages depending on the length of the storyline and its passage of time.

Wrap-up: Students set up a display of lunar flip books for a hands-on school exhibit. Mr. McBride challenges the class for extra credit to create a jingle that sums up something they learned during the lesson. Mr. McBride leaves the class off with the following questions:

- What do you think happens to earth's orbit because of the moon? What would happen to earth's orbit without the help of the moon?
- Can you guess how the moon affects the tides? ocean life? the climate?
- How might the phases of the moon be important to fishermen? To farmers?
- How do you think the moon's phases were crucial in ancient times to determine the seasons, months, and years?
- Do you think it's possible to tell time by looking at the moon?
- During which moon phase are sunrise and moonrise about the same? Sunset and moonrise about the same?
- Where did the expression "once in a blue moon" come from?

The teacher may divulge the answers to these questions or divide the questions among the class and have them research the answers for the next lesson.

LESSON: STEREOTYPING

Topic: Challenging assumptions. **Title:** How do stereotypes affect your life? **Grade:** 5–12. **Time Frame:** 45 minutes to 1 hour

Objective: By seeing how they make false assumptions about strangers and even people they know, students will realize how stereotyping affects their lives and society.

Opening motivation: Mrs. Lindsey calls into class a guest the class doesn't know well, for instance, another teacher in the school (or secretary, janitor, a student from a different grade). Mrs. Lindsey asks the class to fill out a chart answering the following questions: What subject does this person teach? What does he do as a hobby? What music does this person like? What kinds of books does he read? Where does this person live? Where does he shop for clothing? What is his favorite store?

Mrs. Lindsey exhibits the identical chart on a PowerPoint filled in by the guest. She asked the class which answers they guessed correctly, which were similar, and which were totally out of the ballpark. At this point the guest may say a few added words about himself before leaving the classroom.

Presentation: Mrs. Lindsey hands out a sheet with an advertisement, a political statement, short poem, lyric, cartoon, and a quip by a comic, that all contain group or national stereotypes. The class discusses each item on the sheet. The class defines the word stereotype and Mrs. Lindsey asks: How valid are stereotypes? How are they created? Are stereotypes fair? Why or why not? Are some stereotypes harmless? Are others harmful? How so? Do stereotypes affect you personally? How so?

Reinforcement: Students write true and false statements about themselves. Mr. Lindsey encourages them to write true statements that might surprise the class, for example, "I like to dance." Or "I take karate classes." Volunteers read their statements to the class and the class guesses which are true and false. The volunteer corrects them when necessary. Mrs. Lindsey asks the class to consider why they were surprised by some of the true statements.

Wrap-up: For journal writing, Mrs. Lindsey might ask the class whether they think ads, TV shows, movies, and video games should be restricted in how they present characters.

For extra credit, students write how stereotypes affect them either personally or in the way they judge or view individuals or groups of people.

No Teaching Guide Is Absolute

Samuel Taylor Coleridge defines poetry as "the best words in the best order." I love that definition! If you think about it, the definition qualifies any good form of writing. The effect of our writing depends on our word choice and the myriad combinations with which we express them. Coleridge's definition of poetry got me thinking about the definition of a good lesson plan. If it's not the best words in the best order, I'd say it's the best *ideas* in the best order! Just as no poet can tell another poet, "Okay, you choose the words or lines and I'll give you the order," no educator can dictate the framework for your lesson plan. Educators have to organize ideas in a structure that best fit their style of communication.

So, while a lesson has to contain substance and flow, there must be a hundred ways to plan the same lesson!

Let your lesson embrace a natural rhythm. Let it be a fluid expression that penetrates quickly into the unconscious and delights your students with its revelations. On this note, never let yourself fall into a rut by religiously following one guide, whether in this book or another. My guide works well for many, but the clever teacher may or may not stick to it. She does what comes naturally or what works best in her classroom. In retrospect, she might find that her teaching style models a guide she read somewhere, and that's fine. Still, if her method follows no framework familiar to the educational world, who's to say hers isn't valid? New teaching systems are being created every day. Any educator's contrived method may be just as satisfactory or even more innovative than the ones that exist in the books.

Can one deviate from the order of the five-step guide above? Of course. Numerous variations of this guide are not only possible but preferable when the circumstance calls for it. What kind of variations are we talking about? Variations that tailor to the class's needs. Let's take a look at examples of what I mean.

Omitting a Component of the Guide

Using her intuition, the teacher may easily exclude the opening motivation if she knows the class will find the presentation particularly engaging. Similarly, she might skip the reinforcement when a presentation is well accepted or omit a wrap-up when her reinforcement achieves the lesson. In other words, it is possible for a lesson to be missing a component or components of this guide. In fact, a lesson may consist solely of a presentation and wrap-up, or an opening motivation and presentation, or a presentation and reinforcement.

Allowing for Spontaneity Within the Guide

The guide keeps you grounded so that you don't go off on tangents, but when you get an idea smack in the middle of the lesson, go for it. For instance, sometimes a discussion is going so well that it's worth prolonging for the entire period. To the contrary, you may find the need to curtail a debate if it becomes too heated. Occasionally, you might decide upon additional practice exercises for one class or skipping a quiz in another. Seldom does a lesson come out exactly as planned and that's often a good sign.

Perhaps most importantly, give yourself permission to change up your lesson plan when inspiration strikes for some creative fun. Let's take a look at what I mean with a real example from the classroom.

One Thursday, Mr. Blake and his class were performing Act III, Scene Two, in *Julius Caesar*, or, rather, Mr. Blake was playing an inflamed Antony trying to impassion four plebeian readers while the rest of the class followed along lethargically in the play. Tired of his one-man show, Mr. Blake got a sudden inspiration to get the whole class involved. Dividing the class into four groups, Mr. Blake had each group take on the role of one Citizen and recite his lines in unison. "Now," Mr. Blake said, "Give it all you've got! I want the principal to come checking to see what the noise is all about."

What a transformation! The gusto with which the groups shouted and ranted jolted the play to exuberant life. When the class came to a scene where the crowd shouts, Mr.

Blake suggested half the Citizens use growling voices, and the other half, high-pitched tones. What a clamor! As expected, Mr. Blake did get the principal's attention and when she came into the room, the class cheered wildly for themselves.

The superb teacher becomes a chameleon, adapting to the needs of his class. Classes take on personalities. There are classes who are hams and love when the teacher sits on the sideline as they carry on roleplay and most activities. Other classes liked the security of the teacher conducting the lesson. Yet other classes thrive on doing group projects. Your class will guide you more than any guide will. As long as your lessons strengthen learning, it makes no difference how faithfully they stick to your original plan.

ADJUSTING THE LENGTH OF A LESSON

The lesson that continues the next day. Since pacing the lesson is one of the hardest aspects to control, the teacher may end up teaching one and half lessons in one period, or just the opposite: having to continue the same lesson the following day. In either case, the lesson is cut into different dimensions. As long as the teacher doesn't rush a topic or break off the lesson mid-concept, she need not worry much about the cutoff time.

The lesson that extends over multiple days. As expected, broader objectives can't possibly fit into definite time slots. Discussing a novel or a period in history, or working on a project, may take more time. In this case, the objective of the lesson may extend over many lessons. Here too, the teacher doesn't worry about beginning the lesson with an opening motivation and so on, but continues wherever she left off the previous lesson. For a lesson that extends over multiple days, the components of the guide seldom balance. The lesson of one day might include only a few components, repeated components, an inflated component or even just a single component of the guide.

Lessons That Don't Follow the Conventional Guide

LESSON: POETRY

Topic: Didactic poem—"If" by Rudyard Kipling. **Title:** What's your advice to humankind? **Grade:** 8–12. **Time Frame:** approximately 4 hours

Day 1

Objective: By studying Kipling's poem "If," students will determine which behaviors the poet thought his son should live by and write a similar didactic poem.

Opening motivation: Mr. Pratt asks the class, "What are some good rules to live by? What counsel would you give to someone younger than you? Someone your age? An adult?" He asks the class to jot down their ideas.

Presentation: Mr. Pratt introduces a famous poet, Rudyard Kipling, who writes a poem giving advice to his son. ("If" by Rudyard Kipling, https://www.poetryfoundation.org/poems-and-poets/poems/detail/46473.)

Using the Smartboard, the teacher plays George Horn's musical typographical narration of "If." Then, Mr. Pratt divides the stanzas of the poem among groups in the class. He points out how paradox characterizes the tone of the entire poem. Groups interpret their lines and discuss which points of advice resonate with them. The teacher calls on two students from each group to share their group's interpretations and evaluations.

Wrap-up: For homework, Mr. Pratt asks the class to write their own advice poems mimicking the paradoxical nature Kipling's poem and rhyme scheme of the stanzas. Students may, like Kipling, write about behavior that "makes one a man" (or woman), or they can narrow the focus and write their poem about the character traits that make one a good parent, student, daughter, sibling, neighbor, leader, police officer, etc. To illustrate, Mr. Pratt hands out "If" poems former students wrote demonstrating both versions of poems.

Day 2

Reinforcement: Students group to give each other honest feedback without letting personal biases interfere with the evaluation of the poem's content.

Wrap-up: Students enhance the visual appearance of their poems by adding background images, pictures, and photos.

Day 3, a Week Later

Wrap-up: Mr. Pratt has graded and returned the poems. Students have put the final tweaks on them. Now, volunteers read their poems before the class and/or school assembly. Mr. Pratt collects the poems and publishes them in a booklet for the class. A student sample follows.

IF, by Chaya Mindy Perlstein (grade 11)

If you can bite your tongue and guard your words
  Despite the urge to sting
If you can speak with dignity and honor
  Have compassion for each living thing
If you can stand proud when those around you
  Resort to the lowest degree
If you can help those disadvantaged and poor
  And not become deaf to their pleas
If you can respect the opponents who vie for your place
  And do not belittle or shame
If you can rise to the top with substantial success
  But remain humble despite all your fame
If you can lower your tone while speaking with foes
  Be assertive, yet calm and contained
If you can hit failure and roadblocks galore
  And still keep your eye on the aim
If you can think ahead and plan the future
  With a logical, clear state of mind
If you can realize the gravity of your expectations
  And to the consequences you are not blind
If you can be accountable for your actions
  Be responsible all day, every minute
Then dear leader, you can guide our country
  and all the citizens within it.

Lesson: World History

Topic: The Vietnam War. **Title:** Was the United States justified in entering the Vietnam War? **Grade:** 9–12. **Time Frame:** multiple days

Day 1

Objective: Upon learning about America's role in Vietnam, students will decide for themselves whether the United States could justify its involvement in the Vietnam War.

Opening motivation: Mrs. Archer poses the following thought-provoking questions: How far would you go to fight for your country? If you thought your country was losing the war, would you still fight on?

Mrs. Archer plays a few popular songs that raised patriotic feelings during the Vietnam War. For each song, students interpret the songwriter's message.

- "The Ballad of the Green Berets"—1966, Barry Sadler, for the sake of America
- "What We're Fighting For"—Dave Dudley, 1966, for the U.S. flag, to protect America from other countries taking over
- "The Fightin Side of Me"—Merle Haggard, December 1969

Presentation: Acquainting students with pro-war activism during the Vietnam War, Mrs. Archer demonstrates the causes and effects of the Vietnam War on the board. She then turns students' attention to the following material and footage:

- Excerpt of President Dwight D. Eisenhower's press conference explaining the "Domino Theory," April 7, 1954
- Excerpt of President Kennedy's news conference responding to a question on American's involvement in South Vietnam, February 7, 1962

Short video clips of presidents defending the Vietnam War:

- President John F. Kennedy presenting six proposals to the United Nations for the New Disarmament Plan on Vietnam, September 25, 1961
- President Lyndon B. Johnson appealing to a crowd assembled at Johns Hopkins University in his "Peace without Conquest" speech to support the country's war effort, and about the views of the American government, April 7, 1965
- President Richard Nixon moving the majority of Americans in his speech "The Silent Majority" to support his Vietnam War strategy, November 3, 1969

In a chart, students write the main idea of each document and speech. Afterwards, students compare their charts with each other.

Reinforcement: Mrs. Archer asks the class to discuss the following with their peers: Were politicians merely playing politics, or was war necessary?

Day 2

Opening Motivation: To set the mood for a discussion on anti-war activists during the Vietnam War, Mrs. Archer plays Peter Seeger singing "Where Have All the Flowers Gone?" (Pete Seeger and Joe Hickerson, 1962) while she draws the main subjects of the song on the board. The song consists of questions and answers along with the chorus, "When will they ever learn?" Mrs. Archer pauses for the class to predict the responses to the song's questions before giving them away in her drawings. By the end of the song, the drawing comes back full circle—a chain of events shows young girls picking flowers, girls grown up and marrying young men, young men becoming soldiers, soldiers going to their graves, the graveyards strewn with flowers.

The class discusses the song's theme, which is the futility of war. The class discusses whether or not they agree with this theme. Mrs. Archer mentions that many songs like these were composed or sung in protest of the Vietnam War. To model another anti-war song, she plays the most humorous and vicious Vietnam War protest song, "The Universal Coward" by Jan and Dean from "Folk 'n' Roll" 1965 and the class decipher the lyrics.

Presentation: Mrs. Archer guides students to find primary source material online (and in the school library) that protests the Vietnam War. Besides photographs, video clips, students must find at least one written primary source. Students write down a summary for the materials they select.

Students group to share the most significant items from their research. Concurrently, Mrs. Archer makes her rounds checking students' research and providing additional input. Students draw a timeline for their materials.

Wrap-up: Groups decide which materials to show the class the next day. Group members fill in the names of these materials in the correct area of a large timeline the teacher hangs on the wall. Among their primary sources in their presentation, students must include one document.

Days 3 & 4

Presentation: Mrs. Archer chooses representatives from each group to portray two of their group's findings on the timeline via handout, narration, or Smartboard viewing. The audience, meanwhile, writes down the main ideas depicted in each presentation.

At the end of the presentations, the class might have seen a variety of materials. Photographs:

- A young Buddhist monk who lights himself on fire in protest, Saigon, October 5, 1963 (http://www.vietnampix.com/fire1.htm)
- A farmer holding the body of his dead child as South Vietnamese troops look on, March 1964 (http://www.nytimes.com/imagepages/2013/09/05/arts/05VIETNAMjp1.html)
- Jane Rose Kasmir, an anti-war activist, holding a flower above a guard's bayonet during the 1967 march on the Pentagon
- American soldiers taking a break in a bunker where they displayed a sign that read, "Home is Where You Dig," 1968 (http://www.archives.gov/education/lessons/vietnam-photos/National Archives Identifier: 532482)
- A shell-shocked woman coming out of the Siege of An Loc in the photograph Siege of An Loc, South Vietnam, Barbara Gluck, 1974

Written materials:

- An article by Henry Kamm from the *New York Times* on March 16, 1968, describing the My Lai massacre
- Excerpts from Gareth Stevens's *The Vietnam War: A Primary Source History (In Their Own Words)* 2006; pages 16, 18, 24, and 25
- A U.S. Marine's letter to his parents
- A soldier's letter to his history professor at the University of Wisconsin–Madison
- A Vietnamese peasant describing a three-day chemical attack near Da Nang

- Defense Secretary Clark M. Clifford dialogue to Stanley Karnow about skeptical war plans
- Vietnam War veteran John Kerry's testimony before the Senate Foreign Relations Committee, April 22, 1971

Live footage:

- Live fighting at Vietnam (www.Militaryvideo.com)
- The song "For What It's Worth" performed by Buffalo Springfield, 1967
- A march in Central Park toward the UN building in New York City, April 15, 1967
- A march to the Pentagon, October 21, 1967

Wrap-up: Mrs. Archer poses the following questions: Why do you suppose the media projected the sentiment of anti-war demonstrators more than the arguments of those who favored the war? Why do you think it's important to study historical events from different perspectives?

Day 5

Reinforcement: By the show of hands, students state whether they believe the United States could justify its involvement in the Vietnam War. The class forms small pro- and anti-activist groups and prepare to roleplay Vietnam War demonstrations. Using specific examples from the knowledge they've gleaned, groups create banners in defense or protest of the war. Taking turns, the opposing groups march about the room holding their banners (and chanting their beliefs). Each side gets a chance to challenge the other's banners with intelligent questions. (If an overwhelming majority of students share one belief, the teacher divides the class into two demonstration groups and tells students on the "wrong side" of their belief to play the devil's advocate.)

Wrap-up: Students take their seats. Reflecting upon their lessons on Vietnam, Mrs. Archer and her class discuss the following: What message did the Vietnam War send the world? Did it leave a legacy for the United States today?

For homework, students get to choose one of the following assignments:

1. Thomas Jefferson once stated, "The tree of liberty must be refreshed from time to time with the blood of patriots and tyrants." Using their knowledge of the Vietnam War (and further research if you wish) defend or oppose Jefferson's quote in a formal essay.

2. Identify the symbols in each of these four political cartoons published during the Vietnam War and the message the cartoonist relays through the symbols and caption. Mention how you would change one cartoon to make it more powerful or ironic.

3. Write a one-act play about any occurrence during Vietnam including at least three actors. Be sure to keep true to the people's attitudes of the time.

4. Play the online Vietnam War game—*Jungle Warfare, Vietnam 65—Into the Jungle or Platoon*. Critique its design, taking into account how well it portrays the events of the Vietnam War and the skills necessary in combatting the enemy.

LESSON: EARTH SCIENCE

Topic: Auto pollution. **Title:** Are we breathing safely? **Grade:** 7–12. **Time frame:** 4–7 lessons

Objective: Students will learn about auto air emissions and surmise how to keep greenhouse gases from escalating in their environment.

Opening motivation: Mr. Vasquez asks the class to write down the number of people in their households who commute to school or work (or elsewhere) each day and the number of family vehicles used for the commute. On the board, the teacher charts the data he receives from the class to show how many people in the class' households depend daily on family vehicles versus other modes of transportation. Together with the class, the teacher figures out the AVO (average vehicle occupation) of the class's households by dividing the number of people traveling by the number of vehicles.

Presentation: Mr. Vasquez asks students to guess the average number of people occupying a car in the United States in the past year according to the United States Department of Energy. Next, Mr. Vasquez asks the class what this number means and the problem it implicates.

Mr. Vasquez shows the class photographs of polluted atmospheres and oceans throughout the United States. He explains that unfortunately, the automobile is the leading contributor of air pollution. A gallon of gas releases 22 pounds of carbon dioxide. 76% of the carbon monoxide in the earth's air comes from cars. 30% of nitrogen oxide in the air comes from automobiles.

Why is air pollution so harmful? The teacher explains that:

- pollution damages air and water quality.
- carbon monoxide doesn't allow the blood to work at complete capacity to carry oxygen to the brain, heart, and other body organs.
- carbon dioxide and other gases add to the greenhouse gases and raise the temperature of atmosphere and melting ice caps.
- toxic emissions deplete the ozone layer and magnify the greenhouse effect, allowing more infrared rays to penetrate the ozone layer.

How does air pollution cause the United States billions of dollars every year?

- It raises blood pressure
- It causes respiration difficulties
- It increases risk of heart attacks and strokes

The class finds the latest AQI, air quality index, online for local areas and others. Students brainstorm ways they can reduce the number of vehicles such as by biking, walking, carpooling or using mass transit.

A mechanic visits the class to talk about maintenance tips that save fuel—getting periodic engine tune-ups, changing dirty air filters, tightening the gas cap, emptying extra weight from the trunk, and keeping tires well inflated. Students guess driving tips that cut carbon dioxide emissions, such as avoiding abrupt starts and stops, warming up the car no more than 30 seconds, planning a route to an unfamiliar destination so that fuel isn't wasted by idling or doing extra driving (or remaining idle to make calls or redirect the GPS).

Presentation: Next, in a virtual design lab online, on *Discovery Education*, students design a fuel-efficient vehicle of the future, choosing among many factors: the vehicle's size, shape, energy source, and motor size. Once students complete their design, the computer evaluates the vehicle's weight, material cost, and selling price. Then, students test drive their vehicle on a virtual road at a selected speed and distance and get the result of the vehicle's drag force, fuel cost, and carbon emissions, among other data.

Analyzing the data, students keep revising their designs for better efficiency! Without knowing much beforehand about a vehicles' design and performance rate, students can figure out through experimentation which design factors contribute to pollution problem and which can reduce it. Students print the test results of their final vehicle design—the one that best supports the criteria for the most cost efficient, fuel efficient, capable car.

Reinforcement: In groups, students compare their final vehicle designs. Each group votes on the best design of the bunch based on the data provided. (If students can't decide, they call in an objective evaluator from another group.) Next, the groups take turns promoting their prize vehicle, by projecting the blueprint of the vehicle's design on the board and explaining to the class why the vehicle is the best design for the future market.

Wrap-up: Mr. Vasquez underscores the pollution problems facing our environment. Students write personal resolutions. Then groups discuss how they can educate the greater public about fuel efficiency. One group offers to hand out information in the school corridor during the next PTA meeting. A second group proposes writing brochures for the school. A third group volunteers to give a slide presentation at a Drivers' Ed facility. A fourth group sends ideas and data to vehicle engineers, suggesting how the engineers can build cars that better serve our planet.

What Happens after You Teach a Lesson?

So, you've carried out your lesson. Do you set it aside, for better or worse, and move on to the next lesson? Not so fast, my friend. Reflecting upon the success of your lesson can help you hone it for other classes and teach you tricks for all future lessons! Don't forget to ask yourself these questions in the aftermath of the lesson:

- How would I assess the overall lesson? Did my students follow well?
- Was something lacking from my lesson? Could I have given a better explanation? A simpler analogy? clearer instructions? Could I have promoted greater discovery? A hands-on experiment?
- What was the class' attitude? The level of participation? Which questions interested them the most? How many students were heard during the lesson? Who didn't get to share her piece? Did anyone seem frustrated?
- Was the lesson well-paced? Did I allot sufficient time for each component of the lesson? Did I allow ample time for questions? reflection? discussion? Did I push too many agendas into this one lesson?
- Was any part of my lesson tedious? Could I detect boredom? Were my students mentally disengaged during activities?
- Was *I* bored with any part of the lesson? Did I have to feign my enthusiasm?
- Did I make sure to reiterate crucial information? Did I sound too repetitive?
- Was my wrap-up too tight? Did I stir a desire for further learning on this topic?

- Did I reach my objective?
- How can I improve this particular lesson? Do I need to be more meticulous in my research? procedure? organization?

What Were the Highlights of the Lesson?

Perhaps it's even more important to evaluate what went well during your lesson so that you can duplicate that success. For instance, if your class apparently enjoyed chanting or singing, you can plan more of those activities for future lessons. Therefore, ask yourself: what did I do right? What were the highlights of this lesson? What gave life to the lesson? What worked well? Which part of this lesson made me proud? How can I duplicate this success?

Can't spot the highlights? Ask the experts—in this case your students! Any of the following questions will enlighten you immediately to the good parts of your lesson:

- What was your favorite part of the lesson?
- What made you enthusiastic?
- What held your suspense?
- What made you proud of yourself?
- What would you like to do again?
- Did you learn a new life lesson?
- What part of the lesson made you think of something in a different way?
- What part of the lesson changed your mind about something?
- What did you discover?

Gauge Students' Knowledge of Topic: Add the E to the KWL Chart

The KWL Chart, created by Donna Ogle (1986), asks children to write what they *know*, *want* to know and what they've *learned* about a topic. Before listening to, viewing, researching, or reading information, students fill out KW columns, stating in the first two columns "What I **K**now" and "What I **W**ant to Know." The exercise draws the students into the lesson with increased anticipation. Reading the KW columns also helps the teacher assess the students' experience with the topic. She might correct wrong information in the K column so that students don't begin the lesson with false notions. After the lesson, students fill in the last column, "What I **L**earned" to reinforce the knowledge they've gleaned. The teacher checks the L column for student understanding. Especially important, this last column shows the teacher whether or not she has met her objective.

The following is a KWL Chart filled out by fifth grader, Nicky Romero.

KWL Chart, Topic: Fire

Before the Lesson:

What I Know

> A smoke alarm can save peoples' life.
> It is possible to smother a small fire with a blanket, dirt, or sand.
> When your clothes catch fire, you need to stop, drop, and roll.
> You never open doors that are too hot to touch.
> Water does not put out a grease fire.

What I Want to Know

Why does fire sometimes have blue in it?
What's a first, second, and third degree burn?
How come my brother can put out a lit candle with his finger and not get hurt?

After the Lesson:

What I Learned

I learned the following information about fires:
- The majority of fires start at home in the kitchen.
- Gases are easiest to burn because gas and oxygen mix easily.
- A small flame can grow into a large flame in seconds.
- The blue color in a flame comes from molecules that are produced during combustion.

I learned how to do the following:
- how to prevent fires.
- how to put out a fire with a fire extinguisher.
- how to differentiate between a first, second and third degree burn.
- how to treat first degree burns on my own and how to treat second and third degree burns while waiting for professional medical attention.

I like to have my students fill out this KWL chart, but in addition to Ogle's columns, I add an E to the chart to represent what I *enjoyed* learning. Therefore, in my class we have KWLE Charts. Knowing they will be filling in this information puts students in a positive frame of mind during the lesson as they look for the fun moments. At the same time, anticipating feedback of the E column gives the teacher the incentive to design her lesson for optimal impact. Furthermore, reviewing the class's E column after the lesson helps the teacher revise her lesson to better meet the needs of her students the next time around.

Here are Nicky Romero's responses for "What I Enjoyed":

- I enjoyed guessing the fire hazard in each scene of the video.
- I enjoyed watching Robert and Cynthia "create" fire hazards in the class.
- I liked the song we learned using the acronym P.A.S.S. Pull, Aim, Squeeze, Sweep.
- I liked using the fire extinguisher to put out the fire!

Skimming Nicky's KWLE chart and others, and seeing, let's say, that everyone enjoyed guessing the fire hazards and using the fire extinguisher, the teacher can make a note to highlight those two items in her future lessons.

WHERE DO YOU GO FROM HERE?

Revise your lesson. If you can do so on the spot, great! If not, make a note of future changes you want to make. Are you disheartened that things didn't go as well as you planned? Don't be! You can always work out a better plan. Teachers learn master teaching through systematic problem solving. Just knowing this should give you encouragement and confidence in your teaching.

Brainstorm and play around with new ideas. Even veteran teachers who can pull a fantastic lesson out of their hats will tell you that they constantly revamp lessons to keep them fresh, to meet different standards, to accommodate the needs of a particular class, or just for the fun of it!

Do you teach parallel classes? Then you have the advantage of experimenting with the same lesson two, three, four or more times a day! Be flexible so that you can improve lessons on the spot. In one class, you might decide to begin the lesson from a different vantage point to see if it gives the lesson more "oomph." For another class, you might cut out or modify an activity that got too wild in your previous class. Having paced yourself too slowly in one class, you'd want to zip up the pace in another.

When you digressed from the original lesson plan, take careful notes of what went well and why it went well. To review every aspect of the lesson, ask good note takers if you may borrow their notes. At home, through revising and "cutting and pasting" you might change the lesson. Sometimes, it's just a matter of "rearranging the furniture" to give the lesson a fresh perspective. At other times, you might leave the format but jot down a possible variation for a task. As you work on revamping your lesson, insert reminders such as, "Remember to do the experiment near an open window or on the playground."

Don't discount one variation of a lesson over another if you think they can both work. Try them both in different classes. In fact, over the years, you might collect many effective ways of executing the same lessons. What a thrill it is to have so many choices!

Adopt an invincible attitude. Don't be afraid to take risks. The more trials you allow yourself in the beginning of your career, the fewer mistakes you will make in years to come! When you adopt an invincible attitude, no complication is unsurmountable. You tell yourself, "Ha! if this isn't the answer, then I will try something else." You turn into a solution-seeking daredevil and get striking results. Over time, you become so experienced in hunting for answers that you find yourself plowing easily through the blizzard to your destination. Any master teacher will tell you that he credits much of his achievement to his buoyancy and effort.

As your lesson plan unfolds, the adventure begins. Launched as a theory, a lesson takes on a shape largely molded by the educator's enthusiasm, leadership, and ability to elicit students' input. By integrating a rich conglomeration of discussions and activities, the educator truly teaches and the class learns with alacrity. Everything in school becomes fun. Unaware of their teacher's whizzing brain making split-second decisions, students may take the teacher's lesson plans for granted, but they will not take their learning for granted. Ultimately, teachers strengthen students' brain power, enrich their experiences, and often transform their attitude toward learning. No one has greater influence on schoolchildren than an adult who takes the time to cater to students' needs on a daily basis. Outside of parents (and surrogates), teachers make all the difference.

Never doubt this as you enter and leave your classrooms.

13

Liberating
the Struggling Student

"Every child deserves a champion—an adult who will never give up on them who understands the power of connection and insists that they become the best that they can possibly be."—Rita Pierson

Put yourself for a moment into the shoes of the struggling student. You're in sixth grade and your teacher, Mrs. Hamilton, is discussing Isaac Newton's Third Law of Motion. Mrs. Hamilton writes on the board: "For every action, there is an equal and opposite reaction." To demonstrate this law of motion, Mrs. Hamilton lets go of a balloon rocket and it speeds around the room. You don't understand. Why didn't the balloon rocket shoot up like a rocket? By the time you're finished mulling over this discrepancy, you realize that your teacher has been talking the whole time. Now she's saying that the rocket is propelled forward because of the exhaust that pushes against the air. You can see the exhaust in your mind's eye. You would love to be an astronaut and zoom off into the cosmos. This teacher isn't as boring as the others, but she's just as hard to keep up with because you keep missing what she's saying. She's saying too many things.

Now Mrs. Hamilton is discussing Newton's First Law of Motion: An object in motion travels in a straight line. The object remains in motion until it is acted upon by an outside force. You have no idea what this means, but you do pick up a little about what your teacher says about gravity and friction, although you still don't see its connection to the balloon experiment, and you wonder why Newton's First Law of Motion comes after his third and whether or not there is a second law. In the midst of this rumination, you tune back to the teacher because she's speaking about real rocket ships in space! She says that a rocket in space will keep moving in the same direction until it bumps into something or it's pushed into a different direction by an outside force. You wonder what the outside force could be. The teacher doesn't explain, but now she's talking about orbits and calculations and how a spacecraft reaches its target—the moon. By now, everything is a muddle and there's no time to try to sort anything out. You'll never catch up. So, you quit listening and wonder what you're having for supper and what trick you're going to teach Mr. Franklin next. He's your dog. Then, you're startled by the scraping of chairs and notice that the class is out of their seats and pushing their desks to the sides of the room.

Soon enough, everyone is sitting in a cluster on the floor, raising their hands like fans. You slink down and avert your eyes from the teacher's gaze, but it is too late. She calls your name and says to come forward. You rise and make your way to the front of the room.

Everything is in slow motion, but the funny thing is that once you're up there, you feel like you got there too fast. Your teacher hands you a card, a penny, and motions towards the glass on her desk. You haven't an inkling of what you're supposed to do.

The rest of the day isn't much better. Neither is the following day or the day after that. Somehow you find yourself going through the motions, but you're falling further and further behind in class. Mrs. Hamilton takes you aside and speaks to you about paying attention and focusing. She says she's sending a note home. She makes an appointment for you to meet with the guidance counselor. The guidance counselor is kind. He suggests a buddy system and tutoring and wants to meet with your parents. Your parents come down for a consultation. Mrs. Hamilton is there too. You're tested and nothing is wrong with your brain. You don't need special classes, but you're called out of class every Tuesday to work on skills with a lady who smells like scotch tape. And of course, you need to put forth more effort. That's what everyone is telling you.

At this point, you hate school. You begin to get frequent stomachaches, but your mother won't let you stay home. "School is your job," she says. "It's important. You need to go to class and do your best." In response, you think, "What's the use? I'm stupid. Why even try?" Above all, you are sick of the false promises and reassurances. No, when you concentrate you still can't learn. No, you won't get the hang of it, and no, it's not that this is just a difficult topic; everything is hard except computers and they only have that once a week.

Such is the sad saga of many weak students. Their struggles are not much fun to experience vicariously, but excruciating to live in reality.

What can we do for the struggling student?

No group in class is more neglected than the weaker students. As educators, we cannot sit back and let these students flounder. Neither can we ignore them in their seeming apathy. If we are to consider ourselves compassionate human beings, if we are to project ourselves as role models, if we are to fulfill our professional obligations, we must do our utmost to rescue the struggling learners in our classroom. But what's to be done?

Strategies for Helping Students Who Fall Behind

Tune in to warning signs that indicate your student is having difficulty learning. Characteristics of the struggling learner:

- consistently remains unfocused
- seems startled when you talk to her
- gives you an answer out of left field
- finds it hard to follow multiple step instructions
- keeps asking you or others what to do next
- looks tired, depressed, or lost
- walks with heavy steps or slower than her peers
- doesn't respond well to transitions
- has a short attention span
- looks tense during classroom activities
- stands on the sidelines
- is disorganized or messy

- forgets about assignments or supplies
- does a haphazard job at homework
- forgets or fails to follow rules
- has a hard time with multiple-choice
- is a literal thinker
- has poor memorization
- bursts out in frustration
- acts up in class
- avoids reading aloud
- misreads information
- has difficulty making friends

Record your suspicions. When you perceive that a student portrays a number of slow learning characteristics, record what makes you think so. Take down dates. For ex: On September 7, Chloe answered one of six science questions correctly. On September 8, Chloe filled out the rest of the answers as requested but copied them from the book and couldn't tell me in her own words what she wrote. On September 10, Chloe lost her math book again and took a new one from the book closet without my permission. On September 12, when Diego stopped by Chloe's desk to borrow a pencil, Chloe struck out at Diego and slammed her pencil case on his fingers.

Documenting this information gives you something concrete to look back on when you evaluate Chloe's situation or want to present your suspicions of Chloe's learning difficulties to her parents.

Gather background information about the student. Look up past test results and reports. Ask the principal for information. Elicit information from former teachers. Reserve your judgment, but take into account all that you read and hear. Don't brush aside reports of health issues, a dysfunctional family lifestyle, an impoverished home, or an absent parent. Dig deeper. All these factors can affect your plan of action.

Work on first things first. Picture this. You walk into your son's bedroom, nearly tripping over a pair of Nike sneakers. You survey the room with growing dismay. An upside-down slice of cold pizza lies on the radiator. The clean and dirty socks lie in an intermingled heap near the night table. Science fiction novels lay strewn across the area rug, with cookie crumbs powdering them. Crumpled papers litter the desk along with an occasional candy wrapper. A week's worth of t-shirts drapes the bedpost, their jeans counterparts gracing the closet floor and windowsill. The chest of drawers is wide open with a pile of pajamas, belts, and other accessories tumbling out.

You take it all in. Then you go call your kid, gesture at the room, and hand him a broom. Does that make sense? Of course not. The logical thing would be to instruct your son to focus on the bigger things first like getting rid of the pizza, separating the clean and dirty laundry, folding clothing, picking up the books, gathering the trash, placing the sneakers on a rack, etc. Then, and only then, would it make sense to hand him the broom to sweep the floor.

Work this way with the struggling student. There may be a lot to clean up. He may be disorganized, jumbling all his subjects into one notebook. He may not know how to manage his schedule. He may have the attention span of a fruit fly. You might notice the student is a literal thinker, has difficulty memorizing or retrieving information, or expressing himself.

His handwriting may be indecipherable, his spatial reasoning nil. What's the wisest approach? Obviously to work on one goal at a time, choosing the ones that make the most sense for the child.

What if you see red flags but can't figure out how to address them?

Strike up a dialogue with the student. Try to pinpoint the student's weak area by asking him what went wrong when things seem amiss. Once you have an idea of the student's predicament, you can better cater to him.

A real example from the classroom: When Kenneth, a weak student, needed more time to complete his essay, I let him work into the next class. In middle of that class, he raised his hand and once again asked for extended time and I gave it to him. At the end of third period, Kenneth still didn't finish, and what's more, I noticed he only wrote three short paragraphs. Upon asking Kenneth why he didn't complete the essay, he responded, "First I spaced out and then I was listening to you." What do you think I realized right away? That Kenneth got easily distracted. So, I told Kenneth that I wanted him to spend the next half hour working on the essay in the school library and I was going to time him. In those thirty minutes, Kenneth plumped up two paragraphs and added three more logical ones. From the little dialogue I had with Kenneth, I got to the root of his inadequate performance. In the future, Kenneth still needed more time doing the assignment or taking an exam, but I made sure he worked in solitude, in a quiet atmosphere, and with a precise time limit. As a result, Kenneth's work flourished.

Weed out the impractical. Weed out the work that doesn't seem practical for this student. Ask the student, "What's the hardest part for you?" or "What do you wish you didn't have to learn?" Then evaluate whether it's okay to let her drop the task. Not every child needs to create anatomical structures or write his theory on time travel.

Think of the most logical goal. You can't expect your student to tackle math equations if he doesn't know how to add double digits. If your student has a problem with reading comprehension, it's not the time to take care of his lip reading. The Ukrainian immigrant could better spend his time brushing up on his understanding of more simple works than studying Dickens' *Hard Times* with the rest of the class.

Don't try to downplay the student's shortcomings. Your student may be an underachiever, but he is nobody's fool. Telling him that he is bright and will eventually catch up to the class will only frustrate him further.

Use encouraging statements. To help him cope with past disappointment, use encouraging but practical statements. Say statements like, "You're going to like it better in my class because if you need help with your work, I'm going to give it to you every step of the way." This encouragement motivates the disheartened student because it doesn't lay the whole onus on him.

Find out if the student has support outside the classroom. Does this student have a tutor or someone helping her at home? Ask how it's going. Keep in close contact with her tutor/parents/coach, preferably via phone conversation (at least once a week). If the support isn't working, arrange for better support. Free tutors are available in safe environments such as public libraries. Be an advocate for your student!

Give the student small achievable assignments. Boost the weaker student's achievement by letting her tackle small problems which yield instant success. This gives the student the motivation to keep plugging away at more daunting tasks.

Don't only communicate verbally. Write instructions in your student's notebook in clear simple steps. Your writing gives him reassurance of what you want when he cannot rely on his memory. Leave space for his work. Follow up with encouraging verbal and written comments. Keep building on past knowledge.

Be patient with each step. Don't let yourself become overwhelmed by slow progress or by what the student doesn't know. Don't get sidetracked from a goal so that you touch upon one thing and move on to the next. Don't rush your student. Let her work busily but comfortably, and celebrate the accomplishment of each step. Every level you reach with your student will be rewarding. At the end, you'll get much further with patience.

Don't rescue this student from making mistakes. Don't finish work for him or have a more able student "help" him by doing most of the task. Completing tasks for struggling students only makes them feel more dependent and helpless.

Respond to mistakes by saying first what's correct. If you ask, "What is an example of an amphibian?" and a student answers, "a crocodile," you can say, that's a good example of a reptile but not an amphibian. If you ask, "Did you ever see a famous photograph?" and your student answers, "Yes, the Mona Lisa," you can say, "the Mona Lisa is a good example of a famous painting but it's not a photograph." Saying what's correct lends students the notion that they do know something even when they're not on the right track.

Create a mistake-friendly environment for everyone. Mistakes shouldn't have negative consequences. Don't grade classwork, at least not until the student is satisfied with the results. Don't warn the class not to make mistakes unless you're talking about careless ones. Give students a chance to correct mistakes and redo their work.

Train students to think of mistakes rationally instead of emotionally. Disappointed and frustrated by making mistakes, struggling students often give up trying. Train students to think of mistakes not as a verification of what they don't know but as a stepping stone to new information. Respond to mistakes calmly and coach students to help them find their way. When students resolve errors, say, "You see if you look at a mistake rationally, you figure it out so much quicker. You become a problem solver." Keep repeating this message and students will lose half their angst about making mistakes.

Applaud struggles. To foster a growth mindset, Carol Dweck recommends asking the question, "Who had a fabulous struggle today?" To this end, teachers have students drop a marble into a jar on the teacher's desk whenever they've worked out a great struggle. Shortly, the class has a visual reminder that everyone has struggles and they embrace struggles instead of repelling them. You might ask a student or two each day to share their struggles with the class.

Don't expose his weakness to the class. If he doesn't volunteer to do the math problem on the board, don't ask him to do so. If he's a hesitant reader, don't call on him to read instructions to the class. Let him know that his dignity will never be attacked in your classroom.

Accept the student for who he is. No two children are the same. Sometimes plodding students, like all students, have quirks that can test your nerves. Accept this student as a unique individual. Open your affection to his personality. "That's James being James," is a good attitude to take on when a student's quirks or nettlesome habits surface.

Teach clever mnemonics. Students love beating the system with mnemonics that help them get desired results without too much effort. Why not teach these mnemonics to your students? Let's examine mnemonics in math and spelling, two subjects many students grapple with in school.

Pull a fast one on math: Little tricks can help kids struggling with addition or multiplication. For some reason adding or multiplying with the number 9 stumps many students. Teaching the following two mnemonics will have students doing the calculations jubilantly.

- Trick for adding nine with numbers 1–10: Subtract 1 from the digit that isn't 9 and put a 1 before it to get the answer. To demonstrate: 9 + 6? You subtract 1 from the digit 6 and get 5 and put 1 before it. The sum is 15.
- Trick for multiplying 9 with numbers 1–10: Subtract 1 from the factor that isn't 9 and place the number next to it that adds up to 9. To demonstrate: 9 × 3? You subtract 1 from the factor 3 and get 2. You place the number next to it that adds up to nine: 7. The product then is 27.
- Also cool to know: Between 1 times 9 and 9 times 9 the product always adds up to nine. For example, 9 × 4 = 54. 5 + 4 = 9.

Don't stop with this math trick. Loads of others math memory tricks are available online from tricks for multiplying with 12, to estimating fractions, finding square roots, percentage calculation, and remembering the Unit Circle.

Spell it right every time: Are your students terrible spellers? Thank goodness for spell check and dictionaries. But do you wonder how these terrible spellers can ever make a good impression in the world without these helpful devices? Here are solutions that turn correct spelling into a playful achievable challenge for students!

Chunking Words: "Chunking" is a process that breaks down a difficult word into smaller chunks so that spellers can picture each chunk separately in their minds before putting them together to form the word. For instance, if the spelling of the word *committee* is difficult for your student to remember, you might suggest that he divide the word into three small chunks: *com, mit, tee*. He then closes his eyes and sees *com*. If he doesn't see it at first, he might need to open his eyes and close them again and repeat that process until he sees the chunk. Once he sees the image *com*, he goes onto picturing *mit*, and then *tee*. Afterwards, he puts the chunks together to form the correct spelling of the word.

For this chunking method to work, it's important for students to remember not to create chunks with double letters. For ex. *mill en nium*. There's no guarantee one will remember that *mill* has two l's. It's best therefore, to break up double letters of the word—*millennium: mil, len, nium*. The same rule applies for the word necessary. Dividing the word this way: *ne cess ary* might not work for spellers since they have to remember both s's. Dividing the word this way: *ne ces sary* does the trick. Practice this chunking method for the words students commonly misspell, and they won't misspell them again! It's actually exhilarating for students to join the chunks they created to spell words correctly on the spelling test. The spelling challenge becomes an achievable task for everyone.

Note: Words that end with double letters can be broken up by attaching the last letter of the word to the first one or first ones. For example, *embarrass—sem bar ras*. Words that end with double letters and begin with a consonant such as business follow the same guidelines. For example, *business—sb us in es*. The speller just pictures the *sb* in his mind.

Urge students to educate themselves at home. Explain to students that education happens outside the classroom too. They can do their own thing to cultivate their learning. They can volunteer to set up exhibits at religious, recreational or cultural centers. They can get ahead in math, fine-tune typing, or learn more about history by joining free online programs. They can boost their mental sharpness with brainteasers in books. They can start a campaign for river cleanup. They can answer phones at phone-a-thons to raise money for a charity organization. They can seek out people interested in trading skills. For instance, Javier knows how to play the guitar while Anton is great at tinkering with cars. Javier really would like to learn how to fix a car engine. He can trade an hour of guitar lessons for an hour of Anton's mechanic training. Participating in activities outside the school curriculum builds students' learning, gives them added confidence, and an outlet for doing what they prefer rather than what they must.

Make sure your student knows she is responsible for her learning. Underachievers need to keep track of their own assignments and give in their homework on time. Self-discipline lends struggling students a sense of security. Students should have calendars which they can revise and update. Sharing deadlines with the rest of the class, even when the assignment follows a different criterion, makes the weak student feel included as a class member.

A real example from the classroom: As I am about to start a tenth-grade English class, Amy came in out of breath. With difficulty speaking through her windedness, she told me she had run home during recess to get the homework she left there.

"It's good you did that, Amy," I said. "You know I don't like late papers."

"Yeh, I know!" Amy said. "That's why I knew I'd better get it. I didn't want to get a late homework mark."

One late homework mark would not have made a difference in Amy's final average and she knew it. Yet knowing she was responsible to hand in her papers on time like everyone else, Amy took pride in doing just that, even though she had to inconvenience herself.

Resist the temptation to let a student sit idle. Everybody wants to learn and everybody can get some kind of satisfaction out of learning. Never let slower learners sit idle while the class is working on an assignment. Have them work on different goals if the class is doing work beyond their scope. For instance, if the class is analyzing and drawing conclusions about how precipitation trends affect communities, wildlife, and agriculture, the struggling student can analyze and draw conclusions about a flood's effect on communities. If the class is reading passages and writing epigrams about them, struggling students can read a passage and write its theme.

Don't allow students to con you into thinking everything is too difficult. Bear in mind that many underperforming students are adept at trying to get out of work. If you think he can do the job, insist that he does it. If he's trying cover up for laziness by blaming his reluctance on a task he finds too overbearing, challenge his statement.

A real example from the classroom: In my public speaking class, Rina tried to get away with delivering formal speeches, contending that she couldn't memorize them. When I told her that she may read the speech off her paper, she didn't brighten as much as I anticipated.

"The main problem isn't the memorization part, is it?" I probed.

"No," she admitted. "I just don't want to get up in front of the whole class."

There it was. Rina had been masking the real issue, her stage fright. So we worked it out. Initially, I allowed Rina to read her speeches in her seat, then while standing beside her seat, and finally, up at the podium. Naturally, she grumped about my determination to get her to speak before the class, but as expected, she did it and felt proud of herself.

Require the student to answer a major question. To keep the student attentive during class, provide her with one major question she will have to answer on a loose-leaf paper at the end of class or for homework. Seeking the answer to the question will help the student remain focused and alert.

Focus on the subject matter instead of the grade. Ask the student questions like, "How else can you improve as a musician/writer/computer programmer?" instead of "What else do you think you need to work on to pass the exam?" Show students you're more interested in his progress than the grade.

Give instruction, not criticism. The quickest way to get cooperation is to make your student feel capable. You cannot accomplish this if the student feels you constantly disapprove of him. You can correct the child by pointing out what has to be done rather than criticizing him. Instead of saying, "Stop fooling around!" you can choose to say, "You have two more questions to answer." Instead of saying, "You keep smudging your paper," you can say, "If you use the scrap first to get rid of the blackness, you won't smudge your paper when you use the eraser."

When you keep to the mindset of giving students proactive solutions, they feel empowered rather than brow-beaten. They rise much more quickly to your standards and do so cheerfully instead of fearfully.

Don't criticize him for a lack of effort. Don't say, "I need you to try harder." Say instead, "You need to work on your history report for 30 uninterrupted minutes tonight. Please write down what you have accomplished during that time and have your parent sign the paper." Hence, you can lay down the law without using negative words.

Use positive words in coaching. Say, "We're going to tackle this next one!" Instead of "Let's see if we can figure out the next problem." Show kids your confidence in them. Say, "I knew you could handle that reading!" instead of "I can't believe you finished your reading!" Rejoice with their accomplishments, no matter how minute: "Guess what? You're a champ for measuring that sand so carefully!" Make kids feel on top.

Don't discuss the pain in the gain. That puts the student in a worrisome frame of mind. Yes, you want him to work hard, but stressing the hardship is never motivating.

"You have to work hard to get results."
"You still need to complete the next example. Come on!"
"The second chapter is difficult but if you concentrate you'll get what it means."
"I know the test is stressful, but you have to take it."

Don't you feel yourself wilting as you read these statements?
    Let students sense adventure in the undertaking.

"Give it a whirl and let me know what you come up with."
"Take a shot at the next example."
"I can't wait for you to read the second chapter. I'm wondering what's going to surprise you."
"After you finish the test, I'd be curious to know what skill you chose to figure out numbers 5 & 6."

Find your student's academic strength or field of interest. Build his self-esteem through that region. Have the current events buff give the class a weekly news update, the artist, a drawing demonstration, the sports fan, a rundown of the latest moves.

Don't think your student has any strengths? That's not true. You just have to find it. I remember stumbling upon a student's strength in a most startling way. Gathered together at a teachers' conference to discuss a particularly weak student's need for help, my colleagues and I were sharing our experiences with her. One colleague was listening with bewilderment to the ongoing mention of the child's deficiencies. When it came time for her input, this colleague said, "Seldom do I have a child in class so expressive in her writing. She kills me with her poetry." and while we sat amazed, she proceeded to read poems this child wrote that were visionary and profound. The upshot? Everyone has a talent. Sometimes, we have to look beyond our classrooms to find it.

Make sure your student is excelling at something outside the academic arena. Let him see how he can influence parts of the school's agenda. Encourage him to join a sport, to try out for a part in the play, to head a dance program, to carry out interviews for the school newspaper.

Grant your student a voice. Every pet owner has a lot to say about caring for his pet. An immigrant has a lot to share about his culture. Everyone is capable of giving a little talk about something, whether it's about his current experiences, family tradition, or even about responsibilities at home. Allow weak students a voice in the classroom. Having a voice goes a long way in boosting esteem, often awakening the desire to contribute more and to work for it.

Keep a log of the student's progress. Give the student a monthly progress report which includes your observations of his work ethic and character traits. Don't make the report sound like "Big Brother is watching" but rather that you notice his progress and want to celebrate with him.

Give "effort credit." Effort credit refers to points students may receive for showing initiative and working to his capacity. In a monthly meeting, let students show tangible proof of effort they've put into their schoolwork. When tangible proof of effort cannot be produced, students may verbally express the amount of effort they put into something. How much credit do students earn? That depends on the elbow grease the teacher sees invested in the work.

You might decide to extend the opportunity of earning effort credit to the entire class, not only to the weaker students. I like to keep track of the effort credit on a seating chart, jotting down the quality of the effort for each task and the amount of time invested. At the end of the term, along with test grades and my evaluation of the student's class work, effort credit raises the student's average.

The following effort earns students credit:

- Scrap work: outlines, writing drafts, diagrams/plans for projects.
- Homework that wasn't collected.
- Proof of research done on one's own time.
- Proof of hours spent reading.
- Proof of hours spent on learning websites.
- Proof of hours spent receiving tutorial help.
- Homemade flash cards, review questions, or review games.
- Calendars that display goals and deadlines that were met.
- Any initiative the student took in a group project.

In anticipation of the monthly meeting, students set goals for themselves. Students who don't get good grades are reassured that their effort will be acknowledged. When effort counts, weaker students know grades are not all that matters and that they too can be winners.

We have chosen this noble profession as teachers to help all students in both favorable and unfavorable situations. Taking an active role in assisting struggling students doesn't only raise their academic level and transform students' self-esteem for the moment. This positive effect elicits a wondrous chain of events that can channel students' success for years to come.

Charles Dickens in *Great Expectations* voices this notion through his main character, Pip, who speaks about a notable day in his life: "That was a memorable day for me, for it made great changes in me. But it is the same with any life. Imagine one selected day struck out of it, and think how different its course would have been. Pause you who read this, and think for a moment of the long chain of iron or gold, of thorns or flowers, that would never have bound you, but for the formation of the first link on one memorable day" (43).

Let's create the beginning of memorable, promising days for all our students, especially the weaker students.

14

Cutting Competition

"I was, on the whole, considerably discouraged by my school days.... It was not pleasant to feel oneself so completely outclassed and left behind at the beginning of the race."—Winston Churchill in *My Early Life: A Roving Commission*

In his book *Uh Oh: Some Observations from Both Sides of the Refrigerator Door*, the renowned American author Robert Fulghum questions the difference between the self-image in the kindergarten and college classrooms. Fulghum says that when you ask a kindergarten class, "How many of you can draw?" all hands shoot up. What can they draw? Anything. How about a dog eating a fire truck in a jungle? Sure! You ask kindergarteners if they can sing, they say yes. If they don't know the words, it's not a problem, they make them up. They are confident they can dance, act in plays, and play musical instruments. Fulghum maintains, "Their answer is Yes! Over and over again, Yes! The children are confident in spirit, infinite in resources, and eager to learn. Everything is still possible."

Yet, Fulghum says, if you try those same questions on a college audience, a small percentage will raise their hands when asked if they draw, dance, sing, paint, act, or play and instrument. And habitually, college students will qualify responses with their limitations: "I only play piano." Or "I only draw horses." When asked why the limitations, college students respond that they do not have talent, are not majoring in the subject, or have not practiced doing these things since third grade, or worse, that they are embarrassed for others to witness them singing, dancing, or acting. Fulghum asks what went wrong between kindergarten and college. What happened to "Yes! Of course, I can!"

On the Quest: What Happened to "Yes! Of course, I can!"

What do you think happened to "Yes! Of course, I can!"? Curious to discern the answer myself, I set out to try "Fulghum-type" questions on a college audience. At first, students kept their hands down when asked for their talents. Then, interestingly, they began to offer other people's talents: "Eden has a great voice," or "Miriam writes like Gordon Korman!" When I asked the lauded students if their peers' claims were true, they said yes, but just as Fulghum experienced, modified their responses: "I don't have a *great* voice," or "I am just an okay writer." When pressed to tell me why they didn't raise their hands in the first place, students said they thought other people were better singers or writers.

Subsequently, I read Fulghum's excerpt to the class, and although amused with Fulghum's repartee and the experiment I played on them, the class soberly agreed that something along the school journey impairs students' self-esteem. For homework, I asked the class for a written conjecture about Fulghum's question on what happened to "Yes! Of course, I can?" Among the responses, many confirmed my growing conviction that a student's self-image is grossly damaged by competition in the classroom.

Here's how I see it. Before school, every achievement little Sammy does is celebrated. His artwork is hung on the refrigerator. His antics are applauded. His doting parents, grandparents, siblings, and neighbors make him think he is the brightest kid in town. Once in school, however, Sammy begins to notice his skills aren't so hot compared to others. His butterfly drawing isn't as vibrant as Larry's. Susie's glue never smudges. Eric can write real words. A little older, Sammy begins to observe how several kids know more stuff about computers or math or handling a ball on the basketball court. Wanting to measure up to his peers, Sammy stops doing for himself and keeps checking his progress with others.

Now, this isn't all bad for Sammy. Sometimes, kids need to compare their skills to gauge their own. It's good for kids to see where they fall short so they can improve. Nobody should live in a fool's paradise. I don't disagree with that.

The problem arises, though, when the adult steps in and compares Sammy's achievements with others and praises those who are quicker and brighter. The quest for improvement turns into a competition and is devastating to Sammy. What adults say and do have a profound effect on children and their ability to process what they see around them. The typical kid sees the adult's standard as a mandatory goal and decides he must achieve it or he is worthless.

Sadly, educators are at the helm of endorsing competition, by comparing students' abilities and promoting contests. Consequently, confident kindergartners dwindle into uncertain first, second, and third graders, no longer satisfied with meeting their potential and constantly trying to surpass others'. Since the endeavor to outdo one's peers is discouraging for most and unrealistic for many, most students begin thinking they just don't have what it takes to excel. By the time kids reach junior high school, they can quickly tell you what they're *not* good at. They have lost their zest for learning. Few attempt to take risks. Their self-image has plummeted.

Thus begins my crusade against competition in the classroom. Through exploring the many pitfalls of teacher-induced competition in this chapter, I am hoping educators will take heart and eliminate all competitive practices from the classroom. By bringing a collaboration of personal experiences, student testimonies, and documented studies, I contend that competition has no redeeming value. Finally, at the end of the chapter, I present healthy alternatives to competition which motivate students to use their innate abilities and meet their potential while keeping their self-image intact.

The Pitfalls of Competition

PITFALL #1: COMPETITION PLACES A PREMIUM UPON SPEED

When I was in third grade, my teacher held a contest to see which row could pack up first at the end of the day. The row that was ready first got dismissed first, the runners up, second, and so on. As luck would have it, the slowest kid in the class sat in my row—the methodical type who straightened each pencil in her pencil case before putting it away. Well, forget about my row getting out first. No matter how much we hissed and prodded, Sarah just couldn't get her act together and, sure enough, our row always trudged out last. Thus seemed our fate, until Esther, the smart aleck among us, called for a row meeting during recess. In a conspiratorial huddle excluding Sarah, Esther convinced us of the most benevolent way we could help the lagging kid and quickly dispensed our instructions.

Later, we put Esther's plan into action. As soon as the teacher announced our dismissal, we raced over to Sarah's desk and, in short—I'm ashamed to say, packed up for her. I can still see it now. Sarah stood hapless while one girl slammed together Sarah's books and sprinted with them to the lockers. Another girl stuffed Sarah's notebooks, papers, and folders into Sarah's tidy backpack. Yours truly together with an accomplice shoved Sarah's stiff arms into her down jacket, wound her scarf around her neck in an emphatic knot, and pushed her into her seat. Mission accomplished, we all dashed back to our desks to take care of our stuff. We might not have made it out first that week, but we sure did march out a breathless second.

Like many teacher-induced competitions, this one got quick results but at the expense of the child who isn't wired to zip with the program. Methodical people, like Sarah, notice details in everything and need to move purposely to feel grounded. Any competition testing physical speed interferes with this need. Rush the methodical child and she'll be miserable.

Do you wonder how many methodical people you have in your classroom? Notice the children who get completely absorbed in a task, who have more difficulty with transitions, those who are last out the door for lunch, recess, or dismissal. You'll notice five to ten percent of the class fit into this category.

Now, if you're feeling bad for the "slowpoke," you can definitely muster compassion for the next victim on my list—the methodical thinker. The rush treatment inherent in competitive activities and contests completely disregards people who can't mentally speed up their work. How awful for these students to contend with the constant reminder that they don't measure up to their quicker counterparts.

A former student of mine, today a successful CPA, relates the effect "mental sprees" had on her in the classroom. Never quick enough to compete in games, she would give up trying to win any contest. "Most competitive games reward the quickest thinker—the first to shout the answer, the first to finish work, or the first to score the most points at a given time," Tamara said. "I knew the answers, but I just couldn't work it through fast enough and that made me look dumb. I remember spacing out when I came to the board—the agonizing moments while waiting for my opponent to complete the example so that she could get the point and my turn would be over."

Tamara's pain is reflective of many methodical thinkers. Most competitive games disregard methodical thinkers who make up a good portion of the world, people who might in fact be geniuses in regard to figuring, negotiating, investing, inventing, philosophizing, investigating, and problem solving. But since the educator has no time for activities that require methodical skills, the methodical thinkers in the classroom are forced to participate in competitions they cannot win.

Pitfall #2: Competition Creates Anxiety

Methodical or not, all students are met with an unfair disadvantage when they have to operate under tense conditions. The prospect of losing the competition or letting down teammates overshadows the productivity of any contest. An overwhelming number of my students have agreed with this belief, recounting personal anxieties associated with contests in school.

A few student testimonies, in their own words:

"I remember frantically scrambling for a seat when the music stopped and not finding one. Then came the humiliation of being caught standing alone—the odd one out. I can still hear the pregnant pause—the teacher saying, 'Please take another chair out of the line'—and then the music beginning—with the class romping without me."

"I remember competing for the 'dramatic reader' certificate. The competition was down to my neighbor and me. I thought I could beat her easily. But because I was so nervous, my voice came out shaky and the certificate went to my opponent."

"In eighth grade I designed seven posters to get my friend elected G.O. president. I remember quaking inside comparing my posters with those produced for the other nominees. Were mine more eye-catching? Would we win? If we didn't, would it be my fault?"

"We had a contest to see who could memorize the longest poem. I spent a laborious weekend trying to memorize the lines to Keats' 'Ode on a Grecian Urn.' In class, I stumbled over lines and confused words. Although the teacher was kind, I remember my classmates' pitiable looks and the smirks of those who couldn't help but find my recital funny."

"I threw up the morning of the Spelling Bee. I was so nervous I'd misspell a simple word and make a fool of myself."

"To review a lesson, the teacher would snap questions at us individually. The object was to see how many questions we could answer within three minutes. The winner was the one who answered the most questions within that time frame. When the teacher called on me, I just blanked out."

"Oh those dreaded contests before tests! The teacher would divide the class in two teams and go up and down the rows asking questions and keep count of each team's points on the board. The responsibility I felt toward my team was so frightening! I was scared of getting the answer wrong and ruining it for all my teammates."

Oblivious to the turmoil they create with contests, many educators fall under the illusion that the vibrant environment is a learning environment. How untrue. More often than not, the excitement that competitive games generate is a manifestation of anxiety. It's simply (or not so simply) a fight for survival!

Pitfall #3: Competition Induces
Superficial Learning

Because it allows little time for reflection, competition does not give students the chance to learn information well. Unfortunately, I've learned this truth firsthand from my own students.

A real example from the classroom: "Who skipped this first paragraph of page 20 in their reading?" I asked my class one day during a chapter discussion on *Dibs in Search of*

Self. Guiltily, most students raised their hands. "That's okay," I said, "I don't blame you. When I came to this page myself, I thought, 'This looks like a long and boring paragraph.' But since I'm the teacher, I figured I'd better read it and I'm really glad I did. The author provides us with a profound analogy here. I'll tell you what. Read the paragraph now, and I'll give a plus two to the first person who explains the analogy correctly."

The class got busy reading. Fourteen seconds later, seven students their hands. Each tried their luck, but could not accurately state the author's meaning. What surprised me most was the creativity of their embellishments. Then I realized what had happened. So intent on being the first to give the answer, these kids skimmed the paragraph to get the gist of it and made up the rest. Had they spent a little more time reading, I knew many would have gotten the author's precise meaning.

Not one to give up trying an experiment, I told the class, "Read the paragraph again more carefully. This time I'm going to wait for all of you to finish reading. You need to provide the exact analogy. Don't make anything up."

At first, students didn't believe they were going to get sufficient time to read. They kept looking up from their reading at me and their peers. But when they realized I meant what I said, they visibly relaxed and immersed themselves in the task.

After the class finished reading, I said, "Now, I'm going to ask you to write down the analogy. If your analogy is true to the text, you'll get the credit." Five minutes later, I collected the papers and read the analogies aloud. Ninety percent were accurate, and I gave those papers extra credit.

As illustrated, my original mistake was to rush the class by offering credit to the first person who got the answer. Sending my students on a mental spree induced superficial learning. Sending them on a quest for accuracy, though, yielded meaningful results.

PITFALL #4: COMPETITION DECREASES INTRINSIC MOTIVATION, RESULTING IN LOWER PERFORMANCE

Does competition push kids to their best? Apparently not. Numerous studies confirm that tasks presented as contests decrease intrinsic motivation, resulting in poorer achievement than tasks done of one's own incentive. For example, in one study, students were asked to solve interesting puzzles. Half the subjects were asked to compete against each other. The other half were simply instructed to try solving the puzzle within an allotted time. The former subjects performed significantly worse than the latter. In another study, children were asked to maintain their balance on a stabilometer using whatever method they could. Half the children were encouraged to beat the balancing score of other children their age, while the others were encouraged to discover or try out new strategies to maintain their balance as long as they could. Subjects in the competition condition spent less time on the stabilometer than their counterparts in the intrinsic mastery condition.

One can conclude from these experiments that working to beat another person isn't as motivating as working for oneself. When kids work to outdo others, they're acting upon extrinsic motivation, from factors outside the individual. When they work for themselves, they're acting upon intrinsic motivation, the satisfaction or enjoyment of doing the task. The question boils down to this: Do we want our kids to learn with pleasure and master their potential or to work with pressure for lesser results?

Pitfall #5: Competition Hijacks the Focus

With the value placed on meeting a particular goal, kids lose sight of other needs and responsibilities. Some teachers don't even give students a respite from contests; they string them along, or worse, have two to three contests running simultaneously. Unless students can opt out of the contest, competition monopolizes students' minds, preventing them from living the normal course of the day.

Even the competition behind reward charts can stimulate an unhealthy fervor. One of my students wrote about her childhood obsession with beating her classmates on a star chart: "I'd sneak a peek from behind my geography book as my teacher stuck the new stars on the Mad Vocab Chart. I'd tell myself, 'Okay, Abigail got three more, I'm still good. What! Malia got five? Shoot! Now I've got to beat her'—and that would be the focus of my day, or week, or however long it took to get ahead."

Pitfall #6: Competition Places Sole Value on Making It to the Top

When the teacher does any of the following: promotes races, compares students' work, praises only outstanding work, announces top grades, speaks about prestigious colleges, displays only the best work, caters to the talented, or praises winners—he sends the message that the best work is the only work that matters.

Dressing up competition in the guise of play doesn't fool students either. Competitive games don't play fair. Did your teacher ever play games like "Conductor" or "Jeopardy" with your class? Do you remember the same kids winning time and again? That's because very few have the ability to make it to the top. What lesson do these games reinforce for students? That they're never good enough.

Pitfall #7: Competition Squelches Individuality

Combined with feelings of shame, students find their individuality compromised in competitive settings. The voice is suppressed, as well as the soul and spirit. Students who don't thrive in a competitive environment feel they have no right to express themselves. After all, who are they? The losers. Do they matter? Of course not. The effect of this squelching seems to spill over into other areas of life. I've even witnessed students questioning their place in the world because they couldn't shine in a competitive classroom.

Pitfall #8: Competition Doesn't Permit Students to Learn from Their Mistakes

Students who lose contests tend to see where they fall short, but not how they can improve. Attempting to build students' skills with competitive activities is a fruitless prospect without a replay or review of events. Backtracking is not feasible for most contests. What then is the educational gain?

PITFALL #9: WINNING A COMPETITION
FOSTERS A FALSE SENSE OF PRIDE

Okay, so let's say someone proves himself the best in a learning field, what might that mean? That he's most capable? Clever? Brilliant? So what? Did he create his genius? Is he a better person for it? Bill Waterson echoes this message in a Calvin and Hobbes cartoon where an exultant Calvin gloats over beating Hobbes at checkers. Calvin exclaims, "I won! I won!" but then after a while, he says, "Is this all there is?" The cartoon reminds us that there's not much to being the top of the heap. Triumph of this kind is a fickle thing. But unlike Calvin, our children may not come to this conclusion. We have to evaluate whether we want to puff up victors with a false notion that they are better than their counterparts.

Are you convinced yet of the foul nature of competition? I hope so. But maybe you're like thousands of teachers who believe in the following two big myths about competition and use them to defend competition in your classroom. To dispel these myths, I'd like to uncover the truth about them.

The Two Big Myths About Competition

MYTH #1: COMPETITION BOOSTS TEAMWORK

Truth: Competition Destroys the Comradery among Friends

Many educators profess that competition boosts teamwork. Just the opposite. Competition makes students work against each other, unmasking the worst character traits.

How so? First, competition promotes ill will and backstabbing among friends. Similar to the mudslinging involved in political campaigns, fighting burgeons in the classroom when teams are pitted against each other. Behavior in the classroom such as blaming, snitching, and bossing is often a direct result of teacher induced competition.

Second, competition creates a judgmental environment. Since, clearly, competition gives rise to critical judgment, negative energy lingers beyond the game or sport. The reason why kids become such sore losers is because they take the outcome of the game personally. They feel diminished in the eyes of the opponent.

Third, competition arouses envy among peers. There's enough envy to go around without competition aggravating it. Envy takes away one's peace of mind. Envy makes students count others' blessings instead of their own. Sadly, no competition leaves students untinged by envy. How could it when competition magnifies the attributes of a glorified few?

Take a popular contest like Color War, which includes the three drawbacks I just mentioned. For the life of me, I cannot fathom how such contests promote anything but bitterness for the majority involved. I ask my classes every year if they enjoy Color War. Few say they do. Even the winners tell me the prize isn't worth the trouble. Not much different from reality shows on television, competitions like Color War drain the physical and mental spirit. Who needs them?

MYTH #2: COMPETITION PREPARES KIDS
FOR THE REAL WORLD

Truth: Competition Hinders Progress in the Real World

Advocates of competition vehemently maintain that competition prepares kids for the real world. That theory rings hollow. Moreover, studies reveal a negative correlation between competition and achievement in the real world.

It seems that what people view as the competitiveness of highly successful people is really their intrinsic motivation to master a skill and their positive attitude to work hard. Business leaders of major corporations scored high on mastery and work and low on competitiveness, as did successful airline pilots and supertanker crews. In fact, competition seems injurious to successful careers. Competitive scientists, for example, produce more superficial results than their non-competitive counterparts. Therefore, what students need most to face the competitive world is not a competitive edge but a desire to learn and a healthy relationship with learning. I'm inclined to agree with Ayn Rand who said, "A creative man is motivated by the desire to achieve, not by the desire to beat others."

So, let's say you're thinking about cutting competition in your classroom. How does you get started? With changing your mindset.

Getting Started: Reducing Competition

Even if you're one of those die-hards who can't drop competition cold, the following table depicts methods of reducing competitive talk in the classroom. The first column of the table presents competitive strategies as the motivating force behind the teacher's instructions, comments, or praise. The second column offers non-competitive healthy alternatives.

Competitive Strategies and Healthy Alternatives

Competitive Strategies	Healthy Alternatives
Counting physical and/or mental speed—	**Showing the value of process, method, or thought—**
"Let's see who can set up his easel the quickest."	"Let's see if we can set up our easels so that they're nice and steady."
"When you see your answer, run to the Smartboard and tap your choice."	"Take a minute to think of the answer. Then raise your hand and I'll call on someone to tap his choice on the Smartboard."
"Let's see who's the quickest to write 6748 in expanded notation."	"Who can tell me the steps to writing 6748 in expanded notation?
"Let's see who's the first to find a pattern in this sequence of numbers."	"After you find the pattern in this sequence of numbers, can you tell us the skill you used to find it?"
"Raise your hand as soon as you've found the shortest route from point A to point B."	"How would you determine the shortest route from Point A to Point B?"
"Come on, guys. Let's see who's a lightning problem solver."	"Who can shed some light on this problem?"
Pitting classmates against each other—	**Promoting comradery among classmates—**
"The opponent who rings the bell first gets to answer the question."	"If you know the answer, see if you can explain it to someone who doesn't."
"Let's see who can come up with the most synonyms."	"Let's see how many synonyms the class can come up with."

Competitive Strategies	*Healthy Alternatives*
Comparing a student's work to another's— "Once you finish painting the background, your diorama is going to be just as striking as Gordon's." "Why don't you take a look at Bob's robot? See how sturdy it's standing?"	**Treating a student's work as its own entity—** "Once you finish painting the background, your diorama is going to be striking!" "Your robot is tilting. What do you think you can do about that?"
Comparing classes— "This class is much smarter than the other sixth grade." "I didn't have to remind the other class to bring in their permission slips."	**Treating the class as its own unit—** "This class can master anything!" "I shouldn't have to remind you to bring in your permission slips."
Alluding to goals attainable by few— "Claire, you're headed for Harvard!" "You're an amazing musician, Jim. I wouldn't be surprised if you got into Juilliard."	**Keeping the student's options open—** "Claire, you have the aptitude to pursue any career!" "You're an amazing musician, Jim. You'd mesmerize any audience."
Applauding ability— "Wow, Martin, look at how many books you've read!" "I'm so proud you got a 95% on your economics paper, Arlene!"	**Praising effort—** "Wow, Martin, look at how many hours you spent reading!" "I'm so impressed with all the research you did for your economics paper, Arlene! You provide good insight into the high level of China's monetarization."
Pointing out the best— "Aidan used the best vivid imagery in his setting. Here is a sample." "And Tim, you're the winner for coming up with the most creative paper!"	**Praising many people's accomplishments—** "I like how people used vivid imagery in their settings. Let's take a look at several samples." "I like the creativity of your paper, Tim, the playfulness of your dialogue, Quince, the lay out of your chapter, Lacey..."
Ranking the student's work according to the class's ability— "Charley, I think you got the highest average in the class." "Donna, you've got the top grade on your algebra test!"	**Focusing on personal ability—** "Charley, you're doing some of your best work." "Donna, I knew you'd master factoring! Now you're ready for the next step."
Displaying the best— "I'd like to display the best poems on the bulletin board." "I'd like to exhibit the best history projects in the showcase."	**Displaying everyone's work—** "Once you revise your poem, please tack it on the bulletin board." "Let's take turns exhibiting the class's history projects in the showcase."
Choosing a few to perform— "Tryouts for the chorus/play/dance for *Count Dracula* will take place at 3:15 p.m. in the auditorium." "Lydia, Blake, and Hailey, you're good at rapping. Why don't you try writing a rap for the class on the nominative and objective case of pronouns?"	**Letting all students perform (even if they're not talented)—** "Please sign up whether you'd like to be in the chorus, play, or dance of *Count Dracula* and meet the production heads at 3:15 in the auditorium." "In groups, I want you to think of a creative way you can present the nominative and objective case of pronouns to the class."

Designing Activities without Competition

Think you can't have fun without competition? Think again! What's the key? Designing activities that absorb the class (or volunteers from the class) in new enjoyable skill based tasks.

The following educational activities require no teams, keep no score, and provide no tangible rewards. Would your students like to participate in them? You bet!

NON-COMPETITIVE ACTIVITY 1:
THE ASSEMBLY LINE

Ms. Silver tells the class they will be building sophisticated Lego creations. Using Lego blocks they brought from home, students follow a print-out of instructions to individually build the Lego creation designated for their row (for example: a castle, aircraft carrier, dragon, robot, camera, toaster). Students time how long it takes them to finish their design. Then each row becomes a different assembly line. They're given the task of creating the same Lego design, with each member adding something to the product as it's passed to them. The teacher times how long it takes each assembly line to complete their Lego design. This activity demonstrates the benefits of the assembly line during the Industrial Revolution compared to assembling a product individually. The class discusses the power of mass production and how the assembly line changed production in the United States.

NON-COMPETITIVE ACTIVITY 2: STYLES OF EXPRESSION

Mr. Russo hands four volunteers this couplet by Ogden Nash:

> In the world of mules
> There are no rules.

The volunteers go to separate areas and study how they will recite the poem—which words they will emphasize, how they'll use pause, facial expression, gestures, or other body movement to convey meaning. One by one, each volunteer enters the room, recites the short poem and then takes a seat. The class discusses the attributes of each recital.

After this round, Mr. Russo sends out four more volunteers to study and recite an excerpt from *Moose on the Loose* by Kathy-jo Wargin:

> What would you do with a moose on the loose? Would you chase him, or race him, or stand up to face him? What would you do with a moose on the loose? What would you do with a moose in your yard? Or in your house? How about in your room? Or in your tub? Would you give him two boats? Would you see if he floats? What would you do?

Once again, the class discusses the positive qualities of each recital.

The third time around, Mr. Russo might challenge students to read a longer poem or excerpt. The purpose of this activity is to learn different styles of expression.

NON-COMPETITIVE ACTIVITY 3:
COMICS AND QUOTATION MARKS

Mr. Young hands out to the class a comic strip void of words. Students develop a witty dialogue for the characters that use quotation marks correctly. Volunteers offer their comic strips for the class's viewing. Mr. Young places their comic strips on the overhead and the class reads the dialogue, checking for accuracy in sentence structure and punctuation. Then Mr. Young shows the class the cartoonist's dialogue for comparison. Whoever wants, hangs up their comic strip on the bulletin board under the original comic strip.

NON-COMPETITIVE ACTIVITY 4:
A PUZZLE OF EVENTS

For a unit review, Mrs. Cunningham has students create American Revolutionary War puzzles depicting events ranging from the Sugar Act to the Boston Tea Party. Each group of students receive their event and a 24 × 36 cardboard sheet. They plot ideas for their puzzle on a blueprint before transferring the information to the cardboard sheet. Using simple materials such as markers, gel and glittery pens, students design their own sketches and drawings to create a collage that highlights the main occurrences of their event. Carefully, they cut out puzzle piece shapes from the cardboard. Next, students swap their puzzles with another group's and put the new puzzle together. Students study the event depicted in their classmates' puzzles and if necessary, ask classmates about information they don't understand. (They might critique the information as well.) Using fun tack, students paste their classmates' puzzles to another cardboard sheet or the white board. Finally, students present their classmates' puzzles to the class describing their contents. Afterwards, groups hang up their puzzle in its proper place on a timeline.

NON-COMPETITIVE ACTIVITY 5:
EPISTOLARY WRITING

Miss Mahana's class analyzes a series of checks ("Ordeal by Cheque," *Vanity Fair*, http://ghsbears.pbworks.com/f/Cheques.pdf) and use them as a blueprint to create a compelling and well-developed story about an incident the check holders' share. Students work on converting exposition into ammunition. They make sure the setting and characters drive the plot forward with motive, clearly defining the conflict and what's at stake. Students present their stories to the class for a critique on how well they implemented guidelines of effective storytelling into their writing craft. After the presentations, which all portray unique perspectives, Miss Mahana broaches a discussion on perspective: what factors influence one's perspective, the difference between perspective and point of view, and to what degree perspective is grounded in reality.

Let Kids Choose Their Own Competition

Is competition outside school ever healthy? Yes, but only the competitions children choose themselves.

The competitive games that kids like playing are the ones they initiate with selected teammates. For example, I know kids who loved racing against classmates who are slightly better runners for the purpose of pushing themselves to become better at the sport. Along the same vein, kids play hours of chess with cleverer opponents (in person or online) to learn new strategies. This kind of competition is a self-imposed challenge, one the student is ready and willing to meet.

Some students also enjoy entering district or statewide contests where they can test their skills on higher levels. When the contest comes from outside the school, where the prize is modest, the competition doesn't become personal. Competing with other writers, poets, singers, dancers, etc. "out there" is a way to get an objective viewpoint even in the form of a rejection. Students who go for these competitions grow from the experience. If they do win a prize for their achievement, the class feels proud of its winner, often boasting that "someone from our school won."

Give students the chance to compete with themselves. Everyone wants to challenge themselves, but at their own pace so they can surmount each level. Permit students to compete with themselves throughout the year, so that they can feel a steady and satisfying growth. To this end, you might allow students to keep revising pieces of writing for continual feedback and a better grade. With this incentive, students work to fulfill their potential, reviewing their past mistakes and honing at least one writing skill. Students will work on the same paper for months just to see where it gets them, consequently coming up with a better result than they ever thought possible.

So Here's My Plea in a Nutshell

I'm afraid that as long as the educational system embraces competition, students' emotional and intellectual growth will suffer. We can't afford to raise a generation of children who think they can't make the grade because they lack ability or talent. Renowned author Alfie Kohn, who rails upon competition in his book *No Contest: The Case Against Competition,* says, "Competition is to self-esteem as sugar is to teeth." What a perfect analogy to think about whenever you contemplate introducing a competitive activity, contest, or game.

Competitive activities are all nice and wonderful until it isn't a game anymore. Crossing that line happens in an instant for many; for those who don't do well under pressure, for those who fear they won't measure up. Therefore, the educator can assume that what she sees as motivation is merely the fear of failure along with the need to impress or outperform others. All educators accomplish in this case is shifting students' attention from learning for mastery to learning for the sake of winning. Surely, we don't want to do that.

And here's what it boils down to: At the end of the day, the student who scored the most points doesn't count, it's the one who had a deep and satisfying learning experience, who maintained individuality, who kept the loyalty of friends, and who wants to come back to school for the next adventure. All this can be lost over petty nonsense like contests. Let's work on eradicating competition from our classrooms so that more children will drop their helpless attitudes and view academic challenges with eagerness!

15

Pulverizing Prizes

"I don't make films to win prizes. I make films to make films."—Norman Jewison

The Peril of Prizes

Over the years, I've seen teachers condition children like sea lions, throwing treats their way to keep them motivated. Did your homework? Good girl, here's a sticker. Set up your project for the science fair? You get to choose a Hello Kitty pencil. Before they know it, teachers have to contend with students saying, "Why should we do this?" or "What do we get if we do this?"—a sure sign that students have lost any intrinsic motivation to do the task. Isn't it ironic then when teachers wonder why their students don't feel a sense of duty to complete their work? You can't spoil kids and expect them to meet your standards. They feel entitled to do little work for a huge payoff.

You'd think after a while, teachers would catch on and stop with the prizes, but they don't. Whenever I speak against using prizes as incentives, a vehement protest springs from the throats of educators who allege that prizes work wonders in getting students to listen and learn. I put it to them, albeit more diplomatically, that they're probably depending on prizes to peddle humdrum lessons; otherwise, they wouldn't need prizes.

Here we come to a great difference between the mediocre and master teacher. The mediocre teacher depends on incentives such as prizes to sweeten her lessons. The master teacher, on the other hand, doesn't need prizes to spur enthusiasm. Her lessons promise fulfillment and the experience proves its own reward. Clearly, teachers who drop the prize crutch and transform boring curriculums into stimulating ones reap optimal results.

Time and again, I've seen this for myself. As long as an activity proves challenging, no extrinsic motivation is needed. The motivation comes from students thinking, "This is going to be fun!" or "I bet I can do this!" And then nothing takes on more satisfaction for the student than setting out and seizing the challenge.

To illustrate, take the following experiment I did in my classroom: During an impromptu speaking class, I challenged students to come to the front of the room and speak for 60 seconds about a random word I'd give them (like fireplace, pretzel, detective). Immediately, volunteers shot up their hands to accept the challenge.

In the second class, to test if a reward would bring forth more volunteers, I produced decorative notepads and announced they'd go as prizes for those who met the speaking requirement. Fewer hands went up than in the first class! But what struck me worthy of greater contemplation was the fact that the majority of volunteers who emerged victorious from their impromptu deliveries forgot to claim their prizes! Flushed with the pride of their exertion, they sat back down in a buoyant mood. It was only after the mood wore off that they remembered, "Oh, right, I get a prize" or "Oh, great, a prize, thank you!" In this case, the prize proved extraneous to my students' intrinsic motivation to challenge themselves.

Now here's the astonishing thing. If I were the type who indulged students with prizes, the class probably would have expressed little interest even when I introduced this pleasurable assignment. Whether or not they volunteered would have been contingent upon how much they wanted the notebooks. Even so, volunteers would not put the same gusto into the task. They'd do a perfunctory job and take the prize, and that would be that. I'm not pulling these assertions out of thin air. According to research, introducing prizes for pleasurable tasks is a detriment to motivation. Multitudes of studies show that incentives such as prizes (tangible or honorary) eventually turn creative play into work, damaging the child's intrinsic motivation to produce or learn.

In one study, a group of children who participated in drawing sessions with magic markers for certificates exhibited less interest in drawing over time and produced lower quality pictures than a group that wasn't offered a reward. In another study, students in a reward group for reading "high interest" books only read the required pages to receive the reward, while peers in non-reward groups read more than twice the number of pages. In yet another study consistent with the result of the latter, subjects given rewards for playing computer games showed less interest in playing them during free time than their counterparts who received no reward for playing the computer game. Clearly, this research shows how rewards diminish the children's intrinsic desire to achieve. It's a heck of a good reason to throw out the prizes.

Furthermore, indulging children with prizes doesn't do them a favor for when they're out in the real world and have to meet a deadline or follow rules. In the real world, you hear, "If you have not boarded the plane twenty minutes before take-off, your reservation is subject to be canceled." The airline doesn't give you a prize for coming early or for making the flight on time. We give children a more practical outlook on life when we don't reward them for meeting reasonable standards.

In fact, I would even venture to say that rewarding students for meeting sensible requirements is downright degrading! After all, for a teacher to think prizes necessary for completing homework or projects, she'd have to have set the bar very low in the classroom! In contrast, when the teacher instructs the class to do work and then leaves them to it, she gives them the notion they're capable of doing the task.

Are All Prizes Futile?

So, if prizes ruin intrinsic motivation, are all prizes out of the question? Not completely. Sometimes intrinsic motivation needs a bit of a jumpstart. A negative past experience could have shut down the will to try anything. For instance, having been confounded in the past by algebra, a student might stubbornly believe he will never understand any math. When a teacher wants to reconcile the student with a subject, she might use an extrinsic reward as bait. Then, once, the student experiences the pleasure of learning the subject, the teacher can discard the extrinsic reward with no injurious effect.

Additionally, prizes might be a good idea for weaker students who find little pleasure in academics and struggle at everything the rest of the class might enjoy. Often, these kids don't feel satisfaction in their small achievements. Earning a prize for each small achievement, becomes a goal, something tangible to shoot for—a conquest to make them feel that effort counts and they're getting somewhere. Again, the teacher can dispense with the prize once the student begins to believe in his learning ability.

WHAT ABOUT EXTRA CREDIT?
HOW DOES IT DIFFER FROM PRIZE GIVING?

Are you thinking that extra credit sounds similar to prize giving? That's really not true. The justification for giving extra credit points is simple.

To begin with, extra credit is for something extra. That being said, it only goes to deserving students who prove that they have deepened their learning. The teacher doesn't give extra credit for mere class work. Furthermore, working for extra credit is also a means of attaining something greater. Students get to build up points toward their grades much like an employer working for a bonus in his salary. Finally, with the promise of extra credit, good grades become a possibility for everyone, narrowing the gap between the natural brains in the class and the hard workers. Extra credit, in turn, applauds effort just as much as innate ability.

AFRAID STUDENTS WILL FEEL LEFT
OUT FROM THE PRIZE FEST?

So now let's say you're beginning to think the argument against prizes is valid. You still might be asking yourself, what if your students are used to getting prizes from previous teachers? Or what if Mr. Reed down the hall gives prizes and your class will become jealous? Concerned your kids will feel like they're missing out on prizes?

I have two ideas for you.

Give surprise prizes. Studies show that when the prize comes as a surprise, it doesn't interfere with student motivation. Therefore, it's all right to give students unexpected prizes to show you're proud of their efforts. A trip to the park after a rigorous week of tests. A dolphin keychain for their graduation to the next swimming level. These prizes promote good will and celebrate learning. But remember not to give these prizes often or hint to them. Once prizes become predictable, students no longer view them as special and fall back to thinking they deserve them.

Give gifts instead of prizes. What's a gift? An expression of affection or appreciation, not necessarily a symbol of achievement. While prizes make the receiver feel deserving, gifts make him feel cherished. So what's the major difference between prize giving and gift giving? Prize giving doesn't create a bond between the teacher and student while gift giving strengthens the relationship.

Give gifts for no special reason. When a teacher gives the class a gift for no particular reason she's in essence saying, "You're a great bunch of kids. I like you. You mean so much to me." It's a personal gesture. Therefore, there's nothing wrong with giving your class little gifts when you are moved to or just because you decided to one day. You might even tell the kids, "I'm giving you this treat just because."

"Because what?" they are sure to ask to which you might reply, "because you're all so wonderful," or "because I feel like it," or "just because." Imagine kids going home and telling their parents, "My teacher gave us this magnetic frame just because." Gifts like this mean more to students than prizes for academic achievement, and they don't spoil the intrinsic motivation to learn.

A welcome tool at first glance, prizes inevitably destroy the zeal interwoven in the fabric of learning. Privately, I have never had a class that lamented the absence of prizes in my classroom. To the contrary, I have witnessed students derive much pleasure from engrossing themselves in learning for the sake of knowing, growing, and achieving. Kids don't need prizes to acquire satisfaction from learning. Theodore Roosevelt once said, "Far and away the best prize that life has to offer is the chance to work hard at work worth doing." Let these words ring true in the atmosphere of your classroom!

16

Purging Pleasing

"The art of pleasing is the art of deceiving."—French Proverb

The Problem with "Pleasing the Teacher"

Pleasing the teacher is the chief motivation behind students' achievement and obedience in the classroom. After all, please the teacher and reap the many benefits: better grades, lavish praise, preferential treatment, and glowing recommendations. Starting from preschool, children learn that pleasing the teacher is the key to a successful experience in school. Almost unconsciously, students set up patterns of behaviors which include paying avid attention in class, completing work to the teacher's satisfaction, asking advice, accepting counsel, showing gratitude, and cooperating with peers. Not bad qualities for a student you're telling yourself! True, but only if the behavior stems from a desire for personal growth, not from a need to please the teacher.

Here are the basic pitfalls of teacher pleasing:

Teacher pleasers don't learn for mastery.
Teacher pleasers depend on praise to lift their esteem.
Teacher pleasers don't think for themselves.
Teacher pleasers squelch their own voice.
Teacher pleasers suppress their feelings.
Teacher pleasers are scared of making mistakes.
Teacher pleasers avoid risk-taking to stay within the safe bounds of correct answers.
Teacher pleasers fall short of their ambitions.
Teacher pleasers become needy.
Teacher pleasers are lost without instruction.
Teacher pleasers have difficulty making decisions.
Teacher pleasers learn to be flatterers.
Teacher pleasers are overly concerned about their reputation.
Teacher pleasers neglect their moral development.
Teacher pleasers spend enormous energy trying to stay on the teacher's good side.
Teacher pleasers have a blurry sense of self.
Teacher pleasers grow up to be dependent adults.

To prevent the above, we must examine students' behavior, asking ourselves the following questions: Does she want to know or does she want to impress? Is the student's behavior genuine or pretentious? Is he respectful or ingratiating? Is he accommodating or attention-seeking? When students exhibit ulterior motives to their behavior, we have to wonder at what expense.

Have any of your students ever made the following type of statements?

"I work so hard for you."
"I stayed up till 2:00 a.m. to write your essay."
"What kind of compositions do you like?"
"Do you want me to revise the paper once more?"
"Is this what you want?"
"My histogram isn't good enough to show you yet."
"You're going to be disappointed, but my neon sign doesn't glow."
"What do you want me to do next?"
"Are you happy with my project?"
"Do you like my painting?"
"I told my mother you know your stuff."
"Guess what, Ms. Johnson, my model came out the best!"
"Look, Mr. Garcia, I'm letting Cindy go ahead of me!"

If any of these statements sound familiar, you have come face to face with a teacher pleaser.

Unwittingly, teachers reinforce teacher pleasing with the following type of responses to teacher pleasers:

"I work so hard for you." *"I know. I can tell!"*
"I stayed up till 2:00 a.m. to write your essay." *"Wow! that's really something!"*
"What kind of compositions do you like?" *"I like compositions about heartfelt moments."*
"Do you want me to revise the paper once more?" *"Yes, I think you should give Aunt Dottie more dialogue."*
"Is this what you want?" *"This is exactly what I want!"*
"My histogram isn't good enough to show you yet." *"I understand. I'll stop by later."*
"You're going to be disappointed, but my neon sign doesn't glow." *"Yes I am. We don't have time before the play to make another sign. Let's see what went wrong."*
"What do you want me to do next?" *"I think you should sketch the sequence of events."*
"Are you happy with my project?" *"Not yet. I don't see any lords in your feudal village."*
"Do you like my painting?" *"I love your painting!"*
"I told my mother you know your stuff!" *"Thank you! That's quite a compliment!"*
"Guess what, Ms. Johnson, my model came out the best!" *"It sure did! Congratulations!"*
"Look, Mr. Garcia, I'm letting Cindy go ahead of me." *"Wonderful! I'm so proud of you!"*

What can a teacher say or do to discourage teacher-pleasing behavior? Follow these guidelines and you're guaranteed success.

- Show displeasure when students try to please you with their work. Inform students that they're working for themselves—not for your benefit or anyone else's.
- Communicate the purpose of the work. Check that students understand the purpose of their work. Ask them what skills they've gained and how these skills will help them for the future.

- Exhibit disapproval of unhealthy working habits. Students who try to impress you with bloodshot eyes have clearly developed unhealthy working habits along with teacher pleasing tactics. Eradicate the student's need to impress you with the unwarranted hours he put into a task by addressing his need for a better working schedule.
- Make sure students own their work. Ask questions like, "How are you doing with your project?" "What about your work doesn't meet your expectations?" "How do you propose to change it?" "How much time do you think you'll need to finish?" When you put the onus on them, students concentrate on meeting their potential instead of impressing you.
- Emphasize the importance of doing one's best. Let students know that satisfaction comes with meeting one's potential. In this way, students have a means of evaluating their progress instead of asking you about it. If they're satisfied, they know they did a good job. If they're not satisfied, they try to determine why and work on doing a better job.
- Throw back the question. When a student asks for a simple instruction, for instance, "What should I work on now?" throw back the question by asking, "What do *you* think you should work on now?" Does your student seem clueless? Help him walk through options. Trigger his thought by asking questions like, "What else do you think you should know about this topic?" "Do you have any questions you'd like to discuss with me?" "Do you want to read up more on this topic?" Similarly, when a student questions, "Is this good enough?" or "Are you happy with this?" throw the question back by inquiring whether or not she is happy with her work or whether there's anything she'd like to improve.
- Remove your bias. When it comes to appraising creative work, refrain from trying to control the outcome. Don't let your preference for a style or arrangement slant your students' direction. Meaning if your students wants to beautify her nature journal with a muted background of daisies, don't suggest a border of chrysanthemums. Likewise, if your student chooses a Velcro board for his solar system don't steer him toward the magnetic one.
- Express your appreciation for variety. Variety really is the spice of life. Students should express their creative selves instead of trying to determine which particular style pleases you. When introducing assignments, speak with delight about numerous ways former students executed the same task. Before giving back projects, laud an array of achievements. Point out the extensive research someone did to display armor throughout the ages. Praise another paper for its authentic dialogue between historical characters. Pay tribute to a student's graphic design of photographs. When you show your appreciation for many skills, students don't feel pressured to excel at one thing but know that they can definitely excel at something.
- Avoid sounding like "the teacher is pleased" when you compliment work. For instance, telling Jordan, "I love your painting!" might give Jordan the impression you're pleased with her painting for meeting your taste. If instead, you point out the accomplishment of her drawing, Jordan understands you're pleased with her technique. Her focus on the future will remain on doing the job right, not on pleasing you.
- Assure your students you like them unconditionally—whether or not their projects flop or they get good grades. Never express disappointment in students' failings if you

know the student put forth the proper effort. What if the student shirks his work? Then express disappointment in the student's laziness, not in the student himself.

- Let the class see you as an imperfect person. Doing so teaches students it's okay to make mistakes. To this end, you might present something you're unsure of for students to scrutinize. For example, when a student asks me to spell a word on the board (the other day it was orangutan) and I am uncertain of the spelling, I'll write the word on the board and ask, "Does this spelling look correct?" to which my students reply, "Yes," or "No," and either suggest a correction, or look up the spelling.

In these instances, I show students I'm not above making mistakes and have no qualms about asking for verification. In turn, my students know I won't think less of them if they stumble along the way. They also know they can show uncertainty before the class without shame.

For instance, once in a presentation, a student informed the class that light travels approximately five trillion, eight hundred sixty-five billion, six hundred ninety-six million miles a year. A classmate called out, "Can you write that on the board?" Hesitating for a second, the presenter wrote carefully, 5,865,696,000,000 stepped back, and asked, "Does this look right?" and the class said, "Yeah." This double-checking becomes normal in class and communicates that as human beings we're constantly learning.

- Express interest in errors. Show curiosity about students' errors to depict your willingness to help resolve them. Give the message that an error is an opportunity to improve, so that students won't hesitate to show you unfinished products. In addition, express curiosity about your own errors. Occasionally, I invite students to help me figure out where I went wrong and how I can correct information. Doing so allows students to see there's no shame in not knowing everything.
- Praise effort over ability. Let's say your students are designing scale drawings of clubhouses to discover the uses of geometry and measurement in the world of architecture. Saying, "I admire the careful detail you put into the blueprint, including the swinging back door," gives students a different message than, "I can see your sophistication in this blueprint!" When you appreciate effort over ability, students concentrate on the process instead of trying to please you with the result.
- Praise action, not only outcome. During meetings with students, praise their actions, not just the outcome, even if it is outstanding. The outcome of anything is really a combination of small successes that culminates into the final product. If the final product doesn't pan out, the success is still there. Point out small successes in the development so students can recognize their value and not feel overly disappointed if the end result doesn't meet their expectation.

For instance, let's say students are creating diminutive sculptures using Creative Paperclay and old paintbrushes. When a teacher just praises the outcome, she feeds the notion that practicing a skill or putting in effort is nothing to reaching the goal. Telling a student, "You handled the coping saw smoothly," or "You were so meticulous about smoothing the Paperclay down onto the handle of the brush," praises the action and makes the student feel that he's doing something right at least part of the time.

What if the outcome gets botched? Help students face disappointment. Boost the student by saying something like, "You worked hard to paint the nose, chin, and ears using 'trompe l'oeil.' I'm sorry the final product didn't work out the way you expected." This statement conveys that you value effort, not only excellent work. You might even decide the student deserves a number of points toward his grade for effort.

- When students flatter, show disinterest. Accepting flattery teaches kids they need to impress to receive appreciation. In face of flattery, keep your expression bland and turn the student's focus back to his work. You might want to use a more direct approach for blatant flatterers by asking them outright not to compliment you.
- Help students acquire humility. Show students how to acquire humility by not boasting about their ability or announcing their good deeds. When students feel the self-respect that comes along with humility, they no longer feel the need to impress. You'd be surprised how even small children can practice this character building trait.

Using some of these guidelines, let's revisit the students' original "teacher pleasing" statements below. Consider how you would answer the statements to offset teacher pleasing behavior. Then look at the italicized responses for comparison.

"I work so hard for you."

"You're working hard for yourself, Amanda, not for me. You're working to improve the math skills you'll need for life. Can you tell me what you've learned about math in this chapter that you can apply to your life?"

"I stayed up till 2:00 a.m. to write your essay."

"Ryan, I have two comments for you. First, you're not writing my essay, you're writing your essay. Can you tell me what skills you've learned while writing this essay? How will these skills help you in your future writing? Second, if you stayed up until 2:00 a.m., you need to manage your time better. Maybe I can help you plan a better schedule next time around."

"What kind of compositions do you like?"

"Jason, don't worry about the kind of compositions I like. I enjoy all types. As long as you keep to the instructions, you may express yourself any way you like.

"Do you want me to revise the paper once more?"

"Do you think you should revise the paper once more? What might you still consider revising? Why?"

"Is this what you want?"

"I think what you really want to know is whether or not you're meeting the criteria. Let's look at the checklist and see."

"My histogram isn't good enough to show you yet."

"Guess what, I like to see an imperfect histogram. This way I get to see your effort and if you need help, I get to give you guidance."

"You're going to be disappointed, but my neon sign doesn't glow."

"I could never be disappointed with you, Julie, because you don't shirk your work. I know you put great effort into this sign and I'm sorry it flopped. Let's see what went wrong and whether we can salvage the sign."

"What do you want me to do next?"

"What do you think you should do? Do you have a plan you want to run by me?"

"Are you happy with my project?"

"What's going to make me happy, Sophia, is if you work to your potential. To measure your potential, ask yourself what makes you proud of your feudal village. Then ask yourself what doesn't make you proud. That's what you still need to work on."

"Do you like my painting?"

"I think you mean to ask me if your painting shows the proper perspective. And it does. Your street looks authentic because your buildings stand in proportion all the way to the vanishing point. This is good art, Frankie. Anyone would want to take a walk down your street!"

"I told my mother you know your stuff!"

"You probably meant to say that you're glad you're learning so many things in my class." (Or more pointedly to the blatant flatterer: *"My job, Gabriel, is to know my stuff. Your job is to learn the stuff, not to flatter me."*)

"Guess what, Ms. Johnson, my model came out the best!"

Ms. Johnson, to the student in private: *"Benjamin, when you announced your neuron model came out the best, you were boasting to your classmates that yours were better than theirs. That makes people feel bad. Keep in mind that everyone is good at different things. You can be grateful that you're good at creating models and you can be proud of your effort. But just because your model came out better doesn't mean you're better than anyone else. Next time you feel like boasting, hold yourself back and you'll feel good for respecting others."*

"Look, Mr. Garcia, I'm letting Cindy go ahead of me."

Mr. Garcia, to the student in private: *"Lydia, I'm sure Cindy appreciated that you let her go ahead. When you do a favor, though, it's best not to announce it. You want to do Cindy a favor for the sake of being a kind person. Once you announce what you did, you're showing you did the favor partly for my approval. You don't want to do that. Next time your do someone a favor, hold yourself back from announcing it and you'll feel proud of yourself."*

Please keep in mind that you might have to continually reiterate these messages to your students. Old habits die hard. Many students have spent years trying to please their teachers. It stands to reason they'll need some time to eradicate this behavior.

Students cannot truly improve their own lives if they're busy pleasing teachers. Let's not allow students to feed themselves a false self-worth by responding positively to words of flattery or adulation. Let's purge teacher pleasing from our schools; the first step in guiding children toward healthy independent thinking.

Promoting Healthy Independent Thinking

"Independence is my happiness, and I view things as they are, without regard to place or person; my country is the world, and my religion is to do good."— Thomas Paine

The most empowering thing we can do for our students is to foster independent thinking. Independent thinking means learning to evaluate criticism without letting it ruin you. It means speaking and acting with one own's mind. It's recognizing that all minds are unique and that it's natural to express different thoughts, ideas, and feelings than others. It means using one's brain to reflect deeply and to pursue the truth. Independent thinking means basing opinions on bona-fide information and personal experience and not on what others tell you. Independent thinking helps students choose the best options for themselves and quells the desire to live outside one's true self.

The following tips help educators inculcate healthy independent thinking.

Minimize the effect of past criticisms. The greatest mistake we can make, I tell my students, is to lose faith in ourselves because of what people say. People are all too often presumptuous in their criticism of our abilities.

To help students disregard crippling criticism, I like to point out a host of famous people who pursued their dreams despite the things people said or thought about them! Criticism that didn't hold people back from accomplishing their best:

- His teachers thought he was hopeless at composing. (Ludwig Van Beethoven, German world-renowned composer and pianist)
- His teacher said he was "too stupid to learn anything," and that he should enter a field where he might succeed by the virtue of his pleasant personality. (Thomas Edison, American inventor of the incandescent light bulb and over 1,000 other inventions)
- Fired from the *San Francisco Examiner* in 1899, he was told by an editor, "I'm sorry, … but you just don't know how to use the English language." (Rudyard Kipling, English journalist, short-story writer, poet, and novelist)
- Dismissed from drama school because she was "too shy and reticent to put her best foot forward." (Lucille Ball, American actress and comedian)
- Fired from a newspaper because he "lacked imagination and had no original ideas." (Walt Disney, American entrepreneur, cartoonist, and pioneer of the American animation industry)
- Performing poorly in school, he was dubbed "a boy with low intelligence" who stuttered

and spoke with a lisp. (Winston Churchill, British prime minister, 1940–1945, 1951–1955)

- Failing to land a role and almost giving up on acting when a director called her "too ugly." (Meryl Streep, American actress, winner of three Academy Awards)
- Turned down by a recording company that said, "We don't like their sound. They have no future in show business." (The Beatles, legendary rock band)
- He was told after his first performance: "You ain't going nowhere, son. You ought to go back to driving a truck." (Elvis Presley, legendary American musician)
- Rejected 144 times before finding a publisher for his first book, *Chicken Soup for the Soul.* (Author Jack Canfield, who holds the Guinness World Record for having seven books simultaneously on the New York Times Best Seller list. *Chicken Soup for the Soul* sold more than 18 million copies.)
- Demoted from her job as a news anchor because she "wasn't fit for television." (Oprah Winfrey, American media proprietor, talk show host, ranked as the most influential woman in the world)

Let students ruminate about how many other people in the world could have risen to great accomplishments had they not caved to criticism. Ask students if they're going to allow others' criticism to define their future.

Help students evaluate negative criticism. Encourage students to speak about criticism which stunted their progress or disabled them. Help them determine if they should limit themselves because of it.

Students might ask themselves these questions to evaluate negative criticism:

- Have I asked at least four experts for their opinions of my work? Did these experts have all the information they needed? Were their remarks specific and unbiased (as far as possible)? Could there have been a misunderstanding?
- What remarks did the experts have in common? Is there some truth to it? What does that tell me?

Help students devise a plan of action. Once students have a clearer picture of how much they should value the criticism, they might want to contemplate their next step. Here are questions they can ask themselves in this endeavor.

- How strongly do I want to pursue this project? Do I want to take this on as a hobby? As a possible future career? What kind of fulfillment will it bring me? Am I doing this for myself or for others' approval? Will this endeavor help me grow?
- How might I improve my work? Which books or materials do I need? What classes might I have to take? Which tutorials can I watch?
- Do I believe deep down that I can reach my goal despite the rejections I received so far? Are there internal factors holding me back from going forward such as laziness or fear of future rejection? Are there external factors such as financial expenses? How can I get help with this?
- What's my game plan for the future? Can I write a to-do list?
- If I realize this particular undertaking is currently not working for me, what can I take from this experience? How else might I invest my time?

Use strategic words to alter students' belief systems. One of my favorite true stories by Piero Ferrucci in *The Power of Kindness* displays how words can alter our belief system. Before a workshop, someone points out to Ferrucci a man who has a brilliant sense of humor. Ferrucci approaches the man and tells him, "I hear you have a talent for making people laugh." Looking totally surprised, the man says nothing of the compliment but sure enough regales the workshop with jokes. After the workshop, Ferrucci tells the one who introduced him to Mr. X that the latter was definitely a jocular guy. Ferrucci is then astounded to hear, "Hang on, whom did you think I meant? I was talking about that guy over there." Ferrucci mistakenly thought Mr. X was the witty subject while really it was Mr. Y.

Why did Mr. X all of a sudden become funny? Because Ferrucci tapped into his humorous side. Mr. X probably thought, "Me Funny? Okay, maybe I am if someone thinks so." And he gave his humor a shot. Our words have the power to activate hidden qualities, whatever they may be. We might never know the impact, but sometimes we get to see it first-hand like Ferrucci.

You can alter students' belief systems by putting notions in students' heads that they can do something with a latent ability or talent. For instance, let's say you see that Carla is good with numbers and design, you might ask her if she ever considered reading about architecture. If you note that Ambrose moves with grace, you might ask him if he ever took dancing lessons. While Carla might not have ever considered a career in architecture and Ambrose never fathomed dancing, they now believe they have potential to do design buildings or dance. Planting these notions induces students, especially those stigmatized as learning impaired or discouraged by previous setbacks, to start believing in themselves. Once people believe in themselves, they start thinking for themselves and accomplish great feats.

Optimize students' abilities. How do you do that? By expecting the best. Don't be afraid to push students to their mental capacity. Everyone's mind is much better than they think. Those who've learned helplessness might give you a hard time at first, but they'll change their attitude once they see self-made progress. Oliver Wendell Holmes asserts that "the mind is a mansion, but most people are content to live in its lobby." Prod students forward. Don't let them get stuck in the lobby of their minds! There's no contentment there.

Treat students like professionals. Tell your class, "This is what you have to know as a scientist/writer/gymnast/mathematician." Convey that you view them as professionals and they will rise to that standard. When they skip a step in the scientific method, don't say, "You skipped a step in the scientific process." Tell them, "As a scientist you don't want to skip a step in the scientific method. You need to go back to that." All of a sudden, students start thinking, "Maybe I have the qualities of a scientist." They become much more resourceful in their thinking.

Don't share skepticism. Build autonomy by showing belief in students' potential instead of sharing their skepticism.

Once I warned my students that they could not get published if their essays contained wordy sentences. In response, a girl snickered, "Yeh, right, we're all going to be authors," and the class laughed along. But when I didn't share their skepticism and went further by naming former students who actually did become bona-fide authors, my students sobered in surprise. From that moment the class transformed into earnest writers, often rewriting their papers five or six times before being satisfied with the outcome. At the end of the term, students approached me to say that they hadn't realized their writing talent until they took my class. And all I did was awaken the possibility that they could become authors one day.

Transmit the idea that there is no "one way" the brain thinks. Impress upon students what an intrinsically complex muscle the brain is by showing how no one's operates the same. Truly amazed by this, I frequently end off class discussions pointing out how one question or comment triggered so many different thought patterns and reactions. This acknowledgment encourages students to think freely and impart their true thoughts.

Have students believe in their unique makeup. Convey to students that everyone, including yourself, has different strengths and creative styles. Making comments like, "You're a confident public speaker," or "I see you're great at lip syncing," or "You make flawless cartwheels!" gives students pride in their individual abilities. Feeling like individuals, students know they don't have to outdo others and can concentrate on honing skills relevant to them.

Celebrate the quest for knowledge. Absorb the class in an intriguing puzzle or problem. Show how gratifying it is to get down to the core of a matter. Broach topics for discussion that call for probing. For instance, you can have a discussion with your class about the mystery of the Loch Ness Monster and challenge the class to get to the bottom of it!

Coach students to seek the truth. Urge students to pursue the truth and not to mistake what they hear through the grapevine as self-evident. Teach students the difference between eyewitness reports, rumors, and gossip and how to evaluate their worth. Tell students to "practice disbelief" before accepting information as the truth.

Train students to seek answers for themselves. Educate students on how to find the best sources online that provide credible information. You might stress how questioning knowledgeable people is also an expedient way to acquire substantial information for school or personal purposes. Even pedestrians can prove helpful. For instance, before shopping for an electric skateboard, my student Lucas stopped teenagers using electric skateboards in the park and asked them the following questions: What brand is your skateboard? Where did you buy it? What different styles are offered? How much does your skateboard cost in comparison to similar ones? Do you like the way your skateboard is wearing? Do you like the way it feels? Do you feel in control? Can the wheels become loose? How would you know? How long does it take to charge the skateboard? How fast does it go? Did you have any accidents with it? Do you think there's a better brand out there? Why is it better?

In ten minutes, Lucas had the answers he needed. Lucas knew that asking users about their electric skateboards was a much smarter approach than going to a sports equipment store and inquiring about them from a salesperson. He figured salespeople push products and tell you about them in theory, but owners can tell you about them in practice! This pursuit for facts strengthened Lucas's belief in his ability to figure out information for himself.

Let students take the initiative. When students need to seek information, let them take the initiative before giving your suggestions. This exercises their independent thinking.

Here's a case in point: Once a kid wrote a narrative about an underside part of her aunt's car falling off on the highway, causing the car to break down. I asked her to be more specific.

"What's the brand of the car?" I asked.

"An Audi," Lily said.

"What's the name of the part that fell off?" Lily didn't know. When I repeated that the narrative needed that information, Lily said she'd go home to find out. The next day she said neither her aunt nor her uncle could tell her the part that had to be replaced by the mechanic. I didn't respond, but waited expectantly. "Oh, yeah," my student said as the solution dawned on her, "I guess I can stop by the repair shop on the way home today and ask the mechanic for the name of the part."

"Good thinking," I said. And that's what she did. The mechanic, pleased with her interest, not only confirmed the name of the part—the carburetor lid, but also sent her home with a coupon for an oil change to give her aunt.

Challenge students to back up their opinions. Training students to support their convictions helps them filter ideas they may have haphazardly picked up from others. You'd be surprised how often students use a cliché or catchphrase in their speech without thinking what it means. Expect students to render their true thoughts.

Urge students to disconnect from sources of conventional thinking. Disengaging from or reducing the time students spend on TV, blogs, and newspapers reduces the level of devotion we give it. Instead of getting caught up with what the "Theys" say, students can think candidly about topics. Thinking about one's opinions before checking out the media also accustoms the mind to think first before accepting a conventional outlook.

Hold the individual accountable for his behavior.

"But *everyone* was talking!" protests Daniel.

"And if everyone were jumping off the roof, would you do that too?" his teacher replies.

As a kid, I always thought this retort annoying, but now decades later, I kind of like it. Although the analogy is way off between talking in class and jumping off a roof, it drives home the message that no matter what, people must act for themselves.

Think about it. Why don't students act for themselves? Why do kids render themselves blameless for engaging in misdeeds prevalent among classmates? Because we don't hold them responsible for thinking on their own. Let's rectify that.

Communicate to students that they must account for their behavior. Don't go easy on a student just because he's in good company (or rather bad company!). This means we hold Emma equally responsible for bullying even when her friends bully too. We expect Caleb to answer for ignoring the spilled apple juice even though he points out that two of his buddies did the same. We demand pristine homework from Wendy, no matter if she claims that William and Wanda got away with not doing it. Requiring students to check their behavior individually builds integrity and compels them to think and act on their own.

Show consideration for your student's train of thought. Be patient while listening to students. Hear them out. Don't rush their pace. Don't interrupt your students' train of thought to correct their usage or to make your own comments. Listen without praising or modifying words. This allows students to finish their thoughts without telling you what you want to hear.

Give choices. With a choice before them, students get to reflect on their strengths, preferences and interests. Once they make their choice, students automatically take ownership of their work and relay a greater interest in learning. You might exercise students' independent thinking by giving them choices throughout the week.

For instance:

- Answer 4/6 questions from this part.
- Check the extracurricular activity that appeals to you most.
- Choose Assignment A or B for homework.
- Would you prefer learning about the effect of social networking on teen culture or the effect of the media on teen culture?
- Would you rather research climate change and glacial melting or climate change and hurricanes?
- Do you want to give your presentation on Wednesday or Thursday?
- Choose an enrichment activity from the file cabinet.
- You might find a prop you can use in the costume closet.
- Choose any article from the pile that appeals to you and prepare to discuss it before the class.
- You may hand in your blog now or tomorrow before class.
- You may do this assignment alone or with a partner.

Convey respect for pace and accuracy. For example, instead of saying, "You should be able to revise your paper in twenty minutes," you might say, "Revise your paper for twenty minutes and show me the difference." Similarly, instead of saying, "As soon as you've finished the worksheet, you may go out to recess," you might say, "As soon as you've worked on the review sheet and can show me three examples you did accurately, you may go out to recess." These statements permit students to absorb themselves in their task instead of rushing to finish. Consequently, students work for accuracy which is important for their autonomy over learning.

Ask students to share mistakes. Set aside a designated class (at least once a month) where all students share a mistake they made, how they made it, and what they learned. Let students learn from and respect each other's thinking process.

Don't be winner-oriented. Why does a student put effort into writing? Is it because she gets a kick out of finding the right words? Wants to create something beautiful? Or wants to get a good grade? Sadly, the latter is the usual case. Let me present two kids. Maddie comes home and says she had a great day because she won the debate, got the top grade on her math test, and beat her teammates at soccer. Heather had a great day because she learned how to play a new tune on the flute, read an exciting story about dolphins, and is in the process of solving a really difficult riddle with a friend. Maddie equates success with outdoing others, while Heather equates success with the joy of pursing knowledge.

Those who view learning as work that gets judged, marked, and celebrated (or not) can't learn for themselves. We educators want to establish a classroom attractive to the second kid's learning. Steering away from competition and ranking, kids learn to think as individuals, to appreciate learning, and to broaden their breadth of knowledge.

Don't praise intelligence. In six studies, by Claudia Mueller and Carol Dweck, fifth graders were given an exam and told they did well on it. Some were told, "You must be smart at these problems," while the others were told, "You must have worked hard at these problems." In a subsequent test, the children were told they didn't meet the previous standard. The children formerly praised for intelligence blamed their setback on their lack of ability, while those formerly praised for effort, blamed their lack of effort.

Next, when presented with a choice of tasks, the children praised for intelligence chose tasks they knew they could accomplish, while the second group chose tasks that presented a challenge. Afterwards, those initially praised for intelligence were more interested in knowing the others' performance rating rather than the strategies or new information they learned.

Clearly the appraisal of intelligence hinders intrinsic motivation. Refraining from praising intelligence allows children to hold onto their natural curiosity and enthusiasm for learning. They feel autonomy over their work versus a need for praise.

Be a coach, not a fixer-upper. Don't do too much for students by the way of correcting their mistakes. Fixing feeds dependence. I know a teacher who would criticize an essay and then fix it for the student. What did students learn from this exchange? That they were powerless to revise the essay themselves and that their teacher was the savior. Not a healthy message for our young people.

Value spontaneity. Spontaneity is marked by reactions unhindered by external stimulus. Most crucial to independence, spontaneity lets students work through ideas in accordance to their natural thought processes. Therefore, when Zachary has a spontaneous idea (within practical means), let him run with it. If he asks for permission to run a fund-raising sale, start a class newspaper, or play Beethoven's "Ode to Joy" at Open School Night, give him your blessing.

Spontaneity promotes risk taking, cultivates flexibility in thinking, and unleashes raw talent. In this state, the student sets out to tackle the initiative with immeasurable enthusiasm. If he needs help, he turns to the teacher. If the project doesn't work out, he learns from the experience and moves on. But if the teacher crushes spontaneity with words of caution ("Are you sure you want to do that?") or suggests alternatives ("I think you should do this instead") the student begins to doubt his initiative and rely too much on the teacher's opinion.

Don't hover. Feeling a looming presence prevents students from thinking freely and doing their personal best. Ever wonder why you bungle with an audience watching you dance or squeeze into a parking spot or shoot baskets? You're trying too hard to impress. Likewise, many students tense and make mistakes with the teacher hovering nearby. Obviously, you want to stop by to check on students' progress, but remember to move on quickly so that students can work without feeling self-conscience.

Alternatively, you might have students approach your desk to show you their progress. This allows them to take the initiative when they're feeling more confident about their work.

Don't pressure students to impress you academically. When the teacher puts on the pressure for her class to please her academically, she stifles her students' independent progress. I found this out some time ago after grading a batch of quizzes. Disappointed that the answers didn't sport the same smooth flow as those in previous quizzes, I asked my class what happened.

"You did it," one of my students said bluntly before she could catch herself.

"What do you mean?" I asked.

"You scared us," she replied. "You said, 'Dazzle me again everyone! I can't wait to see your answers!' I guess we were so busy trying to dazzle you that we couldn't think for ourselves."

"Oh," I said, "Really?"

The class all looked at me in silent accord. Really.

"I think so," admitted another student. "I felt like everything I was writing was going to be judged."

"So you felt under pressure and couldn't do your best?" I probed.

"I guess," she said, and the class agreed.

So there I had it. What I thought were motivating words stunted the class's potential. Pleasantly surprised by their fluency in previous papers, all I wanted was to hold my class to that standard. What I failed to realize is that most kids do not need prompting before a quiz. Naturally, they will do the best they can. A teacher might want to warn them to look out for little things likes fragments and punctuation. But urging students to do a dazzling job isn't something concrete they can work with and places an unfair burden on their minds. Worse, it turns the focus on pleasing the teacher instead of thinking hard for the sake of coming to a satisfactory answer.

Independent thinking is pricelessly rare. Yet, independent thinking is crucial for one's human development. Independent thinking is necessary for competence, purposefulness, strategizing, theoretical thinking, and a high moral standing. How do your students measure up? Do they use their own minds?

Promote healthy thinking and watch this happen: Students who have fallen to the wayside of unfair criticism will brush themselves off and forge ahead to contribute something worthwhile. Students steeped in the conventional pit, mimicking other's views, working for grades or recognition will emerge with a new sense of obligation to seek the truth and make the right decisions. The atmosphere of the class will pulse with curiosity and a desire for self-challenge and self-improvement.

18

Cultivating the Critic

"It is the mark of an educated mind to entertain a thought without accepting it."—Aristotle

Just How Critical Is Critical Thinking?

It is not unusual for students to go with the flow instead of thinking for themselves. Programmed to copy and memorize information from crisply confident instructors, students don't pause to ask themselves, "Does this make sense?" or "Can this be true?" While observing classes across America, what disturbed me most was students' willingness to accept everything at face value. Their main concern: "Do we have to know this for the test?" Sometimes, I believe, if teachers were to inform their classes that NASA sent a rhinoceros to the moon in 1708, students would obediently take down that information.

Teachers who permit passive acceptance in the classroom squelch curiosity, turning students away from intellectual pursuits, possibly even weakening the class's moral compass. One major goal in my classroom is to get students to think more critically, to question the givens, to be more skeptical of information they read, hear, or think they know. This appraisal brings students to truths they would have not recognized otherwise. Once trained to pursue the truth, students take the initiative in the classroom (and eventually in society) by pointing out errors, suggesting a better method of doing something, or standing up against injustice.

Taking a Critical Look at Well-Known Information

To impress students with the need for critical review, I continually present them with information they take for granted and ask them to form an opinion.

For instance, let's take a critical look at Freytag's Pyramid, a well-known diagram used in literature to describe a story's plot.

Remember how your elementary school teacher drew Freytag's Pyramid on the board to label the parts of the story? As a kid, I never liked this diagram. Basically, it told the reader that the anticipation of a story rises to the climax and plummets from there. To my mind, the diagram didn't do good stories justice. Think about it. Did a good story ever disappoint you? Was any part of the plot anticlimactic as the diagram suggests? Of course, not. No, not for one moment did I believe in the integrity of Freytag's Pyramid.

And yet, as a diligent student, I copied Freytag's Pyramid into my notebook, telling myself it must be correct since the teacher drew it on the board. All the same, as the years rolled by through junior high and high school, my bias toward that diagram grew as I spotted other incongruities between it and patterns of stories. Therefore, when I became an English teacher, I decided, that's it. I'm going to have my students question the validity of this diagram. Thus began my first lesson on critical thinking in the classroom.

For an introduction to literature, I drew Freytag's Pyramid on the board. Evidently familiar with it, my eleventh graders chimed in with me as I labeled each part of the diagram.

"I can tell you're very familiar with this diagram," I told my students. "What do you think of it?" Students looked at me blankly. "Do you think it aptly portrays the pattern of a story?" I asked. More silence. "Do you see any discrepancies between the pattern of the diagram and the stories you know?" I probed. After taking another long hard look at the diagram, students began to exclaim, "Oh!" and urgently raise their hands. What they had to say blew me away.

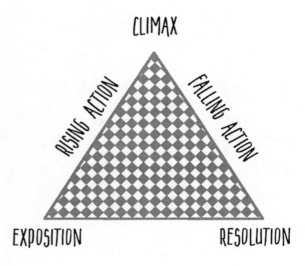

"Stories don't always begin with an exposition," Alana offered.

"How might a story begin differently?" I questioned.

"With a conflict," Alana said.

"And the author can keep feeding the exposition within the conflict," added Kayla.

"So the exposition can be found in the rising action of the story," Malka said.

"And the author might use expositions throughout a story, introducing different settings and characters," exclaimed Simi. "That's what we learned last year, so I don't think the exposition belongs only in the beginning of the diagram."

The class fell silent, registering this information.

"I also question Freytag's decision to use a pyramid," Bella brought up. "Who says there's such a sharp rising action in all short stories? Sometimes the suspense rises more gradually."

"Or sometimes the suspense builds until the very end of the story like in O. Henry stories," Lila chipped in. "The climax appears at the end. In those stories, there is no *falling action*!"

"But most stories don't end like O. Henry stories," Rachel remarked. "The climax is usually in the middle or toward the end of the story."

"Still, the diagram shows that the main climax is found only in the middle of the story," Lila persisted.

"And one more thing," Adel said, "the sharp decline in this diagram doesn't work."

"Why not?" I asked.

"Well, why is there such a sharp decline after the climax of the story? The way down to the resolution can happen slowly or there can be bumps along the way. The diagram makes the falling action look too fast and certain."

"I think it's true that there might be one major climax in a story," said Miri. "So I agree with the climax's position at the peak of the pyramid. But there could also be a smaller climax leading to the main climax and other climaxes following the main climax. Maybe the diagram should illustrate that."

"I totally agree," Judy piped up, "And now that I'm thinking about it, the term 'falling action' for the decline sounds so anticlimactic, like the action falls flat or something. The 'falling action' in this diagram makes the story look like it's void of suspense from the climax to the resolution."

"That's what actually bothered me most about this diagram when I was in school," I admitted to Judy. And then addressing the class, I asked, "How would you modify the diagram?"

The class contemplated for a moment.

"Maybe the diagram should resemble less of a pyramid and more of a mountain or mountain range," Bella suggested.

"You can't really create one diagram that fits for every story, though," Rachel mused.

"Maybe each story should be plotted individually," Simi said.

"I agree with Simi," said Miri.

"Why create a diagram at all?" I asked.

"Maybe it would be interesting to see how the author plotted his story, so we could copy the method if we wanted to in our own writing," Tammy suggested.

"I think that's an idea," I answered. "It might be interesting to plot a diagram for each story we read this year. Should we give it a shot?" I questioned.

"Why not?" the class said. "Let's do it."

There I had it. In fifteen minutes, my class discredited a plot diagram they had accepted for many years. And they felt good about it. Coming to new truths is always empowering. My anticipation was for my students to continue using their critical eye in examining other content.

Important note: I'd like to emphasize that critical thinking doesn't mean looking to pounce on the bad. Although critical thinking can expose fallacies and bad reasoning, it first calls for fair, systematic assessment. When we promote critical thinking, we're asking students to examine the content, subject, or problem with an open eye and come to reasonable conclusions.

Using Literature as a Model for Life

While we're on the topic, I might add that literature is an excellent subject for critical analysis. Since authors pattern characters' behavior after real people, students glean many truths about life by studying characters' behavior and the author's intention within a storyline.

The following critical questions apply to most literature. How about choosing a set of these questions for critical review after reading assignments? You'll soon see students examining literature more closely and coming to mature conclusions.

- What motivates the main character to face the struggle or the challenge? What does this character lack? What is his mistake? What is his strong point? What would you do if you were in the character's situation? Think of one of your friends in this situation. What do you imagine he'd do? Why? What do you think would happen if everyone in your neighborhood took on the character's behavior?
- Do you empathize with the main character? How would you treat him? Do you admire this character? What advice would you give him? Would you want to be his friend, his brother/sister, son/daughter? Why or why not? How do other characters treat this main character? Do these characters treat the main character fairly? How so?
- How necessary is each character to this plot? What would happen if the author removed one of these characters from the storyline? Which character(s) are irrelevant to the plot? Why? Do you think the author should have incorporated other characters? Which type of characters and which type of behavior? How would these characters change the course of the story?
- Can you relate to the events in this story? Do you think they are realistic? Have the characters changed your mindset in any way? What do you suppose is the author's message? How true is this message? How important is his message? Might you have changed a part of the story to convey another message? Do you understand yourself or others any better through this storyline? What lessons did you derive from the story? Which did you take to heart?

SCRUTINIZING THE AUTHOR'S OPINION

Sometimes within a story, authors state personal convictions through their characters' narration or dialogue. How do students respond? Do they consider these opinions? Understand them? Accept them? I like to urge students to weigh these opinions. The discussion that follows sharpens students' critical thinking. For instance, here are excerpts from *A Separate Peace* by John Knowles which suggest blatant convictions. When I teach the story, we ruminate about Knowles' opinions together, sometimes calling them brilliant and other times, off-base. Generally, I'll prepare questions following each excerpt to get the discussion flowing. Take a look at what I mean.

Opinion excerpts and follow up questions from *A Separate Peace* by John Knowles:

"As I said, this was my sarcastic summer. It was only long after that I recognized sarcasm as the protest of people who are weak" (15). Do you believe sarcasm is the protest of people who are weak? If so, how would you describe the protest? the weakness?

"Everyone has a moment in history that belongs particularly to him. It is the moment when his emotions achieve their most powerful sway over him, and afterwards when you say to this person 'the world today' or 'life' or 'reality' he will assume that you mean this moment, even if it is fifty years past" (40). Does this idea strike a chord with you? Do you have a moment in history that belongs to you? Do you think you are too young to appreciate this idea? Do you think your parents can identify with this idea?

"Everything has to evolve or else it perishes" (125). Do you think this theory is true? Can you think of examples that uphold this theory or dispute this theory?

"Because it seemed clear that wars were not made by generations and their special stupidities, but that wars were made instead by something ignorant in the human heart" (201). Do you think wars spring from ignorance? If so, how would you define this ignorance? If not, what aside from ignorance might create war?

ANALYZING INTRIGUING QUOTES

Of course you don't have to be reading a classic to come across someone's convictions. Did this ever happen to you? You're at home flipping through a catalogue, or looking up something online at work, or reading the ads on the subway when you come across a quote that resonates with you. You think, "Hey, I never thought of that before! How clever!" Or maybe you think, "What? Something is off here."

What do you do with these quotes? Here's a suggestion. Why not begin a collection of intriguing quotes and share them with your class for analytical discussion? Just as you urge students to examine authors' opinions, you can have them run through intriguing quotes and ask themselves, "What is this quote saying? Do I agree with it? Can I give examples from everyday living that dovetail with this quote? Does this quote apply to me?" Here are examples of intriguing quotes you can share with your class.

"Expectation is the root of all heartache."—William Shakespeare
"Love is an irresistible desire to be irresistibly desired."—Robert Frost
"Most of the trouble in the world is caused by people wanting to be important."—T.S. Eliot
"The difference between a successful person and others is not a lack of strength, not a lack of knowledge, but rather a lack of will."—Vincent T. Lombardi
"No snowflake in an avalanche ever feels responsible."—Stanislaw Jerzy Lec
"You are no better than you should be."—Francis Beaumont
"Friendship is like money, easier made than kept."—Samuel Butler
"The soul of conversation is sympathy."—Thomas Campbell
"The mass of men lead lives of quiet desperation."—Henry David Thoreau
"Ignorance is always afraid of change."—Jawaharlal Nehru
"Good enough, never is."—Debbie Fields
"The trouble with most of us is that we would rather be ruined by praise than saved by criticism."—Norman Vincent Peale
"Life isn't about finding yourself. Life is about creating yourself."—George Bernard Shaw
"Courage is not simply one of the virtues, but the form of every virtue at the testing point."—C.S. Lewis

Quotes from world leaders also require analysis since we tend to readily accept leaders' words. Let students take a look at these quotes and ask themselves, "What is this quote saying? Does it have valor? How so? Does it contain flaws? How might my opinion differ?"

Famous quotes by world leaders:

"Any man worth his salt will stick up for what he believes right, but it takes a slightly better man to acknowledge instantly and without error that he is in error."—Andrew Jackson, 7th President of the United States, 1829–1837

"The mission of the United States is one of benevolent assimilation."—William McKinley, Jr., 25th President of the United States, 1897–1901

"No nation is fit to sit in judgment upon any other nation."—Woodrow Wilson, 28th President of the United States, 1913–1921

"The only thing to fear is fear itself."—John F. Kennedy, 35th President of the United States, 1961–1963

"Accept everything about yourself—I mean everything. You are you and that is the beginning and the end—no apologies, no regrets."—Henry Kissinger, Unites States Secretary of State, 1973–1977

"Any woman who understands the problems of running a home will be nearer to understand the problems of running a country."—Margaret Thatcher, 1st female Prime Minister of Britain, 1979–1990

"Spying among friends is never acceptable."—Angela Merkel, Chancellor of Germany, 2005–

"Part of being a winner is knowing when enough is enough. Sometimes you have to give up the fight and walk away, and move on to something that is more productive."—President Donald Trump, 45th President of the United States, 2017–

EVALUATING ADVICE QUOTES

Many quotes give advice that motivate and guide us. Franklin D. Roosevelt said, "When you come to the end of your rope, tie a knot and hang on." Vincent Van Gogh stated, "If you hear a voice within you say 'you cannot paint,' then by all means paint, and that voice will be silenced." Introducing quotes like these, witty or scholarly, gives students much to contemplate. They wonder about how valuable the advice is for society and for themselves. Here are examples of advice quotes my class deem worthy of discussion.

- "In waking a tiger, use a long stick."—Mao Tse-Tung
- "Strive not to be a success, but rather to be of value."—Albert Einstein
- "Remember not only to say the right thing in the right place, but far more difficult still, to leave unsaid the wrong thing at the tempting moment."—Benjamin Franklin
- "If you can't convince them, confuse them."—Harry S. Truman
- "Always forgive your enemies; nothing annoys them so much."—Oscar Wilde
- "Never trust the advice of a man in difficulties."—Aesop
- "You must welcome change as a rule, but not as your ruler."—Denis Waitley
- "Beware the fury of a patient man."—Publilius Syrus
- "What you cannot avoid, welcome."—Chinese proverb
- "Never say never because limits, like fears, are often just an illusion."—Michael Jordan
- "No matter the situation, remind yourself, 'I have a choice.'"—Deepak Chopra
- "Be the change you wish to see in the world."—Gandhi

SCRUTINIZING ADAGES

Inspecting quotes further, I exhort students to examine beliefs blindly accepted by society. For example, we take for granted that adages express a truth, but do they? I like to ask students to take a critical look at adages and ask themselves, "Do these make sense?"

Take a look for yourself!

Examples of adages:

- "Absence makes the heart grow fonder."
- "Familiarity breeds contempt."
- "Only the good die young."
- "A bad excuse is better than none."
- "Silence is golden."
- "All's well that ends well."
- "You can't judge a book by its cover."
- "Better late than never."
- "When there's a will, there's a way."
- "You're never too old to learn."
- "If you can't beat them, join them."
- "Practice makes perfect."

QUESTIONING GIVENS

In the same vein as questioning adages, my class enjoys questioning givens, the social norms we accept. Of course, many social norms are a valid and sensible part of our daily lives. Common sense tells us we need these norms to coexist in harmony. For instance, we follow sensible norms when we wait on line in the grocery, give up a seat on the bus for the elderly or disabled, refrain from littering streets or cutting our nails in public.

Other social norms, however, might prove debatable once we scrutinize their rationale. The following are a list of social norms my class brainstorm. We quickly rate each norm from 1–4 in degree of importance. Then we talk about the reason society adopts the behavior and whether it makes sense to us. It's a fun exercise that really gets the class speaking candidly about the values they willingly or grudgingly accept.

Examples of debatable social norms:

- Accepting cereal solely as a breakfast food
- Designating dessert for the end of a meal
- Attending proms
- Social drinking (of alcoholic beverages)
- Celebrating New Year's Day
- Celebrating birthdays/giving birthday gifts
- Making a wish and blowing out birthday candles
- Bringing hostess gifts to a dinner party
- Having graduation ceremonies
- Wearing a tuxedo/evening gown to a black-tie affair
- Eating out at restaurants
- Tipping hairstylists, gas attendants, valets, or delivery people
- Opening doors for women (and other chivalrous acts)
- Not asking adults their age
- Being an ardent sports fan
- Eating turkey on Thanksgiving
- Following a trend (for example, wearing a particular hairstyle)
- Worshipping celebrities
- Asking celebrities for autographs

- Aspiring to look model thin
- Aspiring to look fit and muscular
- Teaching children about Santa Claus
- Teaching children about the Tooth Fairy
- Not speaking a different language someone in the vicinity doesn't understand
- Not telling a secret in public
- Filling in awkward silences
- Beating around the bush instead of telling someone how you feel
- Using terms of endearment on others (for example, "honey," "sweetie," "darling")
- Carrying out the exchange of "Hi, how are you?" and "I'm fine. How are you?"
- Engaging in small talk
- Praising people publicly (for example, honoring people at formal occasions)
- Not reprimanding other people's children

QUESTIONING OUR BEHAVIOR IN SOCIETY

After we question social norms, I want my students to discover startling revelations about their own behavior in social settings. Here's when I test student responses to group norms in behavior experiments. The following experiments I've concocted demonstrate the strong tendency of human nature to comply with authority, reciprocate with flattery, and conform under pressure. The goal of these experiments is to have students question or analyze motives to their behavior. Try these selected experiments with your class and you'll have them thinking more deeply about their behavior in society.

Questioning Compliance

Call a more reserved student to the front of the room and instruct him to yell, "I love school!" three times on the top of his lungs (other good substitutes: "I love my mom!," "I love my teeth!"). Uncomfortable with the request, the student will hesitate, but keep urging him to do your bidding until he complies. Afterwards, ask the student why he listened to you. ("I had to because you're the teacher" is the usual reply.) Then have a discussion with the class about whether the student made the right decision. Discuss the difference between dutiful, respectful, and fearful compliance to authority. As a result of this experiment, students examine their motives behind their compliant or noncompliant behavior.

Questioning Reciprocity

Arrange a set-up where you ask several students to pay genuine compliments to classmates during recess. After recess, tell your class about the set-up and ask the recipients of the compliments to raise their hands if they returned compliments. Next, ask these recipients to think whether they returned sincere or insincere compliments. Then, ask the compliment givers how they felt receiving compliments in return. Define reciprocity and discuss how necessary it is in society. Discuss with students how to determine whether reciprocity is altruistic or self-serving. (You might discuss ways one can accept a compliment with grace without feeling the need to reciprocate.) As a result of this experiment, students evaluate their motives behind future reciprocation.

Questioning Conformity

Push aside all furniture in the classroom so that you have a large space in the middle of the room. Inform students that for sixty seconds they may express themselves freely within that space. They may stride about, dance, sing, converse or do anything else with respect to their peers. After a minute or two of watching this free expression, invite the class to take a seat on the floor. Ask students to raise their hands if during the activity they joined in with another person or group (dancing, flapping about, doing jumping jacks, etc.). Ask joiners why they joined. Ask non-joiners why they didn't join. Define conformity on the board. Ask students what they discovered about themselves and others during this activity. Were they conformists or nonconformists? When is conformity good? When is conformity bad? As a result of this experiment, students examine their motives behind their conforming or nonconforming behavior.

You might also want to show a re-enactment video of the Asch experiment where the subject feels pressured to give incorrect answers to conform with groups' responses (the Asch Experiment, https://youtu.be/qA gbpt7Ts8). Students witness how people willingly ignore their convictions to stay within the good graces of their peers. What a powerful video to cement the influence of peer pressure.

Keep Having Critical Discussions

By now your students have immersed themselves in critical discussion. I can't overemphasize its value. Did your students ever beg for a class discussion? Mine have. And that's not because they just want to shoot the breeze. On a constant search for meaning, students want to keep delving into the reasons behind society's core ideas and values. The good news is that critical discussion can revolve around any unit of study. Over the years, I've collected an ever-growing list of questions for discussion. Occasionally, I post these springboards at the beginning of a lesson to stimulate inquiry or to gage students' knowledge on a topic. Alternatively, I assign these springboards as journal topics or writing prompts prior to a planned discussion. Of this you can be sure: No matter how you use springboards for critical discussion, students will gladly engage in them.

Springboards for critical discussion:

- What is normal? Who decides?
- How do people lose sight of their priorities in life?
- What is the kindest deed one can do for another?
- How might a person be existing but not living?
- How crucial is routine to people's lives?
- Which defense mechanism do we use on a daily basis? How does it help or hinder us?
- Is war a rational response to economic or social differences? Is war a rational response to terrorism? Are nuclear weapons necessary in the world?
- What is your position on capital punishment?
- What is your role as a citizen?
- How can we bolster the economy?
- How have immigrants changed the social and political conditions of the U.S. today?

- What is your definition of heroism?
- What do you believe is the greatest sacrifice?
- How do people acquire moral integrity?
- When do people rebel?
- Is it always right to stand up for what is right?
- What reform movements are needed today?
- In what sense can a young person feel caged? A grown up? An elderly person?
- What makes someone prejudiced? Will you be passing on prejudices to your children? Do you think the world will ever be free of prejudice?

THE FRINGE BENEFITS OF CRITICAL DISCUSSION

Taking part in passionate discussions, students begin to appreciate that their classmates believe just as strongly as they in their opinions. They also realize that it's okay for people to disagree. Ultimately, students comprehend that sometimes there isn't a way to make things right for everyone, even if there should be, even when people cry out for justice.

Bringing the discussion closer to home: Teachers can also exercise students' critical reasoning by broaching discussions that matter strongly to students in their immediate lives.

Examples of critical questions that bring the discussion closer to home:

Springboards for younger children: Does everyone crave power? How do students try to get power? Do you think it's healthy to seek power? Do you view playing in sports leagues a learning experience? Do you think school should make joining sports mandatory? At what age should children be allowed to cross the street by themselves? Why? Do you think the best should always go to the guest? Do you think you should have to eat everything on your dinner plate? Do you think your parents should permit you to eat junk food whenever you want? Should you have the right to choose your own clothing when you shop? What is the responsibility of a babysitter? Which rules seem unfair to you in this school? How would you change them? What rules would you make for teachers? When is it important to exhibit curiosity? When is it inappropriate to display curiosity? What are healthy ways to express anger? If everyone finds something funny and you don't, is there something wrong with you? Does it ever pay to get hurt? Is it ever right to hurt others?

Springboards for older children: Do you think schools should ban cell phones from school? What do you think about mandatory school prayer? Should parents spank their children? Establish curfews? Prohibit violent video games? Insist on maintaining family traditions? Is it your responsibility to help care for your younger sibling(s)? To babysit? To do chores around the house? To keep your room clean? To eat dinner with the family? Are your parents obligated to give you spending money for clothing? For eating out with friends? For games? For books? For vacations? For school trips? Do you think your parents had an easier time growing up than kids do today? Do you think parents should be more in touch with their kids' lives? What's the difference between self-esteem and haughtiness? Should one always tell the truth? Should you always play to win? What do you think is more powerful in helping people, words or actions? Do you think there's a problem with a lack of modesty in this school? What constitutes immodest dress, speech, or behavior? Is it disturbing to you? Why? Which aspect of immodestly disturbs you most? Do you think modesty is praiseworthy? Why or why not?

There are fringe benefits to chewing over issues close to home. Critical discussion of this nature allows students to notice that some of their classmates have strong convictions. They also realize that others are more tolerant with their families and friends, more flexible, compromising, forgiving, and understanding. As the teacher attempts to flush out truths, students can discern whether their stance is virtuous. Perhaps more importantly, students perceive that everyone has struggles, big and small. They feel more empathy. They evaluate biases more carefully. Getting used to conversing candidly during these discussions, students learn to speak without letting their ego interfere. All this exposure is integral to their character development.

Debate Poll

A fun addition to analytical discussion, the Debate Poll has a dual role. First, it takes quick note of those who agree or disagree with certain opinion statements. Students who agree with the opinion statement sit in one area. Those who disagree sit in another. The undecided stand on the edges of the room. Next, a debate ensues as students produce arguments to uphold their opinions. During the debate, students switch seats if they adopt the opposite opinion and the undecided take seats once they've made up their minds. Participants in Debate Polls see in practice how rhetoric sways people's opinions. Since the Debate Poll is great for a gamut of topics, you can use this activity several times a year.

Opinion statements appropriate for the Debate Poll:

- People are mainly out for themselves.
- Nothing is a coincidence.
- Some people need more personal space than others.
- Stereotypes will disappear in time.
- Liberals are open-minded people.
- No man is indispensable.
- Legalizing drugs would decrease crime.
- Middle-class people are happier than wealthy ones.
- Party animals have a rebellious streak.
- The music industry is ruining ethics.
- Everyone craves praise.
- Wearing animal fur is cruel.
- Immigration in America leads to economic ruin.
- Devoting your life to assist others is the only way to live.
- People die without fulfilling half their desires.
- Tougher gun control laws will prevent shooting rampages.
- Our words create our destiny.
- Governments should bail out small businesses.
- Watching TV ruins creativity.
- Schools should permit the military to recruit at high schools.
- Daydreaming is a waste of time.
- Man is responsible for global warming.
- The government should have a say about our diets.
- Change always come along with inconvenience.

Combating Faulty Advertisements

Nothing sways our students' opinions more than advertisements. While advertisements aren't inherently bad, marketing has gotten far craftier nowadays thanks to marketing research and sophisticated technology. Advertisers use anything from price decoys to misleading promises to brushed models to boost sales. They capitalize on fear and make us feel inadequate if we don't purchase their products. In your aspiration to create smarter, sharper thinkers, raise an awareness of the manipulation in marketing. To this end, you can ask students about their experience with advertisements and their influence. You can bring in misleading advertisements and analyze how advertisers play with our minds and control our emotions. Then, you can give students points to ponder and a list of activities that drive the message home.

Try these questions on your class and sharpen your students' consumer skills! Questions for student contemplation (and discussion):

- How did advertisements affect you when you were younger? How do they influence you now?
- Have you ever purchased an item that didn't live up to its promise? How did you feel about it? Can you describe what was faulty about the advertisement?
- How do advertisements manipulate our choices and spending habits?
- Do some advertisements/commercials make fools of people? How so?
- Which advertisements in general appeal to you? Why?

Questions for discussion about particular faulty advertisements:

- Which of the advertisements on the board appeal to emotion rather than common sense or judgment?
- Can you pinpoint the tactics these advertisers use to manipulate consumers?
- What are the underlying messages of these advertisements?
- Which of these advertisements do you trust? Which do you mistrust?
- How will you reevaluate advertisements in the future?

Points to ponder:

- Are TV commercials more or less powerful than other types of advertisements? Why?
- What makes a good commercial/advertisement?
- What type of commercials/advertisements would you create for a good cause?
- Do some billboards affect the social or moral fabric of society? How?
- What can we do about media manipulation?

Activities to drive the message home:

- Bring in an advertisement that attracted your attention. Discuss its appeal. What questions might you have about the product?
- Bring in an advertisement for a product along with the actual product. Discuss whether the advertisement is true to the product.
- Bring in an emotionally charged advertisement for show and tell. Analyze its appeal with the class.

- Bring in an advertisement or taped commercial that downplays inconveniences or hazards. Analyze it with the class.
- Create an honest advertisement of one of your favorite products (for example, Cocoa Puffs) and then one that exaggerates or glorifies the value of that same product.
- Create an enticing, deceptive advertisement for a product you dislike. In a caption, provide the truth you purposely concealed.
- Invent an alluring product such as a new shampoo. Illustrate a misleading advertisement for it. Remember to use persuasive tactics to manipulate the consumer.
- Write a jingle depicting what you've learned about advertisements.
- Read scholarly articles on faulty advertising. Write a paragraph discussing a new marketing ploy used in advertising.
- Devise a plan to combat a faulty advertisement. (Suggestions: Speak to the heads of customer service departments, write complaint letters about disappointing merchandise, return a purchase and point out how the company's advertisement misrepresented it, organize boycotts of stores or products if customers aren't reimbursed and/or advertisements aren't corrected, call up TV stations to protest their harmful portrayal of body images or sensationalism of products.) With the permission and assistance of your parent, carry out your plan, taking written notes and taped or video footage. Present the outcome to the class.

I once saw a cartoon featuring a teacher who says to his class, "I expect you all to be independent, innovative thinkers who will do exactly as I say!" Sadly, the cartoon depicts the mindset of many educators today who discourage critical thinking because it interferes with the ideas and values they want to thrust upon students. However, independent thinking is crucial for a working society. We don't want to foster a robotic society that adopts the next person's thoughts. We owe it to our children to teach them critical thinking so that they can live with integrity, recognize adversity, and make the proper choices.

19

Restocking the Shelves
of Our Book Bankrupt Society

"I cannot live without books."—Thomas Jefferson

Try this. Throw out the following question to any class: "What can't you live without?" Students will rattle off items such as smartphones, laptops, iPads, video games. Unfortunately, books seldom make it to the list. Next, ask the class to show by the raise of hands, "Who likes to read?" How many hands do you think you'll get? You guessed it. Not the greatest showing.

Kids these days apparently have no trouble living book-free lives. Sadly, our children would rather glue themselves to TV and iPads than pick up Sherlock Holmes, *The Wind in the Willows*, or even *Harry Potter*. Entertainment technology: Flashes of lights and graphics, quick dialogue, and racing movements have launched children's brains into a vibrating addictive zone. A 2010 Kaiser Foundation study found that children 8–18 spent more than 7.5 hours a day tethered to entertainment gadgets. That's not to mention the time spent on the phone. My students admit they find it difficult to carry on a conversation outside school without continually checking their phones and responding to texts. This overstimulation makes real living and reading slow in comparison. What a laugh to try to get a brain hardwired for speed to sit back and enjoy a book. When one's in a perpetual fast lane, he doesn't have patience for cruising.

Why Read?

"Reading is to the mind what exercise is to the body," said Irish author Sir Richard Steele (1672–1729). By tossing books aside, our children haven't only lost one of the most enriching pastimes, they have lost a whole way of thinking. Sporting an array of topics, books get students to be introspective about their lives, goals, relationships, and political standings. Readers ask themselves: How can I contribute to my neighborhood like the Babysitters Club? How can I implement Gary Null's advice to take better care of my body? Am I involved in a dysfunctional relationship as defined in this article? Would I have had the guts during the Cultural Revolution to protest my innocence like Ji-Li Jiang's father in *Red Scarf Girl*?

How else does reading work the brain and benefit us? Reading, like any mental stimulation, forges new synapses in the brain and strengthens existing ones. It improves focus and concentration. Students learn how to craft prose by reading clear rhythmic sentences. Reading exposes us to proper grammar and pronunciation, which expands our mental dictionary. Inevitably the words we come across make their way into our vocabulary. Being articulate and well-spoken boosts confidence and aids students in interpersonal skills, ultimately affording them better jobs and promotions.

Besides the robust intellectual gain, reading gives the brain more pleasure than other pursuits. Here's what kids don't realize. Movies and TV have painted the picture for us. Books allow us to imagine them. The imagery we conjure in our minds is much more striking than those given to us on a screen. Reading exercises the creative part of the brain that forms pictures from words. If kids would give reading a chance, they'd see that the vicarious joy our brains get from imagining vivid plots surpasses the cheap thrill offered by animated films. How do we know this is true?

Research suggests that reading about specific visual, motor, and conceptual features activates the relevant area of the brain associated with performing that action in real life. For instance, fMRI (functional magnetic resonance imaging) of participants who read that characters "went through the front door into the kitchen" showed increased activity in the temporal lobes, the part of the brain responsible for spatial scenes. Likewise, when participants read that a character "pulled a light cord," the fMRI indicated increased activity in the frontal lobes associated with controlling grasping motions. The result of this brain imaging suggests we get absorbed in books because our brains create a virtual reality for ourselves.

So what do we have here? Proof that reading improves cognitive function and offers a gratifying experience. What other pastime can beat that? Our children once knew the joy of the reading. Let's give it back to them.

How to Whet the Appetite for Reading

This is a doable challenge; developing interest in reading takes little time and costs no money. Follow the ideas below and you're guaranteed success.

READ TO YOUR CLASS

Out of practice in reading, many students may find picking up a book intimidating. Before shoving books into their hands, try reading to them. This activity exposes hesitant readers to the same rich and engrossing books others read fluently on their own. Inevitably, listening to books quiets the mind and increases children's appetite for books.

Reading to children isn't only for younger audiences. Even older children enjoy listening to a wonderful book. This thought takes me back to an August afternoon in the not too distant past. I am reading *Madeline* to my three-year-old niece. Her thirteen-year-old brother romps into the room and plops himself on the adjacent leather couch, staring up at the ceiling and making believe he's not listening to me reading the rhyme. But he is. His stillness gives him away. So does the darting glances he keeps giving in my direction, to say nothing of the smirking at the corners of his mouth as I read, "To the tiger in the zoo, Madeline just said, 'Pooh-pooh.'"

Which brings me to another point. Don't worry if the book the class chooses for you to read aloud is a bit below their level. As long as the book is more sophisticated than one your students can write, it will teach the class something in its appeal. More importantly, the opposite is true too. Worried your book choice is too intricate for some students? Don't be. As long as your students speak the English language, they are capable of understanding books more complicated than you expect.

Read to your class a bit at a time. Reading a chapter or two per session creates a bit of a tease, but a good one. Once enticed by the plot, students get curious about the outcome of a story and want to hear more. Their imagination takes over as they guess future ventures and happenings. Kept in suspense, impatient listeners may even get a hold of the story and finish it themselves. I remember how a tenth-grade class of mine practically had a tantrum when I took a break partway through reading an abridged version of Daphne du Maurier's novel *The Scapegoat*. Before the week was over, my students smugly told me that the class didn't need me to complete the story. They found copies online and finished it on their own! What could be better than that?

LET CHILDREN READ ALOUD

What's the point of children reading material aloud? Certainly, the concentration during the reading dramatically increases comprehension. But that's not all. Readers get to express their voice which strengthens confidence and proves great practice for public speaking. Moreover, oral reading builds fluency as students learn to assimilate new words and word patterns. For these reasons, oral reading can become quite a celebration in your classroom.

Do kids want to read aloud? Ask most kids and they'll happily comply. Basking in the attention, they'll read anything—a page in a reader, instructions on a work sheet, the rules for the fire drill. The more kids read aloud, the more they become comfortable reading. Just make sure to stick to volunteers for this reading exercise. You don't want to push children before they're ready.

Another word of caution. Use several different readers for longer texts. Why? Unless the reader proves exceptionally skilled in pacing and vocal expression, the class won't forebear a lengthy reading session from one person. They'll get distracted or impatient and read ahead.

PRACTICE DUET READING

Also known as the Neurological Impress Method, this method works for hesitant readers. Invite a hesitant reader to read aloud with you or a peer. The student's bland voice expression or reading handicap such as stuttering will blend in with the more powerful voice in the duet and give him and listeners the illusion that both readers are doing a fine job at reading. A California study showed that after practicing duet reading for five weeks (3.3 hours) students performed significantly better in oral and silent reading fluency and on comprehension assessments (https://eric.ed.gov/?id=EJ692257). The method also works well for several students reading together at a time.

While you might not have much time to invest with your students, any duet reading time is surely beneficial in increasing students' fluency of reading and confidence level, not to mention giving readers a fun experience!

Encourage Reading Aloud at Home

Students can read at home with apps such as *Show Me* to record themselves acting out a story to an imaginary or real audience. Taking center stage on their own home turf, many students do a better reading job and enjoy the feeling.

Utilize Audiobooks

Listening to audiobooks, even the classic "boring" ones, increases students' interest in their plots. Spicing up *Hamlet* proves easy with professional actors performing the bard's play. The actors' expressive voices together with the soundtrack make the scenes come vibrantly to life. Playing scenes of play or chapters of a book increases suspense and sets the student's mind on an imagination spree. Happily, I've found that playing portions of audiobooks promotes an interest in reading the book. In fact, all I have to do to stir the appetite for a particular book is to play a chapter of it for the class!

Encourage Play Acting

During one of the tours I took in Israel, the tour guide had our group reenact the battle between David and Goliath in full costume. A 60-something gentleman played Goliath to the hilt and I took the part of David. We had great fun reading from the text while our "armies" cheered us on. But more interesting than seeing the adults enjoying themselves was watching how a teenager, reluctant at first to read part of the narration, got visibly and audibly more animated as he played his role.

I see this happening often with students in the classroom. Acting enlivens students, often reticent ones, and absorbs them in the plot. So why not use plays to reenact a scene in history, roleplay a concept, or dramatize literature? Online short scripts can cover a multitude of topics. For example, in *Plays, Scripts for Young People*, scripts range from fact-based stories about "Rosie the Riveter" ("Everything's Coming up Rosies" by Christina Hamlett) to a portrayal of the importance of the seasons ("The Miracle of Spring" by Helen Hanna) to an epic tale ("Beowulf," an adaptation by Eddie Mcpherson). You can find historical plays in old Junior Scholastics and literary plays in anthologies. An ardent fan of drama, I implement plays into my literature curriculum. My students have great fun acting out the jurors' roles in Reginald Rose's *Twelve Angry Men*, the various live and dead roles of characters in Thornton Wilder's *Our Town*, and the complicated characters in Shakespeare's *Macbeth*. As students become more adept at acting, don't be surprised if they ask to perform for a wider audience in school or without.

Make Silent Reading a Pleasant Experience

I'm in touch with students' reluctance to read dry information. I also don't blame them for disliking boring, archaic stories. What I find most astonishing, though, is watching students thumb through the pages of a what I consider a truly sensational reading selection and hearing them cry out incredulously, "What? We need to read eight pages?"

"Yes," I say, "Why don't you give it a chance?" All the while, I'm thinking, "Why aren't they excited?" I was the kid who waited with bated breath for the new anthology the first day of school so that I could read it from cover to cover. So, when students count pages, I can't relate. I have, however, simple ideas for making reading a more welcoming experience:

Rules for presenting reading material:

- Give reading material relevant to students' lives or interests.
- Expose students to pleasant, large fonts that appear less intimidating.
- Make sure there's clean and ample space between sentences and paragraphs.
- Define new words students will find in their reading material.
- Teach students to recognize topic sentences where they can glean essential information.
- Teach students how to derive the meaning of unfamiliar words from the context.
- Train students to visualize a story as if it were a movie and to play it back mentally. This visualization tunes them into the sequence of the story.
- Encourage students to ask you questions about idioms, explanations, allusions, or analogies they don't understand.
- Help students make inferences and predictions based on photographs, cartoons, excerpts of recordings and videos. Then teach students to employ these skills when reading.
- Let students follow along with a recording of the reading material.

INCREASE ANTICIPATION FOR READING

How do you get students to truly anticipate reading? By taking advantage of these strategies:

Say an eyebrow-raising statement. To promote healthy enthusiasm for reading, you might pique your students' interest in the reading by saying an eyebrow-raising statement like, "After you've read this article you're going to understand why there are so many criminals in the streets" or "After reading these two chapters, you will understand how bionic braces might transform our walking in the future." Alternatively, you might provide a collage of pictures or photographs for students and say, "After you read chapter 22, you'll be able to label these photographs."

Use an Anticipation Guide. An Anticipation Guide is a pre-reading strategy (Frank Smith, 1978) that asks students for their opinions related to themes or concepts in stories. Students check off and discuss whether they agree or disagree with statements and anticipate reading the material to learn the author's viewpoint. Students automatically take charge of their reading and focus on its content. After reading the material, students can revisit the statements and see whether the book changed their perspective.

The following illustrates an anticipation guide for *The Little Prince* by Antoine De Saint Exupery:

Before reading *The Little Prince*, write whether you agree or disagree with each statement.

- Children know more about people than adults think. _____
- Adults are less superficial than children. _____
- We should judge people by their actions. _____

- We should judge people by their circumstance. _____
- Loving others is more important than being loved. _____
- People seek approval. _____
- When a person dies, he is gone forever. _____

Incidentally, teachers can use anticipation guides for any reading topic. For example, for subjects such as history, science, health, or economics, teachers can write true and false statements and students can guess their answers based on previous knowledge or logical thinking.

The following illustrates an anticipation guide for ancient Egypt:

Before reading the chapter on ancient Egypt, write whether you think these statements are true or false. (For your interest, I filled in the correct responses.)

- Most ancient Egypt pyramids were built as tombs for pharaohs and their families. (True)
- The Great Pyramid was built by slaves. (False)
- The ancient Egyptians rode camels. (False)
- Egyptian women had equal rights with men. They could buy, own, sell, and inherit property. (True)
- The king of Egypt could never be a woman. (False)
- Egyptians believed that by preserving dead people's bodies through mummification, people's souls would live on in the afterlife forever. (True)
- Both Egyptian men and women wore makeup. (True)
- The ancient Egyptians invented paper, locks and keys, pens, and toothpaste. (True)

Provide a Booklist of Positive Influence Books

Look for traits such as integrity, responsibility, courage, self-control, and compassion. You're in luck when choosing young adult fiction. Ranked by the Association of American Publishers in 2011 as the fastest growing publishing category, young adult fiction is quick to change students' perspective. The plots, which sometimes have greater sophistication than adult books, have substance and often deal with critical life issues instead of mere cruelty or empty romance. Young adult books are frequently books students come back to as adults. For instance, you can't beat books like *The Outsiders* by S.E. Hinton and its hauntingly powerful view into the thoughts and feelings of teenagers. That's good reading for anyone.

Help Students Read Widely

Don't make the mistake of only sticking to a couple genres in your curriculum. Kids' interests vary. Some like gory stories, sci-fi, mysteries, or historical fiction. Others gravitate to comedies or real-life stories or even self-help guides. Kids who complain that reading is boring simply have not found what appeals to them. I assure you that everyone can gain an interest in some genre of reading. They just have to find it. Remember there's no accounting for taste. What students get hooked on might be a genre unattractive to you. Have an open mind. Afford students the opportunity to explore many genres and read those of their interest. Anthologies therefore come into good use in the classroom. Schools tend to provide one anthology to a grade. I suggest scouting for a list of additional age-related anthologies and ordering copies for the school or class library.

What about the classics? You may teach a classic or two in school, but don't be a stickler for the classics unless they're your students' choice. Remember, you want to entice students to read, not obligate them to plod through a book. Turn to the classics that students universally enjoy. For instance, a staple of English curriculums for generations, *To Kill a Mockingbird* by Harper Lee, wins students' hearts. It's not for nothing the book has sold over 30 million copies worldwide and was voted UK's best-loved book and the most inspirational book of all time in dozens of polls worldwide. Though exquisitely written, some classics just don't measure up to students' expectations. Therefore, don't push *Moby Dick* or *Wuthering Heights* if you can't drum up enthusiasm for them.

Use Primary Accounts versus Secondary

Primary accounts, real accounts, always attract more intrigue and empathy than secondary ones. For instance, *To Be a Slave*, a Newbery Honor Book by Julius Lester, offers a compilation of personal testimonies of former slaves who were shackled, beaten, separated from their families, and finally emancipated. Reading these true accounts, students can feel more genuinely what it was like being a slave in the American South. Similarly, reading "Dear Ma and Pa" letters from a disillusioned son trying to find gold in California during the Gold Rush is much more real and effective to a student than plodding through the events of the Gold Rush in a history book. And then there are those astounding survival stories written by survivors. Take Juliane Koepcke, the miracle girl—the sole survivor of a plane crash in 1971, who, still in her seat, plummeted two miles from the sky into the Amazon rain forest. In *Reader's Digest*, Koepcke recounts her harrowing experience, including the eleven days she spent in the Peruvian jungle before she was rescued. Reading Koepcke's words draws the reader personally into the experience.

Ply Students with Current Articles

The articles need not be about any particular subject matter. During the course of the year, share your fervor for mountain biking, traveling, building, designing. Keep students abreast of current events, the latest in technology, the new study that's going on at the Mayo Clinic. Once students latch onto a subject, go for it. Bring in reading material that pertains to that subject. And then drop the subject once interest wanes. I know a tenth-grade teacher, Mr. McCormick, who each morning divides the *Wall Street Journal* among groups of students and has them inform the class about the daily news. It's not surprising that Mr. McCormick's students go on to subscribe to the *Wall Street Journal* long after they leave his class.

Present Excerpts from Books

A brief dialogue, monologue, or illuminating paragraph can pique students' interest into checking out the book. Once sensitized to good excerpts in literature, my students submit their favorite excerpts to my list.

Here are tiny excerpts that both my students and I find fascinating.

"I am well in body although considerable rumpled up in spirit, thank you, ma'am," said Anne gravely. Then aside to Marilla in an audible whisper, "There wasn't anything startling in that, was there, Marilla?"—L.M. Montgomery, *Anne of Green Gables* (fiction)

"I intensely disliked my father's fifth wife, but not to the point of murder."—Dick Francis, *Hot Money* (mystery)

"Perhaps I haunted her as she haunted me; she looked down on me from the gallery as Mrs. Danvers had said, she sat beside me when I wrote my letters at her desk. That mackintosh I wore, that handkerchief I used. They were hers. Perhaps she knew and has seen me take them. Did she resent me and fear me as I resented her? Did she want Maxim alone in the house again? I could fight the living but I cannot fight the dead."—Daphne Du Maurier, *Rebecca* (classic novel)

"Not every thirteen-year-old girl is accused of murder, brought to trial, and found guilty."—Avi, *The True Confessions of Charlotte Doyle* (historical fiction)

"There are days when I wish I didn't live in a stupid boardinghouse, when I wish I could wake up like a normal person without listening to a thousand cuckoo clocks, without running into Mr. Penny in the hallway before he has shaved, without having to make Miss Hagerty's breakfast. Some days I would like to smash Mr. Penny's clocks and Miss Hagerty's dusty knickknacks. And I would like to sit down at breakfast with my mother and my father and no one else and also not have to look at Angel Valentine who is more beautiful than I'll ever be."—Ann M. Martin, *A Corner of the Universe* (juvenile fiction)

"When people are insulting you, there is nothing so good for them as not to say a word—just to look at them and *think*. Miss Minchin turns pale with rage when I do it, Miss Amelia looks frightened, and so do the girls. When you will not fly into a passion people know you are stronger than they are, because you are strong enough to hold in your rage, and they are not, and they say stupid things they wished they hadn't said afterward."—Frances Hodgson Burnett, *A Little Princess* (juvenile fiction)

"A low mood is not the time to analyze your life. To do so is emotional suicide. If you have a legitimate problem, it will still be there when your state of mind improves. The trick is to be grateful for our good moods and graceful in our low moods—not taking them too seriously. The next time you feel low, for whatever reason, remind yourself 'This too shall pass.' It will."—Richard Carlson, Ph.D., *Don't Sweat the Small Stuff ... and It's All Small Stuff* (nonfiction, psychology)

"The week after my parents vanished I tried to climb the water tower in Ionia, Tennessee. I hoped to see the ocean. It was a hot, windy day, and grit from the cement works pelted my face, making me blink. That morning my sister Bibi had teased my hair to cheer me up, and now, in the heat, I felt it prickled out all around my head like a thistle blossom. Usually it hung down, fine and flyaway and not a good color: beige, the shade of a grocery sack."—Suzanne Freeman, *The Cuckoo's Child* (fiction)

GIVE BOOK TALKS

If you want to excite kids about books while divulging more than an excerpt, you can give a book talk. Basically, a book talk shares what you know about a high-quality book without giving away too many details. To grab the audience during a book talk, mention something exciting about the book and illustrate your meaning by reading excerpts from the book. You might preface a book talk with a discussion or activity. Book talks are especially helpful for a harder sell, such as nonfiction.

The following book talks give you an idea of how to conduct them. The first book talk begins with a discussion and the second, with an activity. You might mimic these styles or develop your own.

Book Talk That Begins with a Discussion

You know, we've become good friends with Charlie Brown this year. What do you think makes him so lovable? (Discussion ensues.) What do you think of the other characters of the *Peanuts* cartoons? Did you ever wonder how Charles Schulz, the creator of these cartoons, came up with his ideas? Did you know that Schulz named Charlie Brown after his good friend who worked with him at Art Instruction Schools?

Let me read to you what Schulz says about his friend in his book, *My Life with Charlie Brown*. (The teacher reads an excerpt from page 15.) Did you know that Schulz said that he came up with cartoon ideas in his saddest moods? He said, "Happiness does not create humor. There's nothing funny about being happy. Sadness creates humor." Do you agree? (Discussion ensues.)

In this book, you also learn how Schulz's strip got started and evolved over time and the way his characters reflect his personality and philosophy. Let me read for example how Schulz came up with the comic strip idea for Sally complaining about the grade on her coat-hanger sculpture. (The teacher reads an excerpt from page 152.) You also might notice from this reading that Schulz writes his book with an easy conversational style that makes you feel like speaking right back to him. If you want to check out this book, I'm going to put a few copies in the class library.

Book Talk That Begins with an Activity

Before I give this book talk, I need four volunteers to share a brief personal story with the class. Two volunteers will recount true stories and the other two will make theirs up. The audience is going to watch and listen closely and guess which stories are real and which are fabricated. Who'd like to give it a try? Thank you, Hayden, Julian, Ruben, and Vanessa. Please leave the room and discuss among yourselves who will tell the true and false stories. Then come back inside and we'll begin. (Volunteers leave, reenter, and tell their stories.)

Now, by the show of hands, who can guess which people were telling the truth? Which people were fibbing? How did you know? (Discussion ensues.) Would you like to learn the signs that tell you whether or not somebody is being genuine? Would you like to become an expert human lie detector? This book, *Detect Deceit: How to Become a Human Lie Detector in Under 60 Minutes,* gives the reader practical techniques for detecting deception. Let me read to you a couple techniques Dr. David Craig discloses in his book. (The teacher reads the techniques.)

So how might these techniques help you in life? Would you like to read other techniques to help you detect a crafty salesperson? A con artist? A potential bully? A disingenuous candidate for political office? Who would like to borrow this book over the weekend?

A word of caution: As you decide upon a book for a book talk, check the book carefully for unsuitable references. Before lending the book to your students, you might want to rub out some inappropriate words or paragraphs. If the book is peppered with innuendoes, violence, or cruelty, reconsider using the book. Often, the favorable part of a book doesn't outweigh its negative influence.

INCORPORATE FREE VOLUNTARY READING

In *The Power of Reading,* Stephen D. Krashen advocates FVR—Free Voluntary Reading—a program that allows for class reading time every day unaccompanied by instruction or follow-up questions. Krashen's vast research heralds reading for pleasure as the foundation for advanced levels of reading proficiency. Mostly, types of FVR calls for silent reading or self-selected reading and discussion. According to Krashen's collection of studies in schools across the globe (in countries such as United States, South Africa and Japan), students clearly benefitted from FVR, outperforming traditionally taught students in reading comprehension, writing style, grammar usage, spelling, and vocabulary. For example, Krashen's close look at the effect of a free reading program on students ages 12–17 in 60 reform schools attests to a 12.8% gain in reading comprehension scores over a 4.6% gain in schools with comparative reading programs.

Krashen also cites a study done in 32 countries (Postlethwaite and Ross, 1992) that heralds free reading as the second of 150 predictors explaining why their nine-year-olds did exceptionally well in reading. (The first predictor was the schools' discernment of parental cooperation.)

By implementing FVR into their curriculum for a mere fifteen minutes a day, teachers see how students start showing a greater interest in reading and read more on their own time. Students who thought reading was a chore now can't get enough of it. No one ever says the opposite—referring to reading as boring or a waste of time. Asked on an end-of-the-year survey to rate the activities they enjoy most, 92% of the classes chose FVR as one of their top four choices out of 25 other activities.

While FVR is not the only alternative or solution to improving literacy skills, and doesn't replace assigned reading or writing courses, FVR stands as one of the best complements to many language arts classes. Try FVR in your classroom and notice the difference yourself.

PROMOTE RESEARCH

Researching information causes students to read or skim much more material than they would ordinarily on their own or for an assignment. Doing research has always gotten a bad rap. And no wonder. Research connotes doing a bunch of investigative boring work. How do you transform boredom to excitement? How do you get students excited about tracking down information and reading about it, even for personal interest?

Let students pick from a broad range of possibilities. Keeping students confined to researching otters or whales is not as enticing as giving them the choice to research any sea creature. (Besides, the audience doesn't want to hear twenty papers about the same animal.) Research papers also tend to take on the doldrums when they're about famous people. Even when you ask kids to choose any famous person, they (or their parents) seem to pick the same ones. How about encouraging students to research less acclaimed people who don't typically make it into the textbooks? Everyone knows Thomas Edison, for example, but what of Samuel Insull, Edison's personal secretary, who among many successes built electrical power stations throughout America, making cheap electricity available to the country?

Along the same vein, Rosa Parks is a name imprinted in the minds of most fifth graders, but not the fearless Civil Rights activist Ida B. Wells, who in 1884, almost sixty years prior to Parks, was forcibly removed from a train in Memphis when she refused to sit in the "colored only" section. And what about Victoria Woodhull, the first woman to run for president of the United States in 1872, 135 years before Hillary Clinton ran for president! Encourage students to research a vast array of unsung people—investors, business entrepreneurs, activists, educational leaders, reformers, philanthropists, poets. This will keep research fresh and exciting.

The worst bankruptcy in schools nowadays lies in the book department. Give students back books and they'll thrive. By the middle of the year, revisit the poll. Ask students what they can't live without and see the difference. True, they'll still clutch their phones to their hearts, but I bet reading will claim second place. Having crept into the fabric of their intellectual and moral minds, books will make a comeback. You'll see!

20

Putting Literacy to the Test

"The real purpose of books is to trap the mind into doing its own thinking."
—Christopher Morley

Now that you've got students reading with alacrity, how can you check students' comprehension of the material? How can you determine their ability to dig deeper, decipher information, and come up with credible results? This chapter presents cutting-edge exercises and assignments that procure huge dividends.

Ready? Let's begin.

Literacy Exercises and Assignments

READING FOR UNDERSTANDING

These are some quick, simple exercises that train students to read for understanding:

- Have students take notes while reading short selections. Let them compare their notes with peers to see if they got the gist of the material.
- Discharge activities where students must follow reading instructions to come up with a satisfying result.
- Ask students to think how they can connect the reading selection to a personal experience or something else they've learned.
- Ask students to write questions next to sentences or paragraphs they find confusing. They can collaborate with peers to answer their questions and then go back and read the text again to make sure they understand it.
- Give students an excerpt and let them predict events that will happen briefly afterwards. Then let them read on to see if their predictions come true.
- Give students an excerpt and let them imagine what events happened prior to that reading selection. Then let them read the prior selection to see if their presumptions were correct.
- Have students work in pairs for a reading assignment where they have to come up with comprehension questions.
- After students finish reading a piece, prepare a summary paragraph for students with one sentence that isn't true to the text. Have students try to detect the faulty sentence.
- Let students enliven a story by drawing a comic strip reflecting an occurrence in the story. This teaches students to delineate the integral parts of the story. Students can

work independently at first and then compare comics. Afterwards, students can team up with peers to place their comics in a chronological order of events.

The following are painless comprehension exercises for tougher reading selections:

PARAPHRASE THE TEXT

If you want students to imbibe more challenging textual material, try out *Paraphrase the Text*. The activity is simple. Working clockwise, students take turns reading a couple paragraphs of the text. The peer to the reader's left interprets the text. All members must agree with the interpretation before the group resumes reading. At the conclusion of the reading, the teacher gives a comprehension quiz to the class.

Benefits of *Paraphrase the Text*:

- The activity strengthens comprehension: Students must concentrate to paraphrase the main points.
- Everyone in the group feels good since his opinion counts.
- The activity increases attention span: Students focus better because they're actively involved.
- The activity makes otherwise "boring" reading fun. The challenge to get the meaning right practically turns the activity into a game!

PLOT SUMMARIES

Nothing puts comprehension to the test like requiring students to summarize reading material in a short paragraph. The task calls for discerning the crucial information and writing it coherently. The endeavor is daunting, but easier with practice. Ask students to summarize articles, short stories, chapters, and long works and watch their comprehension soar! As an automatic bonus to the process, students practice tighter writing. For example, when given a limit of, let's say, 80 words to summarize shorter material and 100 words to summarize a book, students learn to select words carefully because every word counts! Literally!

Curious what summaries look like? The following are examples of students' plot summaries of various reading assignments. Each summary captures the essence of the work.

Did you ever wonder how people get addicted to morphine? Patients recovering from surgeries are often prescribed pills such as morphine for pain relief. Though morphine ebbs the pain, it is also very addictive, more addictive than alcohol and equally addictive to heroin. As their body adapts to morphine, patients take larger amounts to the point where the latter feels he can't survive without it. A medically managed detoxication clears the drug and minimizes discomfort.—Leeron Weinberger (Article: "Addicted to morphine after Surgery")

Pressured by his father's expectations, P.S. studies feverishly for the upcoming Latin exam. During the exam, P.S. is nervous he won't pass, so he cheats, violating the school's honor code. Afterwards, wrestling with his conscience, P.S. thinks of turning himself in. Before he can take action, however, a fellow student, adhering to the school's honor code, reports P.S. to the school administration. P.S. admits to cheating and the administration expels him from school.—Prince Emanuel ("So Much Unfairness of Things," autobiographical short story by C.D. B. Bryan)

Daniel Kahneman explains how everyone has two modes of thinking. "System One" prompts us to act on impulse and emotion with little mental activity. This way of thinking comes to us automatically and can be called intuition. Some mental activities, however, require deeper thought and concentration. "System Two" then takes over forcing "System One" to yield to a more rational thought pattern.—Shira Yagdaren (Daniel Kahneman's *Thinking Fast and Slow*, Chapter One)

Living with stern Aunt Polly, orphaned Pollyanna practices her father's "Glad Game" which entails finding optimism in every situation, no matter how bleak. With this philosophy, Pollyanna exults in the window view of a stuffy attic and finds joy in eating bread and milk as a punishment. Soon Pollyanna spreads joy to the people of her aunt's dispirited town in Vermont. After injuring her legs in an automobile accident, even Pollyanna becomes downcast, but the townspeople buoy her spirits with examples of how Pollyanna improved their lives. Eventually, Pollyanna learns to walk and appreciates her legs more than ever. —Charlotte Roberts (*Pollyanna*, by Eleanor H. Porter)

What's the Main Message

Want students to dig deeper? Calling for a one sentence answer, the assignment *What's the Main Message* has students think critically to discern the essence of shorter written pieces such as editorials, interviews, reports, anecdotes, or poems. In small groups, one person reads the text out loud while other members follow along taking notes. After that, students compare notes, decide upon the main idea, and express it in a written statement. A student from each group writes her group's statement on the board. Surveying the statements, the class votes on the one they deem most accurate. The teacher casts her vote as well.

The benefits of *What's the Main Message*:

- Groups practice analytical skills as they boil down the text to one message.
- The activity piques curiosity since everyone is eager to see the other groups' statements on the board.
- Students exercise evaluation skills as they compare groups' statements on the board.

Here are students' one sentence summaries for *What's the Main Message*:

- The ACLU (The American Civil Liberties Union) believes banning people with disabilities from owning firearms harms their civil rights. (Vania Leveille and Susan Mizner, "ALCU: Gun Control Laws Should Be Fair," *USA Today*, February 20, 2017, http://www.usatoday.com/story/opinion/2017/02/20/gun-control-congress-aclu-editorials-debates/98147914/)
- Wondering how to make a bookmark stick to paper without tearing the paper when you pull the bookmark off, Art Fry got the idea to invent Post-It notes, along with the inspiration to use Spencer Silver's new adhesive for Post Its. ("An Idea That Stuck: How a Hymnal Bookmark Helped Inspire the Post-It Note," *All Things Considered*, NPR West, July 26, 2014, http://www.npr.org/templates/transcript/transcript.php?storyId=335402996)

- Consumer Reports examined My Pillow and declared it, "kind of lumpy, but comfortable" and polled staffers who had different opinions about whether the pillow alleviates sleeping problems. (Celia Kuperszmid Leherman, "Should My Pillow Become Your Pillow?" *Consumer Reports*, November 3, 2016, http://www.consumerreports.org/mattresses/should-my-pillow-become-your-pillow/)
- A cab driver feels that giving a terminally ill old woman a ride and visiting all the places of her youth upon her request before dropping her off at a hospice, was the most important thing he did in his life. (Kent Nerburn, "The Last Cab Ride," http://academictips.org/blogs/the-last-cab-ride/)
- To become a poet, Eve Merriam insinuates you must analyze the essence of something using your five senses and then recreate it when it's no longer in existence. (Reply to the Question: "How Can You Become a Poet?" by Eve Merriam, https://echowrite.wordpress.com/2008/03/03/poems-about-writing-poetry/)

TURNABOUT QUESTIONING

Brilliant in its construction, *Turnabout Questioning* challenges students to come up with good questions in their homework reading that will stump the class or teacher. *Turnabout Questioning* works particularly well for more difficult reading assignments (or for the dry ones). This learning strategy tricks the brains of those who despise memory work. In their critical pursuit for challenging questions, students are actively and almost effortlessly absorbing the information they are reading.

To get students accustomed to the process, the teacher might want to photocopy an excerpt of the reading material for the first few reading tasks and underline the places where good questions can be found.

As an incentive for students to produce higher level thinking questions, a teacher might grant the following extra credit:

- 2 points to anyone who introduces a question no one else came up with (even if someone has a satisfactory answer to it).
- 3 points to anyone who introduces a question no one else came up with and stumps the class with the question.
- 5 points to anyone who stumps the teacher with a question.

The spirit in the classroom is vibrant as students listen, disqualify some of their questions, mark remaining ones in hope of presenting them, and strive to answer the questions asked. Although the class knows that the teacher won't get to everyone's questions and that they might not get any points, they still feel the thrill of the game.

Here's a glimpse of the way *Turnabout Questioning* plays out in a 9th grade classroom. The subject is Chapter 7 of *The Story of My Life* by Helen Keller.

Teacher: "Okay, everyone. Let's begin *Turnabout Questioning* with your questions on Chapter 7." (Hands wave vigorously.) "Josephina?"

Josephina: "Helen Keller says that whenever anything delighted her, Miss Sullivan would talk it over with her as if she were a little girl herself. Can we assume Miss Sullivan was childlike by nature or was she putting on a show?"

Teacher: "Anyone has this question or a similar one?"

Kim: "I do."

Teacher: "Let's hear it, please."

Kim (reading her question): "Was Miss Sullivan really excited about the subjects she taught Helen Keller or was she just acting interested for Helen's sake?"

Teacher (confirming the similarity): "You got it. Who has an answer to Josephina and Kim's question? Lorenzo?"

Lorenzo: "I don't think it was an act. Helen Keller was her big project, and she was making real progress with her. She must have been genuinely delighted each time Helen showed her interest in discussing something new."

Teacher: "That answer sounds credible."

Oliver: "Can I ask the next question?"

Teacher: "Go ahead."

Oliver: "When Helen held frogs, katydids, and crickets in her hand, she says they forgot their embarrassment and 'trilled their reedy note.' How can animals or insects feel embarrassed?"

Teacher: "Anyone else have that question?" (No one raises a hand.) "Oliver, so far you got yourself two points. Can anyone think of a response to Oliver's question?" (The class is silent.) "Okay, Oliver, let's make that three points for you! Congratulations!"

Josephina: "Not five points?"

Teacher: "Nope. You didn't stump me. I have an answer! Helen Keller isn't saying that animals or insects feel embarrassed as we understand the word. She's using embarrassment to mean uneasiness. I think she's suggesting that the creatures felt so comfortable in her hand that they forgot to be uneasy that someone was holding them and just went on being themselves and making their little sounds.... I'm wondering now—What made these creatures feel comfortable when Helen Keller held them?"

Kelly: "She must have been very gentle."

Tom: "Also maybe because Helen liked nature so much, and spent so much time in the woods, she had the smell of nature on her and the creatures felt more at home with her than with other people."

Teacher: "That sounds credible to me! Can anyone tell us why Helen Keller might have purposely chosen the word embarrassment instead of uneasiness or fear?"

Jan: "Uneasiness I think is too mild and fear is too strong. Helen Keller was too gentle to begin with for the creatures to feel full-fledged fear. She's trying to say that they acted at first as if they were embarrassed, like they felt vulnerable at first and then got used to Helen—sort of like a person who's uncomfortable in a crowd but then warms up and has the confidence to speak up."

Teacher: "I hear what you're saying. That analogy is excellent."

Harry: "It could be that Helen Keller felt like the insects were people to her—maybe when she was little she spoke to them and imagined them thinking and feeling like human beings. So maybe she thought that these new creatures were holding back from singing at first because they were embarrassed but then warmed up to her once they saw she wasn't threatening them."

Derek: "That a cool idea."

Teacher: "Next question please? Okay, first Jan and then Ben and we're going to end with Paul for the day."

When do you end *Turnabout Questioning*? After twenty minutes or so, for the purpose of keeping the anticipation alive for future rounds of the activity. When you conclude, have students pass their papers forward to show they've done the assignment.

The type of questions students ask, their depth or lack of it, reveals to the teacher how well the students have grasped the information read. In the best-case scenario, the students have taught themselves the material and the teacher can go on with the next agenda.

COMPARING AND CONTRASTING

Once again, we have a win-win exercise where the students read material and retain it easily while enjoying the effort. For this activity, students practice their critical thinking by comparing and contrasting two reading selections. The texts of the selections must share many facets; for example, a baseline of knowledge, a writing style, particular themes or procedures, time periods, events, character traits, motivations, or conflicts. Students are asked to seek similarities and differences between the two works, writing a minimum of three comparison and three contrast statements.

Customarily, students work with a Venn diagram. A Venn diagram consists of overlapping circles. In the central part of the circle, the student jots down the comparisons between the texts, in the outer parts of the circles, the contrasts.

The Venn diagram demonstrates a student's effort in comparing and contrasting Shel Silverstein's renowned children's book *The Giving Tree* and Clifford Simak's science-fiction story "A Death in the House."

Notice how several comparisons in this diagram relate to the contrasting elements on either side. That's not unusual. Comparisons often come to light when working with contrasts and vice versa. But matching comparisons with contrasts is not a necessary criterion of this assignment, as illustrated in the last two examples of this diagram.

Older or more sophisticated writers might begin with a Venn diagram to gain perspective and then organize their comparisons and contrasts in paragraph form. Writing in paragraph form gives the student more space for detail and elaboration as illustrated in the comparison and contrast below:

> Both the Giving Tree and Old Mose sacrifice their company to make their friends happy. The Giving Tree begs, "Come boy, climb my trunk, swing from the branches and be happy," but eventually realizes that climbing a tree would no longer make his boy happy, so he gives the boy what he wants: his apples, branches, and finally his trunk, although these all mean the boy will part from him. Likewise, Old Mose harbors a fierce hope that the alien will get well again and stay with him, as already the house felt less lonely with its companionship, but when he sees that friendship is not what the critter needed, he enables it to return home, giving up his silver for the cage's repair (Ahuva Sutton).

Reviewing with *Comparing and Contrasting*: The review process is similar to the one for *Turnabout Questioning* in that students receive two points for comparisons or contrasts their classmates do not have and five points for the ones the teacher doesn't have on her list. Ordinarily, I don't volunteer my comparisons and contrasts until the end of class, which affords a greater number of students a chance to state theirs. Then a few minutes before the bell, students listen to my recitation of comparisons and contrasts and mark off any of theirs that remain unmentioned. Next, they pass their papers forward and I check their marked statements to make sure they bear no resemblance to mine before awarding them credit.

THE GIVING TREE

CONTRAST

The Giving Tree starts off happy and ends off melancholy.

The giver in non-human, the receiver is human.

The giver has a soft exterior and a kind heart.

The Giving Tree takes place over many years.

The tree sacrifices its apples, branches, and trunk from its physical being.

The giver's final gesture allows it to achieve the boy's companionship.

At the beginning of the story, the receiver is vibrant and strong; at the end, weak and pathetic.

COMPARE

Both givers are happy at the end of the story even though they are left with little physical pleasure.

Both receivers are not given names.

Both givers exercise unconditional giving.

Both authors use intentional long sentences when they want to slow down time.

Both receivers are demanding.

Both givers are desperate for companionship.

Both receivers have to work to get what they want. The boy cuts down the tree, the critter shows Old Mose how to fix his cage.

A DEATH IN THE HOUSE

CONTRAST

"A Death in The House" starts off melancholy and ends happy.

The giver is human, the receiver non-human.

The giver has a rough exterior but a kind heart.

"A Death in The House" takes place over a couple of months.

Old Mose sacrifices time, effort, and money.

The giver's final sacrifice deprives him of the critter's companionship.

At the beginning of the story, the receiver is weak and pathetic; at the end, vibrant and strong.

Venn Diagram comparing Shel Silverstein's *The Giving Tree* and Clifford Simak's "A Death in the House"

Comparing and Contrasting in younger grades: Comparing and contrasting reading selections might be daunting for smaller children who've had limited practice in critical thinking.

To get younger children's analytical juices flowing, the teacher might first want to compare and contrast items rather than readings; for instance, two dry cereals (Corn Flakes and Rice Krispies) or two sports (hockey and soccer). The teacher might ask, "How are these cereals alike?" and then, "How are they different?" and write the results the class gives her in a Venn diagram on the board.

For these comparing and contrasting prep assignments, the teacher might alert students to questions they should ask themselves, for example, how can one compare and contrast the ingredients, taste, and texture of these cereals? How are the preparation and rules for hockey and soccer similar and different?

Next, the class can graduate to try their skill at comparing and contrasting topics they've learned, for instance, the causes, developments, and outcomes of World War I and World War II.

An even more creative and fun way to practice comparing and contrasting is to write a subjective essay comparing two places such as school and camp, or two people like Grandma and Grandpa. Students might also like modeling ideas after essays they read. In her humorous essay "Neat People Versus Sloppy People," Suzanne Britt pinpoints a moral distinction between the two, maintaining that "neat people are lazier and meaner than sloppy people." The exaggerated account gives students the impetus to write their own amusing opinion essays comparing different types of people. Students come up with titles such as, "Loud People vs. Quiet People," "Emotional People vs. Logical People," "Patient People vs. Impatient People." Like Britt, my students posited startling statements about their subjects such as "Loud people are more sensitive than quiet people," or "Patient people are less moral than impatient people." What rousing debates we have over these essays!

CHARACTER REPORTS

While on the subject of opinions, I'd like to introduce *Character Reports*, which gives students the authority to voice opinions about characters in literature. For this assignment, the class gives characters report cards on their character traits.

How does it work?

After we've finished discussing a book or a few short works, students decide on traits the characters exhibit. For younger classes, the teacher might give a list of traits for selection.

For example: kindness, optimism, generosity, perseverance, bravery, patience, humility.

For each trait, students rate the character from 0 to 4, with number 0 showing the characters exhibits the opposite trait, to 4 meaning the character exhibits the trait to the greatest extent. Once the chart is filled out, students can identify not only which characters share traits, but which ones seem most similar or opposite in nature. Like many report cards, a space for comments is provided next to each trait for evaluators to back up their ratings with references from the story. Given the power to choose traits for characters and evaluate them, students revel in this assignment.

The following table illustrates a student's character report for characters in *Roll of Thunder, Hear My Cry* by Mildred D. Taylor.

Linus Barbieri's Character Report
on Roll of Thunder, Hear My Cry

	Kindness	Optimism	Generosity	Perseverance	Bravery	Humility
Cassie	4	3	3	4	4	3
Little Man	4	3	3	4	4	4
Stacey	3	2	2	4	4	2
Christopher-John	3	4	2	2	1	2
Papa	4	4	4	4	4	3
Mama	4	2	3	4	4	4
Uncle Hammer	2	1	3	3	3	1
Big Ma	4	4	4	4	3	3
T.J. Avery	2	2	2	2	2	2
Jeremy	3	3	3	3	4	3
Lillian Jean	1	1	1	2	2	1
Melvin	0	0	0	0	0	0

	Kindness	Optimism	Generosity	Perseverance	Bravery	Humility
L.T. Morrison	4	3	3	4	2	2
Mr. Jamison	4	3	4	4	4	4
Harlan Granger	0	1	0	2	0	2

(Character Trait rating 0–4, where 0 is least like and 4 is most like.)

This chart can also serve as an outline to help students write an essay comparing and contrasting characters. Students can work on the chart in groups or independently and get up in front of the room to share their opinions with the class. In addition, this assignment exercises students' ability to come up with antonyms for positive traits. If a character isn't brave, he might be cowardly, if he doesn't have humility, he's probably boastful.

On a practical note, *The Character Report* teaches students that not all characters are completely good or completely bad. For most characters, as with people, there's always a possibility for redemption or improvement. The teacher might ask students how characters might redeem themselves or earn a better rating on the next report card. They might provide their suggestions for improvement in the comment section as well.

Incidentally, my students show much more enthusiasm for comparing and contrasting assignments than for any other literary task. Several tell me the motivation is the mental challenge—the elation they feel when the light bulb goes off for them. For others, it's the excitement of illuminating their classmates with their observations. In any case, the assignment proves that exercising the mind is fun!

BOOK CLUB DISCUSSION

Great for any age, book discussions put students to the task of ruminating about books (or short stories) and coming to conclusions about characters, their motives and behaviors. Students discuss events of the plot, insights about life, themes, authors' writing styles, and more. No rules apply for *Book Club Discussions*, however, the teacher might take the following into consideration.

In younger classes, teachers might have students fill out charts together identifying the setting, characters, motivations, conflicts, climaxes, and themes. For classes new to this type of discussion, the teacher might provide springboard questions like: Is there anything interesting about the author's writing style? Who is your favorite character? Why? Which part of the story held the most suspense for you? Why? Would you have changed any aspect of the story? How would you rate the story for its suspense on a scale of 1–10? Explain your rating.

For more targeted discussions during the book discussion, the teacher might supply questions pertaining to the particular story. For example, for the book *Where the Red Fern Grows* by Wilson Rawls, I put forth the following questions: How is Billy different from the other children in his hometown? Is there anything you'd be willing to wait and work for, perhaps for two years? Why would a hunter respect raccoons? Which one of Billy's dogs would you prefer, Old Dan or Little Ann? Why? What does the red fern symbolize? What might you guess about the book's author?

To ensure that everyone gets a chance to talk during *Book Club Discussion*, the teacher might divide the class into small groups or appoint a facilitator whose job it is to hold up a red card when a person exceeds a minute monologue.

The Question Exchange

Students read an assigned story at home and write down one thought-provoking question they have about the plot on an index card. In class, pairs exchange index cards and write down possible responses for each other. Then pairs get together to discuss the responses they gave.

From there, pairs separate and meet with a new neighbor or two to share the responses they gave. Afterwards, students return to the original neighbor to share any new information and to discuss the best possible response to their respective questions. Finally, students help each other formulate a written response to their questions on an index card.

Next, students put all index cards in a box on the teacher's desk. The teacher draws an index card from the box and reads the question. The class offers their opinion before the teacher reads the answer provided on the card. The class gets a chance to agree or disagree with the written response. The teacher continues to draw questions from the box for discussion until the class feels they have a good grounding on the story.

The benefits of the *Book Club Discussion* and *Question Exchange* are many. These assignments:

- help students clarify the plot.
- help students develop literacy skills.
- expose students to new ideas.
- give students a chance to question and explore ideas.
- improve students' ability to think critically.
- lend students a deeper understanding of human nature.
- teach students that there's often more to a story than meets the eye.
- change students' perception or point of view.
- lead to more sophisticated evaluation of future reading.

VRC (Vocabulary and Reading Comprehension)

Sitting untouched for years, my collection of miscellaneous reading materials kept growing. Here I had articles (and excerpts) bursting to be shared, but neither the time in class, nor a way of connecting them with existing lessons. My lessons, as they were, were becoming "too full." First, I considered just handing over the collection to students for their weekend reading pleasure. Then I had a brainstorm: In addition to offering students a good read, why not have them improve their vocabulary and reading comprehension in the process?

So began our VRC take-home assignments, and so it continues today. For each VRC assignment, students receive a booklet of reading material. With the opportunity to get 2 extra credit points a week, students produce questions based on these articles using their vocabulary words within the contexts of their questions. Students devour up to 150 articles a year, all the while exercising their comprehension, reviewing vocabulary, and testing their proficiency at using new words in sentences.

The following illustrates a sampling of students' questions typical of a VRC assignment. The vocabulary words the student incorporated are underlined within the sentences.

Questions derived from "What'll Become of Fred?" by Fred J. Epstein, M.D., and "An Accidental Journey" by Fred Epstein:

- How did Fred's teacher, Mr. Murphy, <u>elicit</u> Fred's <u>latent</u> abilities?
- Which person was most <u>disgruntled</u> with Fred's learning disabilities? Bring references to back up your choice.
- Why must principals be <u>discreet</u> about what they say to students like Fred?
- What characteristics did Fred have that allowed him to reach such <u>prodigious</u> heights in medicine?
- After Dr. Epstein's death, other neurosurgeons <u>superseded</u> his position. Do you suppose the replacements were better or worse than Dr. Epstein?
- How would the world be different if the majority of people were learning disabled? Would "regular learners" seem <u>intractable</u>?
- What kind of life might Dr. Epstein have led had he allowed his disability to <u>inhibit</u> his ambitions?
- Why did Dr. Epstein's hope of publishing a book become an <u>ephemeral</u> dream?
- Do you know of another example where a child with learning disabilities made an <u>innovative</u> discovery?
- Do you think that <u>impediments</u> ultimately benefit or harm people?

For the VRC assignment, you might want to hand out "question stems" to assist your class in creating questions. Encourage students to ask questions using the higher levels of Bloom's Taxonomy. These question stems help students achieve that.

- How did…
- What do you think…
- How do you think…
- Predict what…
- Do you believe…
- How would…
- What would…
- Do you know…
- Do you suppose…
- How does…
- What is the main…
- Should…
- What is the best…
- What is the most…
- Why did…
- What inference…
- Is there…
- Why might…
- What lesson…
- What conclusion…

By implementing VRC into your curriculum, you enhance lifelong skills. Time and again, students tell me they read the booklet and have no intention of doing the extra credit but find themselves toying with questions just because the challenge is there. And get this: Anytime you feel like it, you can use student model questions as a vocabulary review—in the same class, or in another. In fact, in a departmentalized system, you can swap assignments between classes. One class gets to read and make up the questions for an article and then swaps their results with a class that has done the same with another article. This way each class gets to create and review—and all with new reading material. You can work out the details for yourself. You may choose to give the review in class or assign it for homework.

Lately, I've begun to challenge students to find their own articles and submit VRC questions pertaining to them or to hand in VRC questions on any topic they read in any class. As a result, students submit questions on human nature, world events, the environment, economics—you name it.

Here's a collection of questions taken from students' assignment papers on various topics. The vocabulary words the student incorporated are underlined within the sentences.

- Should parents <u>exhort</u> a child to learn how to play an instrument if he or she shows little or no musical talent? Why or why not?
- Do you think the <u>frenetic</u> pace of America <u>dovetails</u> with its endless conveniences? Use <u>cogent</u> reasoning in your explanation.
- Is there no <u>blatant</u> answer to the problem of small town merchants losing business to a <u>voracious</u> competitor like Walmart? How would you <u>assess</u> the situation?
- What is the best way to answer an <u>irksome</u> request?
- How does one politely say no to a request without entangling himself in a web of <u>animosity</u>?
- Do you think <u>feigning</u> confidence is productive or counterproductive? Why?
- As a community activist, come up with an <u>ingenious</u> way to promote recycling.
- What <u>inference</u> can you make knowing that the Hawaiian alphabet has twelve letters?
- Is it an <u>innate</u> characteristic to wonder, "What's in it for me?"
- Do you believe people with self-awareness have greater <u>forbearance</u> towards others? Why or why not?
- What makes Beverly Cleary's books <u>winsome</u> to readers?

Writing Assignments That Evaluate Acquired Literary Skills

Do your students groan when you require them to write a composition? Do they look alarmed with the thought of doing it on their own? Are you constantly looking for creative writing assignments to oust students' belief that writing is drudge work? Then this little section is for you. These three writing assignments excite my classes and provide the teacher with an accurate assessment of the skills students have acquired over the school year.

MODERATING A PANEL
DISCUSSION AMONG AUTHORS

The student chooses three or four writers and constructs a dialogue among the voices. As the moderator, the student asks the "writers" questions, and the "writers" respond in turn. The questions the moderator broaches must apply to all, meaning no "writer" may skip an answer or remain on the sidelines. In responding to the moderator's question or to the other "writers," each "writer" must allude to the expertise true to his/her work(s);

for instance, to his/her plot, characters or writing craft. The moderator can choose to rule with an iron hand or let the "writers" go on rants, but ultimately must smooth disputes to bring the dialogue back on track.

The teacher might provide younger students with a list of pertinent questions; for example, how do you create vivid characters? Which part of your book do you regret writing? What do you believe is important in raising children? Which one of your techniques would you advise the other authors to adopt?

WRITING A BOOK REVIEW

This form of literary criticism induces students to analyze a book based on content, style, and originality. Writing the book review requires the utmost attention to detail as well as an encompassing knowledge of literary or scholarly works. Students must know that a book review is a commentary, not a book report or merely a summary. The book review should give a taste of the plot but not give surprises away.

I require students to use at least five literary elements within their discussion (for example, imagery, conflict, irony, dialogue, characterization) and to make at least eight valid points. For this assignment, students should know how to use transitions between ideas and quote material from the work within their discussion.

The teacher might assist the class in writing the book review by outlining key elements students should take into consideration, for instance, how the main characters affect the story and whether or not the author makes the reader believe in them as people. In addition, the teacher might hand students a list of questions as a guide for their writing. The questions can run the gamut of evaluating the setting to inquiring about facts in the story to assessing the author's writing style. Questions might include the following: Does the author make the reader feel part of the setting? As you write, can you pass on to your reader the sense of the setting and place the author provided? Are the author's concepts well defined? How accurate is the author's information? Is the language clear and convincing? Are the ideas developed? What does the work accomplish?

WRITING AN EXCERPT

Students pretend they wrote a fascinating book or short story. Their assignment is to provide the class with the most intriguing part of that story. The excerpt must leave questions in the reader's mind, therefore the excerpt may not give away an ending. Students can pluck out an event from the beginning or middle of their story, but not too close to the end. (Depending on the age, I require students to demonstrate a number of literary elements or techniques within their excerpt; for example, suspenseful lead, credible voice, suspense, figures of speech, theme.)

The class benefits from discussing ideas for genres and plot development. Let students brainstorm ideas together. Here are several options my students considered and put to paper:

- Basing the excerpt on a true account, personal or not.
- Writing a personal account but embellishing some facts.
- Modeling characters after real people and manipulating the plot.
- Inventing fantastical characters and/or a fantastical plot by giving characters extraor-

dinary powers in an ordinary world, extraordinary powers in an extraordinary world, or more frustratingly, ordinary powers in an extraordinary world.

- Employing famous people from history as characters and embellishing history.
- Plugging famous people from history or present day into a different time period.
- Altering the plot of an existing book.
- Borrowing a fictional character from an existing book and placing the character in a new predicament or life changing experience.
- Joining characters from different known stories to embark upon an experience together.
- Joining a character from a known story with a new fictional character or real person to embark upon an experience together.

Literacy is one of the most crucial gifts a person could receive. "Books are great meals for the mind," says Jen Selinsky. I think that's only true when people know how to imbibe the material. Let's train students to think about what they're reading. Let's make sure they know how to write about it and model language skills in their own writing. Students enter our classrooms with diverse backgrounds and literacy skills. Through consistent assessment, we can make informed decisions about the literacy needs for each student. But ultimately, we want students to enter pages of any reading selection without fear and be able to think about their insightful implications.

21

Testing and Grading
Made Easy

"Certainly, every student and school ought to have standards and evaluation, but who sets those standards, and who writes the test? Whoever controls the test controls the school."—James Lankford

When you see a child studying, does your stomach clench with the haunting memory of quizzes and tests you took during your school days? How did test time affect you? I still have disturbing dreams where I have to conquer a looming test or I'm sitting in class and taking one where I know nothing. What a relief to wake up to the blessed present devoid of this heartache.

How do we give students a reprieve from anxiety while facing a constant rainfall of quizzes, reviews, and tests? How do we rid them of the trauma (yes, trauma!) it wreaks on their psyche?

How do we make test time appealing and meaningful?

Follow the suggestions in this chapter and you will see a huge positive difference in your students' motivation, retention, spirit, and test scores when it comes to test time.

Let's get straight to test time, beginning with quizzes.

Quiz Time

"Ugh!"

"Help!"

"I don't know a thing!"

"We're having a quiz? What quiz?"

These are reactions you might have heard when you announced you're giving a quiz. Which brings us to the first two big don'ts concerning quizzes.

THE TWO BIG DON'TS FOR QUIZ TIME

1. Don't give pop quizzes! Their purpose, I presume, is to make students take learning more seriously. All the same, if students need pop quizzes to keep them motivated, the quality of teaching is poor. Furthermore, these quizzes do not serve as a true assessment of what students know since they intensify anxiety and make students blank out while writing answers. For these reasons, all administrations should obliterate surprise quizzes from the school system.

207

2. Don't begin with a quiz! Aside from you having to contend with all the whining and excuses, here's the problem with beginning class with a quiz. The quiz puts a damper on your lesson even before you begin teaching. Worse, students remain alert for the quiz and then mentally unwind. The sharp focus they need for the new lesson (not to mention anticipation) dissipates. So what do you do instead? Just this:

THE ONE BIG DO FOR QUIZ TIME

Give open-book quizzes at the end of class. Let the quiz mainly be on the new material of the day. This gives students the incentive during class to listen, take good notes, and clarify all questions. With the material fresh in their minds, students do well on daily quizzes and feel an immediate reward for paying attention during class. The burden of reviewing for homework also eases because the quiz already served as the key review. At home, students need only skim their notes of the previous lesson to feel fully prepared for the next day's learning. Ultimately, students retain so much more information because cramming doesn't pay a role in their quiz taking.

The one exception to the rule: Yes, there's always an exception. Quizzes on homework reading is the only exception to this quiz giving rule. Since the reading knowledge is usually a large component of the lesson, the teacher needs to test students' comprehension to ensure they're with her. Otherwise, the lesson has no foundation to build upon.

Want to make sure your students read material without getting tense about an impending quiz? Arm students with a list of questions and state that one of those questions will be on the quiz. Some students may cop out at first and ask their classmates to fill them in on the answers without reading the material. But it's just a matter of time before they learn that it's easier to read the assignment than to memorize answers they don't understand.

Now that we got that out of the way, let's get back to the matter at hand. You're prepared to give the quiz at the end of class. How do you make this quiz more appealing? Here's the answer.

Cater to the creative spirit in everyone! Here are some ideas.

- Provide extra questions and let students choose the ones they prefer to answer.
- Ask fun questions that call for students' opinions, criticism, and evaluations.
- If you give multiple choice, allow students to explain their choice.
- Let students go online, play a game related to the material, and submit their score.
- Select key words from the lesson for example, Sri Lanka and habeas corpus, and ask students to show you that they recognize these words by employing them in sentences.
- Supply students with a quote or a cartoon and have them connect it to the lesson material.
- Challenge your students on the spot to come up with two good quiz questions based on the lesson. Then tell them to swap their questions with a person sitting near them. Students should attempt to answer one of the questions. If they can't, they may answer one of yours.
- Instruct students to draw a character, diagram, or circumstance applicable to the lesson and to explain their drawing.
- Ask students to give the lesson a review—rate the content—why they liked the material or disliked it and to provide concrete information from the lesson in their explanation.

Side point: Want to make the grading of the quizzes less tedious? Don't always have everyone answer the same quiz questions. Distribute various questions throughout the class, and you'll get to read a potpourri of responses which will surely entertain you!

COLLECT ALL OR NONE

To save themselves grading time, many teachers don't collect all quizzes, but only a select few. I always feel this unfair to the student who, invoking Murphy's Law, flubs his answers the one time his teacher asks him to submit the quiz and is pleased with his answers when the teacher doesn't collect the quiz. Do what I do to give students a fair chance. Collect either all or none. When collecting all, give students a one-time reprieve from handing in the quiz. When collecting none, announce that whoever wishes may hand in their quiz for credit.

THE TIME SPAN FOR QUIZZES

For short answer quizzes, I strongly suggest not allowing students much writing time. In fact, I tell my class that they might not have enough time to complete their answers but will receive full credit if their responses are on the right track. Furthermore, students must write complete sentences. They do not have to rephrase the question in their statement, but they need to make sure that every sentence contains a subject and a predicate. There are a number of reasons for this whole arrangement:

Why the limited time? Poorly prepared students have the tendency to ramble on in their written responses hoping they will impress the teacher somewhere between the lines. Knowing that they must provide sufficient material within a limited time improves their studying and writing habits.

Ironically, limiting time also allows students to be more spontaneous in their writing, concentrating on the main criteria for the quiz, which is to give information, not to sound one way or another. The time limit frees students from the onus of trying to sound "sophisticated," and they end up sounding more intelligent.

Finally comes the teachers' bonus. With quiz time taking up a relatively small portion of class, teachers can give quizzes without compromising much teaching time.

Why insist upon complete sentences? Writing complete sentences compels students to focus on the subject—after all, by definition, a sentence must include a subject. Automatically, complete sentences render more accurate information. What is more, the overall response is much more concise and easy to read.

Quiz time is over. You bring the quizzes home to grade. Now what?

BE A LIGHT (AND COMPASSIONATE) GRADER OF QUIZZES

- Check mainly for the content. Don't keep taking off points for the same errors like spelling mistakes or poor punctuation. Reserve the heavier critique on grammar for homework papers that students have had time to perfect.
- Soften the critique with parentheses. Minimize crossing out words. Place parentheses around awkward usage and poor word choice and suggest replacements above the

parentheses. Parentheses show students that their thought is fine, it's only that the words are ill-constructed.

- Notice the good parts. Draw smiley faces next to the good part of answers or write "Nice effort!" or "Nice try" next to mediocre answers so that students see you notice the effort even when the answer isn't fabulous.
- Laugh with students about flop ups. Help them find the humor in things that go wrong so that they don't give up on themselves. Writing something like, "Whoops! You mixed up mitosis with meiosis in this response," conveys a good-humored attitude and teaches students to take blunders in stride.
- Be sympathetic. When the grade doesn't accurately depict the student's capacity or effort, write a little note on the quiz to acknowledge that. For example, "I know that your score doesn't reflect your intelligence or hard work."

So now that we've covered quizzes, we can hop along to the review. Which review are we talking about? The review before the test.

The Review Before the Test

Let's discuss the type of reviews you want to conduct in your classroom.

Here's the important thing to know about reviews before tests: These reviews must call for strategic thinking. That's the only type of review that activates the class and cements knowledge. Reviews that don't involve a mind-challenge waste time. So, drop the reviews where you call on students to spew forth memorized information. These reviews don't motivate the class to do anything but pray you don't call on them. The class either knows the information or doesn't. They can't gain from listening to correct answers without understanding the thought process behind them.

Instead of mindless reviews, challenge the whole class with stimulating activities. You'll have students prepared for the test in no time!

Here are my favorite review activities guaranteed to motivate your students!

CHAPTER REVIEWS

Ever wonder why many authors naturally summarize the main points of each chapter for the reader? That's because a short review reinforces memory and can be used as a quick reference. That said, an accumulation of chapter summaries is a magnificent gift students can give themselves. So why not instruct the class to write chapter summaries, designating different chapters for each row. Then pluck the best chapter summaries from each row's batch and present them to the class for a cumulative review of a topic. If nothing else, the interest in reading their peers' work will serve as a boon to their reviewing!

Here are examples of students' chapter reviews from textbooks:

"Did you ever wonder about the first civilizations? One of the first civilizations emerged in Mesopotamia between the Tigris and the Euphrates Rivers. The initial settlers were the Sumerians who invented the wheel, sailboat, and the twelve-month calendar. They developed cuneiform, a symbol writing on clay tablets. Babylonians later conquered this Mesopotamian area and developed the world's first law code, the Code of Hammurabi. Mesopotamia was eventually overtaken by the Hittites, Assyrians, Chaldeans, and Persians."—Racheli Jacobovits

"Dalton introduced the theory that atoms make up matter. Overtime, the model of an atom changed. In 1897, Thompson performed the cathode ray tube test to prove that electrons are embedded in an atom. Rutherford's gold foil experiment in 1909 proved that a dense nucleus exists in the center of the atom. Later, the Bohr model portrayed the nucleus and rings of orbiting electrons. Today's Wave-Mechanical model shows that electrons move in distinct regions known as Orbitals."—Sarala Kahan

RHYME IT!

This activity can be done as a collaborative effort before an exam. The teacher divides topics or subtopics among groups in the class. Each group reviews the material and summarizes the important parts in rhyming couplets. Following group recitals of their couplets, the teacher or elected class members collect the poems, edit them, and assemble them into one long poem. Voila! A creative review of all the material is born for class distribution! The review is also easier to commit to memory since the mind recalls rhyme and rhythm better than ordinary prose.

Before embarking upon the activities below, students must study information at home. Note: Although several of these activities seem to have a competitive streak, they pose no harm. The contestants are volunteers, everyone has a chance to win, and the prize is extra credit.

STUMPING THE EXPERT

This panel game, an adaptation of "Stump the Experts," is fabulous for reinforcing the learning of lengthy curriculum material.

Rules for "Stumping the Expert":

1. For homework, have students prepare at least three challenging questions on the subject area. Inform students that they will be receiving extra credit if they can stump a panel of experts from the class with their questions.

2. The following day, select three volunteers from the class to act as your panel of experts.

3. Allow students to take turns challenging this panel of experts with their prize questions. The questions are asked to the panel members from left to right. The panel member who answers a question correctly receives extra credit points. If the question stumps a panel member, the same question goes to the next panel member. If the entire panel is stumped, they may collaborate to discuss the answer among themselves. If the answer comes as a result of panel members' collaboration, panel members divide the credit.

4. If the student asking the question is able to stump the panel of experts, she receives extra credit points once she properly answers the question herself.

5. When the teacher decides the experts have had their share of questions, he switches the three on the panel with a fresh selection of volunteers from the class.

Here are are two variations of "Stumping the Expert" that my classes enjoy immensely:

Variation #1 of "Stumping the Expert"

Instead of a panel of experts, the class divides into two teams. Two members of the opposite teams (always volunteers) come to the front of the room and challenge each other with one of their questions. Whoever answers the question correctly receives extra credit and a point for her team.

- If both contestants get each other's answer correct, they both receive extra credit and a point for their team.
- If a contestant is stumped, she may call on a team member to give her a one-word hint. (The hint, of course, may not be the answer.) If, as a result of the hint, the contestant gets the answer, she and the team member receive extra credit. If the contestant does not get the answer, she does not get extra credit and the team does not get points. The teacher poses the question to the class audience and whoever get the answer correct receives the extra credit.
- If both contestants are stumped by each other's questions, the teacher poses the questions to the class audience. Whoever gets the answers correct gets the extra credit.

The game proceeds as long as everyone remains interested. The team that answers the most questions gets to omit one answer from the test.

Variation #2 of "Stumping the Expert"

Instead of a panel of experts, students divide into groups. Students challenge peers within their group with prepared questions. Anyone who stumps the group writes his question down on notebook paper with his name beside it. After an allotted time, the teacher stops the exercise and has a representative of each group approach the front of the class with the list of questions that stumped their group. Any question that stumps the class grants the originator of the question extra credit. The game goes on until all the questions are asked or students lose interest.

In Quest of Questions

1. Volunteers create examination questions as a review of the subject material. The teacher types the questions for the class on a handout. The people who wrote the questions are not named on the handout.

2. In groups, students discuss which two questions are most essential to the subject material. The teacher presses students to keep an open mind and not bias the group to accept the questions they created. When groups come to a consensus, they defend their choices before the class.

3. The class votes upon the two best questions. The questions that receive the highest number of votes wins. The students who wrote the winning questions receive extra credit or may omit an answer from the test.

Who Am I?

This game mimics *What's My Line*, a 1950s game show broadcast on CBS.

1. For a review, a student approaches the front of the room and assumes an identity of someone or something from the subject material (for example, Jane Eyre, Patrick Henry,

Roanoke Island, the Census Bureau, mitochondria). The student reveals his identity only to the teacher.

2. Within three minutes, a panel of volunteers must guess his identity. Panel members speak in turn and may only ask the mystery guest questions that can be answered with a "yes" or "no." For example, "Are you a famous person?" "Are you a place?" "Are you an agency?" "Do you help people think?"

3. If the panel guesses the mystery guest's identity within the time frame, they receive extra credit. If they don't meet the deadline, the extra credit goes to the mystery guest. The teacher switches the panel for every mystery guest.

A Variation of "Who Am I?"

The panel member gets to keep asking questions as long as the answer is "yes." When the answer is "no," it's the next panel member's turn. The panel member who guesses the mystery guest's identity receives extra credit. The teacher may or may not keep to a time frame.

THE EDUCATION COMMERCIAL

The teacher divides the class into groups of three or four. A member from each group picks a slip of paper from a lot. The slips of paper name words connected to subject material. For instance, if the subject material is the Machine Age, slips might name inventions such as the radio, phonograph, high speed printing, the modern battleship, and the freight locomotive. For homework, groups prepare to act out a short commercial for the word they've chosen.

The commercial needs to influence the class in some way, for example, to understand the value of an item, circumstance, development, or social influence. Encourage students to dress up, and bring in props. In class, students get an entertainment review.

Testing, Testing, Anxiety-Free

Now it's test time. Do your students dread it? Do they complain about the memorization? Do they have difficulty recalling facts? Places on the map? Names of people? Names of functions or processes? This memorization, I find, is the main burden for students. Can you remove this burden? Easily. How? By considering open-book testing.

OPEN-BOOK TESTING

Are your tests intelligent? You might think so, but if they don't require deeper thinking, they're not intelligent at all. An intelligent test doesn't harp on facts. It typically doesn't ask for word definitions, fill-ins, matching, or any information that checks for recall.

Open-book tests allow students to look up references: the chronological order of a story, a mathematic or scientific formula, the date or name of a battle, the function of the inferior vena cava. These facts, while essential for building information, don't give away the answer to the test. The open-book test is designed to see what students can do with base information.

The test itself calls for higher order thinking. Remember, it is not a "spit-back" test. Studying for this type of test urges students to think deeper into the material, to notice cause and effect, relationships, and possible innovative opportunities. When answering questions or carrying out tasks for the open-book test, the students must analyze information, build an argument, or design something (as projected in Bloom's Taxonomy, chapter 6) to receive a good grade. The thinking on the test is more intense but much more rewarding.

You can always consider open-book tests when you're testing higher order thinking. The students know they have × amount of time to finish the test so they don't come to the test unprepared. They must have memorized a portion of the material to do well on the test because they won't have the physical time to complete the test if they're constantly checking up information. Instead, they approach test time with the peace of mind that if they forget a name or definition, they can quickly look it up.

Let's take a look at sample questions or task instructions you might find on open-book tests.

Sample questions for a test on *Macbeth* by William Shakespeare (Grade 10):

- How would the play be different if Lady Macbeth killed King Duncan?
- Is Banquo's role more crucial to the plot when he's alive or dead?
- How necessary is Lennox's role to the play? Explain.
- If you were to be the director of a *Macbeth* school play, which aspect of the play might you highlight or cut out to please a modern-day audience?
- Write a good headline that could have been printed during the days of *Macbeth*. Write a few paragraphs that would appear in the headline's column.

Task instructions for a test on physics. Twirling a Top (Grade 7):

- Welcome to the open-book physics test. For this test, you will carry out a task. Please do not share science textbooks.
- Using your knowledge of the following concepts—the Gyroscopic Effect, energy, and angular momentum—design a twirling top. Your top must spin for at least 6 seconds within a 30-cm diameter.
- Before you design your top, choose potential materials for your top from the bins on the yellow table. You may approach the bins as many times as you need to examine, collect, or return materials. You may not speak during this task. Please direct all questions to me.
- Draw a design for your top on paper. Discuss which materials you chose for the crown, shoulder, body, and tip of your top and why you chose those materials. Please discuss at least three materials that you specifically didn't choose for the anatomy of your top.
- Test your top and its spinning quality. If you have time, reconstruct or refine your design for better results. Five minutes before the end of class, test your top one last time. You can still receive full credit if your top fails to spin well if you describe what's holding it back and how you would refine your design the next time around.
- At the end of class, please hand in your top along with your scrap work, final design sketch, and written material.

Sample question for a math final (Grade 6); Topic: Equations (Note: Students must follow a particular protocol for answering this part of the test and getting their peer's and teacher's feedback. But by the end of the year, they know the drill and carry out instructions impeccably.)

A company plans to publish a new sports magazine. The manager estimates that the company can publish 30,000 copies of the magazine for a total cost of $27,000.

Write an equation that one can use to determine the cost of publishing each copy of the magazine.

- Tell what the variable you use represents.
- Solve your equation and find the solution.
- Decide on a reasonable price that the company should charge customers for the magazine and justify your decision.

When you are finished, laminate your paper. Then swap your laminated paper with someone else's. Take a look at his equation and work it out on a loose-leaf paper. Compare your answer with your friend's. Did he set up a correct equation? Do you agree with his reasoning? Why or why not? Please write a response about his equation on your loose-leaf paper. I will be checking this response to see how much thought you put into it.

When your friend has completed your equation, please confer with him to discuss both your equation and his equation. You may ask your friend for help with your equation if you need it or check up rules in your math book. Then, if necessary, you may redo your equation on a loose-leaf paper, explaining where you went wrong. Afterwards, you may approach my desk to hand in your work.

- If your answer was initially incorrect and you revised it correctly, I will give you a similar equation to work out and justify. If you answer it correctly, you will receive full credit.
- If your answer is correct and you didn't revise it, I will accept your paper. If I see you have not completed the equation correctly, I will explain where you went wrong and give you another chance to revise it and work on a new similar equation for full credit.

AN ALTERNATIVE TO OPEN-BOOK TESTS

Does the idea of open book testing still go against your grain? How about allowing students to bring one index card of information to the test? Analyzing what they should put on the index card helps students prepare for rigorous testing. This small "cheat sheet" additionally eases the apprehension of those who have memory difficulty since they can bring factual information with them to the test.

Preparing the Test

Teachers can alleviate a whole lot of their students' anxiety by preparing tests with a bit more consideration for students' test-taking preferences. Here are helpful tips for designing the instructions and format of the test.

THE INSTRUCTIONS

Keep instructions precise and simple. For example, say, "Please use evidence from the document to support your reasoning" instead of "Please supply sufficient evidence from the information in the document that dovetails with your reasoning."

Give one direction per sentence. For example, "Do your scrap work in the space provided in your test booklet. Do not write any scrap work on your answer sheet. Please make sure to transfer all answers from the test booklet to the answer sheet."

Let your directions take on a friendly tone. For example, "Here's a section I figured all you dog lovers will appreciate. Just don't get carried away with the story and forget about the rest of the test. Keep moving on."

Let your instructions take on an encouraging tone. For example, "Think you can tackle the next challenge? I bet you can. Take a deep breath, and answer the questions from this part based on your knowledge of opportunity cost, profit, and comparative advantage."

THE FORMAT

• Don't crowd material on the page. Leave ample space between problems.

• Don't put any visual distractions on the page unless they're necessary for the test examples.

• Prepare extra questions for the test. Students appreciate when they can omit a couple of answers from the test or from a specific part of the test. Give students the option of receiving extra credit by answering all questions.

• Limit the number of sentences students may use to respond to a question. A one- to two-sentence limit are common for short answers. Students like to have limits that help them gauge their time better.

• Make sure all multiple choice questions have one clear answer, but permit students to defend their choice. Perhaps their way of thinking differs from yours but displays logical reasoning that merits credit.

• Here's a little twist to the usual multiple choice question: Give the answer and have the students find the correct question among several!

• True or false statements should be either entirely true or entirely false. Students shouldn't have to worry that part of a true statement might be false. Have students justify the correct statements and modify the false ones so that you get to see their reasoning. (You may do this also with multiple choice.)

• Begin the test with a few easy questions to calm down students who take tests too seriously.

• On the bottom of a new test, ask students to give you input so that you can revise it for future classes if necessary. Here are good prompting questions: How did you find this test? Were you expecting the test to be different? How so? Which questions did you like? Which questions didn't you like? Why? Which ones did you have a difficult time answering? Why? Would you prefer taking a different type of test? What kind?

CHECKING THE TEST

Read your test. Anticipate students' questions and try to clarify anything that's not crystal clear.

Take your test! You might find questions too time-consuming, difficult to answer, or just plain unfair. Revise for clarity. Write sample answers for short answer sections and the like.

Time yourself as you work at a moderate pace. Provide your class with an additional fifteen to twenty minutes to complete the test.

Show your test to colleagues for feedback. Something incongruous might jump out at them that you didn't notice.

Preparing Tests for Weaker Students

Many weaker students stand out in class the first week of school. Those students need modified tests from the get-go. Be careful, however, not to judge students' aptitude by the grades you've seen on their past report cards. Many factors that no longer exist could have accounted for a student's weak performance. Always give students' ability the benefit of the doubt.

How do you evaluate your students' test-taking abilities? How do you modify weaker students' tests? With these easy steps.

First see how all weaker students perform on the open-book standard test. Then evaluate each student's abilities. For added assistance, you might discuss with students what they found most challenging on the test.

For lower than average students: Decrease the content for those who did okay on the standard test but couldn't manage abundant questions. But don't dumb down the test. Slower students need to exert more mental effort per question than their faster thinking peers, but many can master higher level questions if given the time (as discussed in Chapter 6: Blossoming with Bloom).

For very weak students: You might have to narrow the scope and content for those who did very poorly on the standard test, but sprinkle the test with a variety of questions— a few higher-level questions that call for analyzing, evaluating, and creating, and several lower level questions based on remembering, understanding, and applying. Notice which level questions the student can answer satisfactorily, which level is harder, and which is not feasible. Adjust future tests accordingly.

Caution: Don't allow students to get comfortable with easier tests. As students' study habits change, and they get tutoring assistance, many can cope with more challenging tests. Always try to raise the student's level of thinking by superseding lower level questions with higher order ones.

REFORMATTING THE STYLE
OF YOUR TESTS FOR SOME STUDENTS

Students who have weaker cognitive skills or think very literally may never get the hang of your particular testing style. Therefore, you might have to reformat a test to meet their needs. For instance, I concentrate on cartoons, poems, and other interesting texts for my vocabulary tests. While most students think this format amusing and intriguing, some students find deciphering cartoons and poems cumbersome. Moreover, questions on future tests are on cumulative material and hold too many vocabulary words for weaker students to process at one time. Understandably, I've had to turn to a less sophisticated format for testing some students on vocabulary.

Below are two vocabulary tests I devised for students who need straightforward vocabulary tests. Both tests contain opinion-based questions that use vocabulary words within sentences. Notice that the questions do not give away definitions. The difference between the tests is that the first easier test uses vocabulary sparingly within sentences. The second, harder test contains more vocabulary words within sentences and demands more intricate responses. Students can take these tests without stress, but still find them challenging.

Modified Vocabulary Test—Easier Level (Grade 10)

1. What is the most preposterous thing you've ever done?
2. What is the zaniest thing you've ever done?
3. What is one of your tenacious opinions?
4. What do you think is the most laudable character trait in a friend? Why?
5. Do you think indolent people are happy? Why or why not?
6. What makes you feel disgruntled? Why?
7. Name a circumstance that always puts you into a jocund mood.
8. Are you a novice at babysitting? Please explain.
9. Did your enthusiasm for school wane since the beginning of the year? Why or why not?
10. What is an example of an arduous task you deal with each day? Please explain.

Modified Vocabulary Test—Higher Level (Grade 10)

1. Would you rather go on a vacation with a zany, gregarious, or candid person? Please explain why your choice is preferable to the others.
2. What arbitrary consequence might despotic rulers consider an infallible antidote for combating rebellion?
3. Name a circumstance you're coerced to endure which you find either irksome, foreboding, or arduous. Explain why you feel that way.
4. What is a plausible reason one store might have lucrative sales while another store selling the same merchandise doesn't?
5. Is it easier to misconstrue ambiguous, naive, or diabolical motives? Please explain your choice and why you didn't choose the others.
6. Two children sitting in adjacent chairs at the shoe store keep teasing each other. What solution is manifest to their mothers?
7. Do you think an apathetic citizen would act brazenly toward government politics? Why or why not?
8. Do you think teasing a timorous child is callous behavior? Why or why not?

Spare Students' Embarrassment

To spare students the awkwardness of being singled out in front of the class when given special tests, arrange for these test takers to pick up their tests in the school office. In class, hand students the class' standard test as well, and if they have time, let them fill out what they know on the standard test.

Before, During, and After the Test

You'd think you can distribute the test, let students take it, hand it in, and that's that. Right? Almost. Here are some tips for making the test-taking experience as comfortable as possible for students.

BEFORE THE TEST

- Don't photocopy test booklets back to back. Students find it irksome to keep flipping pages and readjusting the booklet to answer questions.
- Change seating arrangements for greater exclusion. For example, you probably don't want to seat students cozily around tables during test time. If necessary, move desks for even spacing.
- Don't switch any one person's seat. Singling out someone this way gives him the insulting notion that you suspect he might cheat.
- Read the test (or part of the test) for the sake of the auditory learners. Did it ever happen that a student asks you to read a question and after you comply, he says "Oh!" with a sudden enlightenment? That's your auditory learner. To see who is an auditory learner before test time, glance up as you're reading something to the class. While most students will be looking down at the reading material, a few will be looking at you. Those are your auditory learners! Auditory learners, even the brightest ones, benefit from hearing the test read to them.

DURING THE TEST

Advise students during the test to:

- highlight key words in the instructions to help them maintain the focus.
- think of the answer to multiple choice questions before looking at the choices.
- read all the choices to multiple choice questions. (The first choice that sounds good isn't always the best answer.)
- skip the questions they don't know and go back to them later so that they don't get bogged down by a few questions.
- label their scrap work and hand it in so that you can see their effort.
- organize their ideas in small phrases or outlines before writing longer answers to help them include the information in a coherent paragraph.

Look around the room. Check out your students. How is the test affecting them?

Give your support. Many telling habits may surface during exam time, such as nail biting, hair pulling, sighing, muttering, nervous rocking, or irregular breathing. High-strung students need a comforting word. Every teacher can develop his own way of easing anxiety. Some like to approach students individually and whisper comments like, "Take it easy, it's just a test" or "Calm down, you're doing your best." A colleague of mine believes that a kind gesture can substitute words, like patting a student on the back or gently squeezing a quivering hand. My sister's professor cracks jokes, "You have nothing to worry about," he once announced to the class. "I took my test this morning and got a seventy-four!"

Don't prowl about! Many educators think that maintaining vigilance during the exam entails circling the room and peering over shoulders as students take the exam. Students will tell you though, that no matter how casual or soft, the teacher's hovering presence or sound-making movements disturbs their concentration. All observation can be done from behind the teacher's desk or from a stationary position in the back of the room.

Take questions during the test. Always provide time to answer questions during the exam. No matter how many times you've reviewed your test for clarity, someone is bound to have a valid question.

Don't take questions right away. First, let the class have twenty minutes of uninterrupted concentration. Say something reassuring such as: "I will begin to answer questions at 3:20 p.m., but I guarantee I'm going to get to all your questions. So, don't dwell on the questions that stump you. Skip them and you'll come back to them later."

When the time comes for taking questions, don't randomly answer questions. Deal with one section at a time. "Any question in the multiple-choice section?" For longer tests, you might work from the beginning to end of the booklet, asking, "Any questions on the first page?" (pause) "The second page?" and so on.

Keep your tone light and friendly when you take questions. Don't come across agitated or impatient with simple or unwarranted questions. Afford equal time to everyone. Never cause the students to feel bad for asking questions.

After the Test

What should students do when they finish the test early?

Students should have the prerogative to occupy themselves with quiet work while waiting for peers to finish an assignment or test. Don't badger your students to do something productive with their extra time. I remember as a kid a most annoying teacher who would yell, "Don't waste your time, people! Don't just sit there; do something!" After a test, "doing something" for students might mean sitting quietly and relaxing. Relaxing is necessary for refueling. My advice is to let students alone. Only enforce the rule that students who finish early may not talk to anyone or disturb a test-taker in any way.

Quell the anxiety of the slower test-takers. Tell them, "Don't worry if people around you have finished the test early. Make the most of the time that's given to you."

Don't allow anyone to leave the room before the bell. When teachers permit students to leave the room after a test, those who are still taking the test feel pressured to hand in their paper. Test takers are also subjected to the growing noise in the hallways. To prevent this added strain, don't let students hand in their papers before the bell. This rule also inspires the early birds to check their tests for careless mistakes.

Grading Made Easy

We spoke about test time, what about all the grading?

Time-consuming and mentally draining, grading written work is the least favorite part of a teacher's job. Considering that it can take ten minutes on average to grade a quiz and twenty minutes to read and correct a two-sided essay (multiply the time by the number of students, 25–30 a class), teachers choose to assign fewer (and shorter!) writing assignments. It's no wonder students don't do enough writing. But who can blame the teachers? As an English teacher, I spent much of my free time after school bogged down with papers. In fact, I even contemplated abandoning my teaching career just to escape the marking!

How do we make grading time easier?

Over the years, I have struggled with different methods of grading essays in hope of curtailing grading time without sacrifice to my students' learning. From all the ideas I have tried, one outranks them all.

HOW TO CUT YOUR GRADING TIME IN HALF

To reduce half your marking time for all essays, give students an oral critique! Speak into a recorder as you read the work. Guide the student as you go along by saying, "Now I'm reading the first paragraph…" Then, read a few sentences in silence and speak your mind. For example: "William, you give some misinformation here. In the story, Tom's paper was caught in the crevice of an ornament, not a brick. Be accurate when you give details of the story."

Read on until you're ready to make the next point, for example: "I like how you conjure the imagery for the reader in the second paragraph. When you describe the moment Tom glances down at Lexington Avenue, the reader can feel Tom's terror on the ledge." Continue reading silently until you see another bump or area of praise: "William, here you write, 'It says while Tom is on the ledge that Tom lost his nerve.' Don't write *it* for a subject, rather define who or what you mean. You mean to say here that the *author* states Tom lost his nerve."

Resume commenting this way, reading and speaking intermittently. As you read silently, the student will use the time to register what you have just said.

The oral critique saves you time for numerous reasons. First, it keeps you focused on the task. The recording is on. The urgency to continue reading and speaking is ever present. You don't get distracted. Second, when you speak, you don't have to worry as much about formulating your thoughts into coherent expression as when you write something down. Third, with the recording you communicate much more at one time because we human beings naturally think and speak much faster than we can write. For instance, when we write comments on students' papers, we tend to omit profound notations because we have no patience to slow down our thought to match our writing pace. You know what I'm talking about if you've ever found yourself revising the sentence structure for a student or inserting the correct punctuation instead of writing what the student needs to change. Speaking on a voice recorder permits you to instruct and explain everything. It's a powerful alternative to writing comments. You don't hand back the paper without any corrections, but with brief memos that make sense when the student listens to the oral content.

At the end of each student's oral critique, I summarize in mere seconds the essay's strong and weak points. Before evaluating the student's next essay, I listen to the summary of the old one so that I can see whether the student learned from her mistakes. If you don't want to take the time to go back and listen, you can have students jot down their previous essay's weak points on headings of new essays.

Given a choice whether they want me to continue the oral critique or grade on paper, my students opt for the voice recording. Asked how they like this audio approach, my students are profuse in their appreciation. For certain, they say the detail of the critique helps them more accurately hone their writing. Additionally, they consider this approach more personable. Listening to my comments, they feel like I'm sitting right there with them as their personal tutor. Even my tone, they note, lends significance to the words. One student put it simply: "A voice is much friendlier than red ink." Moreover, many treasure the personal messages I inject that have to do with their academic progress.

This auditory method, as you might also imagine, is a wonderful boon to the disorganized students, especially the weaker students who need careful guidance. It's a given that it improves everyone's listening skills. Students tell me that after listening to the recordings, they find themselves paying more attention in class.

By the end of the year, equipped with recordings, students can make an accurate assessment of their progress. Parents express overt wonder when they see their teenagers lock themselves in their rooms to review each recording and get to work right away on the revision process. What's more, parents voice their admiration for my dedication. "Wow," they exclaim, "you take the time to speak directly to each student! What commitment! What devotion!" Which is rather ironic, since as I mentioned, the effort an educator puts into the written critique far exceeds the effort one expends for the oral critique. But parents don't realize that and of course, they don't have to know.

To those educators reluctant to try this method, I say you have nothing to lose! When I first introduced this idea to a colleague, she said, "What? Send my voice out there? No way! I'm going to sound like Elmer Fudd." As unconventional as this method sounds, it's the most innovative and rewarding of any method I have implemented in my teaching career. All I ask of you is to give it a chance. When you become accustomed to the oral critique, you may become a speaking pro and decide you don't mind that your voice is recorded for posterity or sounds like Elmer Fudd. Or maybe you won't go for the oral critique, after all. The wonderful thing is that once you begin, you don't have to commit yourself to this approach. You can dub the oral critique an experiment, discontinue the process anytime, and revert to the written critique, even in the middle of grading a batch of papers!

Additional note: The oral critique works for quizzes and short responses on tests. It also almost guarantees that students will review their mistakes instead of just looking at the grade.

ADDITIONAL TIPS FOR GRADING

Require students to type all assignments. Do you squint to decipher handwriting? Even the neatest handwriting slows down a reader. I have cut hours of my time by reading only typewritten work. Require typewritten homework and writing assignments from your students. Granted, you'll hear some grumbling at first, but students will thank you in the long run. In the first place, typing is a quicker form of communication. With practice, even slow typists can type faster than they can write. The speed of normal handwriting is 15 words per minute. A fifth grader can type 25–30 words per minute (http://www.educationworld. com/a_curr/curr076.shtml). In the second place, revising papers becomes so much easier for students via cutting and pasting. And finally, typing is a must for the future anyway, so you might as well give younger children the practice.

Make sure you are rested when grading papers. Sleep deprivation slows you down considerably. When I am wide awake, I can read twenty essays in one sitting. If I'm tired, I fidget after one and take a break for every two.

Check the ambience. Grade papers in a sunlit room. Turn off all phones. Sit in a straight back chair at a table or desk that gives you plenty of arm space and foot room. Keep the temperature of the atmosphere cool. Warm temperatures make one lethargic.

Tackle the harder-to-grade papers first. Grade the weaker papers before the stronger ones so you know the grading will only get easier.

Create a time goal and keep to it. Decide the number of papers you want graded by a given time. To keep your focus, cut your stack of papers into divisions of five. Aim to grade five papers at a time. Put yourself on a timer for each paper (actual or mental) so you don't get carried away with the technicalities of a paper.

Point to the place! Pointing to the place was not just something the teacher made you do in grammar school. It can help you in so many ways. Try this. Go to the library and run your finger across spines of books as you browse shelves. You'll notice how much quicker you can scan the books. Point as you read instructions of a recipe and you won't find yourself rereading sentences. What's the point of pointing? It gives you a focus so that your eyes don't wander or jump all over the place.

Quicken the pace of your reading by pointing to students' sentences—move your finger along at a slightly quicker pace than you read. This keeps your eyes from its lazy pausing and allows you to maintain sharp concentration on the essay's content. No longer will you have to stop to ask yourself, "What's he saying here?" Having remained mentally acute all along, you will pick up instantly what your student is saying (or not saying) without puzzling over it and having to reread paragraphs.

Have students highlight revisions. To save time reading revised work, have your students highlight the parts they've changed so that you can compare the new with the old without rereading the entire paper.

Categorize the papers as you grade them. Instead of mulling over what grade to give each paper, place them in categories of Excellent, Very Good, Good, and Poor papers. Return to the batches after you finished grading all the papers and rate the papers within the batch from the best to worst. For instance, in the Excellent category, decide which papers deserve an A+ or an A and transfer over the rest to the Very Good pile. In the Very Good pile, decide which papers merit an A– or B+ and transfer the remainder to the Good pile, and so on. In this way, you give a more accurate mark based on the class's performance as a whole.

Don't inflate marks. While it isn't advisable to grade strictly, you don't want to inflate marks. That makes students think they're not capable of advancement.

Suppose educators would reconstruct all quizzes and tests to give students the best chance at getting good grades. Imagine if students walked into a class feeling unthreatened by quizzes and tests. What would happen then? Aristotle said, "The aim of the wise is not to secure pleasure, but to avoid pain." I'm not sure students will ever cherish taking tests, but take away the burden, train them to think instead of memorize, let them feel achievement is attainable, and they will never again crumple a paper when they get it back. I'm equally certain that although educators may never take great pleasure in grading papers, adopting the grading methods provided in this chapter will remove the pain and make all the difference.

22

Giving Specific Praise
and Constructive Criticism

"The dream begins with a teacher who believes in you, who tugs and pushes, and leads you to the next plateau, sometimes poking you with a sharp stick called 'truth.'"—Dan Rather

Once I had a conversation with a bunch of students about the feedback they get from their teachers. Here's a few snippets from what they said:

- "It's disappointing when I get a grade, even a good grade, like an A on top of a paper and the teacher writes 'Excellent!' without any other comment."
- "I hate getting back an essay with crossed out sentences and not knowing why."
- "One of my teachers wrote, 'I can see you've learnt a lot from this project.' That comment didn't enlighten to me. I wanted her to tell me what I did right or wrong and where to go from there!"
- "I worked so hard on my family tree. I don't understand why I got a B–. How can someone get a B– on a family tree?"

These students aren't alone. In classrooms across the nation, students receive very little feedback, oral or written, when it comes to their progress. Justified in their frustration, students deserve better.

What's Wrong with Vague Praise

When my niece Basya was in ninth grade, her teacher instructed the class to interview a person who had gone through surgery and to write a report that explained the medical problem, the need for the surgery, and whether or not the operation was successful. My niece decided to interview Dr. Murray Porter, who had received a heart transplant.

Born with a congenital heart disease, Dr. Porter's disease was the overgrowth of the heart muscle. When he was twenty-eight years old, his heart had overgrown sufficiently where he became symptomatic and started getting chest pain. Dr. Porter's heart muscle had grown so thick that it blocked blood flow. At twenty-nine, he had open-heart surgery where they removed and shaved away some of the excess muscle. Regardless, his heart started enlarging, causing its walls to become thinner. As years passed, the contraction of his heart became poor and he suffered heart failure. On January 25, 2004, Dr. Porter received a new heart. On June 2, 2006, my niece interviewed Dr. Porter, who spoke candidly about his medical history, its complications, and life in the aftermath of his heart transplant: how the anti-rejection drugs suppressed his immune system, how he had to avoid people to stave off germs and infection, but most of all how grateful he was to be a recipient of a new lease on life.

Compiling the results of the interview into an eight-page typed report, my niece was proud of its outcome. Having followed my niece's progress of this project, I was naturally curious to see the teacher's comment and critique, and so when my niece got back her paper, I asked to take a look at the feedback. I was quite surprised to see very few comments—a couple corrections of mechanics and a few circled typos. At the conclusion of the paper, the teacher wrote, "100%. Excellent discussion of medical and personal issues involved." That's it.

What could the teacher have delineated in her comment? He could have mentioned why the discussion was excellent—referring to particular parts that lifted the interview out of mediocrity. He could have complimented some of the word usage, the sentence variety, the smooth flow of the paragraphs. He could have helped her avoid future problems with pronoun reference by clarifying the rules or attaching a worksheet discussing the cases of pronouns.

Perhaps what bothered me most was the lack of interest the teacher took in the topic. I mean how often do people come across a heart transplant recipient? And here, a student had interviewed one and the teacher didn't seem to be brimming with wonder or eager to have the student share her firsthand account with the class. I couldn't help thinking of the opportunities lost for my niece's class. Imagine if my niece would have read the interview in class and collected further questions to check out with Dr. Porter. Perhaps Dr. Porter would've agreed to visit the class and give a firsthand account of his experience. How do you see that playing out? Can you imagine the exciting exchange that could have taken place?

Ironically, my niece wasn't taken aback by her teacher's lack of interest.

"Most of my teachers don't write anything," she said. "They just give a grade."

"And is everyone okay with that?" I asked.

My niece echoed a response I've heard from many students: "No, we're not okay with that. We'd love to hear more. But what can we do about it?"

PRAISING RIGHT

Giving specific, descriptive praise means telling the student exactly what she accomplished. The teacher can praise effort, accuracy, fluency, good goal-setting, mastering a skill, creativity, bravery, etc. The point of the praise is to encourage the deed and show the student you're there to assist her further achievements. This encouragement fosters autonomy and a willingness to explore, apply skills, and face obstacles with determination.

For verbal praise, the teacher should speak in a sincere and natural voice.

- Today you worked non-stop on your mural of the Harlem Renaissance. That shows your determination. (effort)
- This week you were able to correctly define ten chemistry terms. That's six more than last week. (accuracy)
- You set the goal in January to run the half marathon and you did it! Congratulations! (good goal-setting)

- You pulled off that radio broadcast without a hitch. When I closed my eyes, I could imagine you were an adult. You spoke with finesse. (fluency)
- You carried out that questionnaire on saving honeybees despite people heckling you. I admire your bravery! (bravery)
- The class appreciated how you used amusing graphics such as the frantic man skating down the skateboard rail to illustrate an inclined plane. From the audience's laughter, I'm sure you could tell your presentation on work and energy really kept the class's attention. (creativity)
- You were able to compute fifteen correct digits on today's math time worksheet. That shows me you mastered the skill even though you were absent when we learned it! (fluency, mastering a skill, effort)
- You charted the path of Hurricane Katrina with accuracy. You captured its power and devastation. (accuracy)
- Having the students read the votes aloud in the process of reaching the finally tally was an excellent tactic to keep the suspense alive! (creativity)
- Your blog for John Adams enlivens the time period. What imagery you create in the street scene! You used so many sensory details that the reader is swept into the experience. (mastering a skill)
- The misty night and halo of light that you painted to surround the mountain peaks serve as a perfect setting for something supernatural to happen. (mastering a skill)
- You presented rules for the candidates that mimic those of a real debate! (accuracy)

For written praise, the teacher should keep to a genuine and enthusiastic tone. Let students look back at your comments and smile.

- You did vast and thorough research on your topic, including every aspect of Tchaikovsky's life and career. Your bibliography looks professional. (effort and accuracy)
- Your precise presentation covered the Four-Color theorem and proved that math can deal with exciting challenges. You had the whole class working their minds! (effort and accuracy)
- The setting of your composition hits the reader with gusto! With the autumn leaves swept up by the wind, the garbage cans banging against each other, and the rain pounding on the skylight, the reader gets a realistic sound impression of the storm. (fluency, effort, and mastering a skill)
- You wanted the reader to witness one of the many "little" upheavals in the routine days of children's lives. You met your objective. By absorbing the reader in the Little Leagues' dilemma, you make it the reader's problem as well. (good goal setting)
- What a good idea to use three different colored arrows for plotting the voltage vs. hours of battery use. The comparison between the three brands of batteries is sharp and clear. (creativity)
- I like how you have the reader imagine many soccer nets overlapping thousands of times in a tiny space to describe the tightly packed fibers of bulletproof clothing. That analogy helps the reader understand the concept. (creativity and accuracy)
- You took the effort to alternate styles in your essay by incorporating compound sentences, complex sentences, and compound-complex sentences. (effort)
- You give admirable attention in your memoir to Ms. Montgomery's shoes, lending the

reader your view from under the table and increasing the anticipation of what will happen when Ms. Montgomery reaches your hiding place. (mastering a skill)
- The clever question in your report, "Do you agree with the saying that 'seeing is believing'?" is really thought provoking. The class is bound to doubt their perception once they try the many exercises in the booklet! (good planning)
- You provide a mass of information in discussing how architecture influenced the fields of philosophy, art, technology, and psychology. (giving sufficient information)
- You delight the reader with Tim's flippant responses to the dragon and his nonchalance in face of its wrath. You touch upon every child's desire to lord power over someone (or something!) (creativity and mastering a skill)
- I like how you clearly explain the concept of density using the penny, piece of foam, rock, and paper clip in your experiment. The experiment is easy to replicate. (clarity)

Constructive Criticism

For criticism to be productive, it must be constructive. In addition to pointing out the error, the instructor must show the proper use, function, or illustration or lead the child to it. For example, nothing is wrong with telling a child that he's confusing the tens and hundreds columns, if the instructor then demonstrates the correct lining up of the digits. The criticism without the demonstration is nothing more than a rebuke. And this rebuke will only lend the student a distaste for whatever he's working at.

ORAL CRITICISM

The following constructive oral criticism specifically details what the student is doing wrong and how he can improve. The teacher points out an inaccuracy, non-fluency, the need for better goal setting, etc. Students experience no hard feelings in this exchange, and to the contrary, usually express appreciation for the teacher's guidance.

Examples of constructive oral criticism:

- Your drawing aptly shows how tobacco use affects many parts of the human body. The sketch of the heart, however, overpowers the lungs. Find a human body diagram with a picture of the organs in the science book and you'll see what I mean. (inaccuracy)
- Your board demonstration was a bit stilted because you kept looking into your notes to find the spelling of each algebraic term. Next time, you might consider hanging up algebraic terms on the board so they're available to you when you need them. (non-fluency)
- What a wonderful idea to use flour and salt dough to form mountains and other landforms for your state. What other visuals or written material will accompany this project? (need for better goal setting)
- From your outline, I can't tell if reading *Into the Wild* by Jon Krakauer empowered or disempowered you. What information from the book would you draw upon to expound on this topic? (insufficient information)
- It looks like you directly copied information from this book about drug legalization or switched a few words around. To avoid plagiarism, you need to paraphrase by

changing the sentence's structure, style, and word choice. Let's see if you can properly paraphrase this information. I'm going to come back in fifteen minutes and check your progress. (mental laziness)

- You demonstrated correctly how the same salt affects the boiling point of different liquids. How about also experimenting to see how different salts affect the boiling point of water? (need for better goal setting)
- A few of your steps for building a sand castle is out of order in this outline. Begin your outline again, imagining yourself getting ready to build a sand castle. For example, what step do you need to take before you arrive at the beach? Work the process from there and show me the difference between your first and second outline. (inept mastery of skill)
- What can you add to your model to expose more accurately how Jacob Riis and Lewis Hine depicted crowded tenements? (inaccuracy)
- Next time, when using the pinking shears, you might want to layer your fabric and cut it together rather than separately so that the edges of all layers are even. (inept mastery of skill)
- Your introduction sounds a bit dull. What can you say to create a common bond with your audience when you introduce Parkinson's Law? (dull arrangement, uncreative)
- Can you tell me how the work divided evenly for this irrigation project? Who set the budget for the materials and decided upon the cost of each material? Who contributed to the design of the irrigation system? Who organized the setup? Who conducted the experiments? Who completed the evaluation sheet? (effort)
- I like how you used warm colors for your gesture drawing and cool colors for the negative space. To give your art work greater volume and form, I'd like you to use more than three colors on the pose. (improving on a skill)

THE WRITTEN CRITIQUE (OR ORAL CRITIQUE)

When it comes to students' written work, teachers make the mistake of having students redo their papers without showing them how to fix mistakes. As a result, students just keep practicing errors, embedding the wrong way of doing things further into their brains. Daniel Amen in his book *Making a Good Brain* puts forth this idea splendidly by asserting that practice doesn't make perfect; it's perfect practice that makes perfect. Amen maintains that the brain doesn't care whether you become a good piano player or not, it just learns the keys the way you practice them. So if you practice the wrong keys, you become perfect at playing badly.

Our students will never accomplish anything if we just tell them, "Use more detail" or "This paper lacks craftsmanship." We must direct them! For example, to address personal narratives that greatly lack detail, here's how Mr. Bishop directs students with his comments: "Emma, you mention how frightened you are in the elevator during the blackout, but you need to use greater detail to reinvent the trauma of the experience. I suggest drawing the reader into the elevator with you. What were you doing during that hour? What were you thinking? How were you feeling? What were your physical sensations? What about the atmosphere? Could you see at all? Did the elevator get stuffy? What sounds did you hear? How did you know when the firemen came? How long did you it take them to remove the elevator door? Were the firemen speaking? What did you hear them saying? What were you doing while they were working?"

Here's another example of how Mr. Bishop tries to pin the student to an experience: "The account of your fall happens in too much of a blur, cheating the reader of the true events of the terrifying experience. Close your eyes, Henry, and envision the fall in slow motion. Here are some questions that might jog your memory. Were you alone upstairs? What was the time of day? What were you doing right before you lost your footing? How did you lose your footing? What do you remember about your fall? Was the staircase carpeted? Did you try to catch yourself? What details did you notice as you were falling? When you landed, what was your first thought? Your second? Before your parents came running—what did you hear? When you first saw your parents, what do you remember about their facial expressions, body language, or dialogue? What was your reaction to their concern? How were you feeling emotionally? Do you remember saying something or moving in any particular way?"

Now Emma and Henry have direction. They might not take Mr. Bishop's exact suggestions, but they now know where their narratives lack detail and get the idea of how to go about incorporating it. Had Mr. Bishop merely written to them, "Your paper needs more detail" or "The reader can't feel your experience." they wouldn't have any real guidance. Vague comments accomplish nothing. They only make students feel poorly about their writing ability and frustrated when it comes to revising papers. They don't know how to begin improving skills, let alone raising the writing level.

Do you always have to write (or say) full-fledged paragraphs when giving constructive criticism? Not at all. Sometimes a one- to three-sentence comment works just fine. And depending on the quality of work, you might only have to make these comments sporadically during the course of your reading. The following are examples of short criticism extracted from students' compositions and essays on various subjects. I purposely provide numerous comments in this section because teachers constantly ask me for them. The comments touch upon an extensive array of faulty areas.

Constructive written (or oral) comments:

- You start off trekking down the hill, only to present a dialogue between yourself and your father. Then at the foot of the hill, your mother starts speaking, which in my opinion, sounds quite spooky. Where was she all the while? What was she doing? (inconsistency)
- How can the Russian government violate the rights of American citizens? What exactly do you mean to say? (confusing meaning)
- You didn't use numbers in your abstract on percolation to describe your results. Substitute vague words like "most" and "some." (vague usage)
- President Nixon could not have passed Project Independence in 1980. He resigned as president in 1974. Please check your dates carefully. (inaccuracy)
- What's the emotional cost versus the financial cost? When investing in stocks, the reader needs to know this information. (insufficient information)
- What is a typical mean bus driver? Remember how we discussed "show vs. tell" in class? Here's a good place to show the bus driver's behavior or other people's reaction to him, so that the reader can sense his meanness. (failure to implement skill)

- Your report on how the Energy Crisis affected Americans until today is lacking since you haven't done any research on the years since 1979! What about the Alaskan oil pipeline? Shale oil of the Dakotas? Fracking? Ethanol? Add more current information like this to your report. (insufficient information)
- How did the tuna sandwich, water bottle, and history textbook all fit into your character's manila envelope? (illogic thinking)
- In this sentence, the pronoun *that* has no clear antecedent since it refers only to the idea of the previous statement. How would you revise this sentence to eliminate the unclear reference? (grammar problem)
- Your paper will glow once you describe how terrestrial and aquatic food webs are interconnected. (missing connection)
- In your discussion on Confucianism as an ethical system, it's not enough to explain how it influenced the Chinese attitude toward life. Give examples of how it set patterns of living and standards of social value. Show how it provided the background for Chinese political theories and institutions. (didn't meet criteria)
- The length of your hiking trail and maximum gradient doesn't seem to match with the information on the topographic map. Look closely at the hiking trail you mapped on the topographic map. What information do you need to take into account? (inaccuracy)
- Provide fresh sensory detail. The sun shining into her bedroom sounds blah—How about the sun reflecting slats of sunlight across her faded bedspread? Do you see what I mean? Weed the tired descriptions I underlined from your paper and substitute them with fresh ones. (uninspiring word choice)
- Besides newspapers, what other forms of mass media did the American public rely on before the radio? (insufficient information)
- In your summary of the TedEd Talk "Why Doesn't Anything Stick to Teflon?" you were supposed to stick to summarizing the video's information about Teflon and its extraordinary properties. You digressed to include personal benefits. Please remove this information and watch the video again to incorporate the points you missed in your summary. (didn't meet criteria)
- Is the faded wallpaper an accurate sign of the building's age? Might there be a better indication? (poor evaluation)
- It doesn't make sense to say that the Salem Witch Trials occurred in the late seventeenth century, a time when witches were killed for practicing witchcraft. There were no witches. What word can you substitute for witches in the sentence? (incorrect information)
- At the end of your weather report, you write, "All in all, expect a beautiful summer day." What information in the map contradicts this statement for a particular region? (contradictory information)
- Don't just mention that McCarthy accused Owen Lattimore and Louis Budenz. Identify the accused and what McCarthy accuse them of doing. (didn't meet criteria)
- If your character's fingers were numb, then it's understood that he can't feel them. Check your paper for other redundancies. (redundancy)
- Don't just mention that President Eisenhower and Prime Minister Winston Churchill carried out Operation Ajax. What was the operation? Describe it. (insufficient information)

- If your character's music is on full volume in the first paragraph, you can't have him turn up the volume in the second. Revise for consistency. (inconsistency)
- "Mind over matter" is a phrase that means the use of willpower to overcome physical problems. It has nothing to do with your reference to illusion in your experiment. (incorrect information)
- Plotting your own graph based on events happening in the classroom made the bystander effect come alive. Humanizing your bystanders with names instead of numbers would make the graph sound more credible. (polishing necessary)
- You make the reader wait too long. You write a sequence of events that run the course of two days (and three pages) without your characters encountering a conflict. The key as a writer is to get to the conflict without delay. (uninspiring information)
- The Brain Trust was not formed to handle immigration. Please research the function of the Brain Trust. (incorrect information)
- Your paper on aerospace engineering gives a general idea why engineers must know viscoelastic behavior of polymers, but I would like you to discuss in detail how engineers use this knowledge to design aircrafts, rockets, and spacecraft. (didn't meet criteria)
- You mixed up the 1948 Blockade of Berlin and the 1961 Berlin Wall. Please untangle the information and set the record straight for each event. (incorrect information)

When it comes to their progress, students hunger to know where they stand. They want honesty. Our fundamental job as educators is to mentor students. Receptive to feedback and not as vulnerable as adults, young people grow immensely with guidance. Educators should provide students with a constant feedback loop where students work to high standards, come back for feedback, set new goals, and so on. By the time students graduate from high school, they should view themselves as lifelong learners. We convey with our specific praise and constructive criticism that learning is a continuous delightful process. What healthier message can we give our students?

Bibliography

Aaron1912. (2008, June 9). "The Roaring Twenties—Dance Craze." YouTube. Retrieved from https://youtu.be/yNAOHtmy4j0.

"Addicted to Morphine After Surgery." (2017). Retrieved from http://www.morphineaddictionhelp.com/addicted-to-morphine-after-surgery.

Afrodrumming. (2012, July 24). "Oldest Native American Drumming Video Ever." YouTube. Retrieved from https://youtu.be/igmpvrRQIkI.

Aggy007. (2009, September 1). "Sir Nicholas Winton—BBC Programme *That's Life* Aired in 1988." YouTube. Retrieved from https://www.youtube.com/watch?v=6_nFuJAF5F0.

Amen, D. (2006). *Making a Good Brain Great.* New York: Harmony.

Anderson, L.H. (2002). *Thank You, Sarah.* New York: Simon & Schuster Books for Young Readers.

Anderson, L.W., & Krathwohl, D.R. (Editors), Airasian, Peter W., Cruikshank, Kathleen A., Mayer, Richard E., Pintrich, Paul R., Raths, James, & Wittrock, Merlin C. (2000). *A Taxonomy for Learning, Teaching, and Assessing: A Revision of Bloom's Taxonomy of Educational Objectives (Abridged Edition).* New York: Longman.

Aronson, B. "Famous Failures: 23 Famous Failures to Inspire You." Retrieved from http://www.bradaronson.com/famous-failures/.

AT&T. (2014, January 7). "Texting While Driving Test Course | AT&T." [YouTube]. Retrieved from https://youtu.be/gKhS9IJ4EHA.

Balme, James. [Tvpresenter4history]. (2010, December 29). "The Anglo-Saxons in Britain." YouTube. Retrieved from https://www.youtube.com/watch?v=Vzxiz3Kw9eI.

Bang, M. (2004). *When Sophie Gets Angry...Really, Really Angry.* New York: Scholastic Paperbacks.

Barbd Dar. (2010, September 30). "Nick Vujicic I Love Living Life. I Am Happy." YouTube. Retrieved from https://youtu.be/zJD1w_fpWqo.

Barnett, M. (2012). *Extra Yarn.* New York: Harper-Collins.

BBC. (2012, July 11). "The Korowai Tribe (Amazing Tree-House Builders from BBC's *Human Planet.*)" YouTube. Retrieved from https://youtu.be/X0lG0duiOLQ.

BBC News. (2014, August 6). "Train Rescue: Passengers Tilt Train to Free Trapped Man in Australia—BBC News." YouTube. Retrieved from https://youtu.be/lIQxrArMI7M.

Beanz2u. (2006, February 10). "First Moon Landing 1969." YouTube. Retrieved from https://youtu.be/RMINSD7MmT4.

Bentley, W.A. (2000). *Snowflakes in Photographs.* New York: Dover.

Berk, R.A. (2009). "Multimedia Teaching with Video Clips: TV, Movies, YouTube, and MTVU in the College Classroom." *International Journal of Technology in Teaching and Learning,* 5(1), 1–21. www.sicet.org/journals/ijttl/issue0901/1_Berk.pdf.

BigFishMad. (2013, January 13). "1200lb Black Marlin Cairns Grander Hot Shot Charters." YouTube. Retrieved from https://www.youtube.com/watch?v=OmdBbTNdwR8&feature=youtu.be.

Biography.com Editors. (2016, August 4). Lucille Ball Biography. Biography.com. Retrieved from http://www.biography.com/people/lucille-ball-9196958#related-video-gallery.

Bloom, B. (1983). *Human Characteristics and School Learning.* New York: McGraw-Hill.

Bloomingdale Brothers. (1886). *Bloomingdale's Illustrated Catalogue.* Mineola, NY: Dover.

Bradley, J. (Photographer). (1979). "Harold Whittles' amazed reaction to hearing for the very first time." Retrieved from http://imgur.com/gxcGEgB.

Breyer, S.G., O'Connor, S.D. (Annenberg Foundation Trust at Sunnylands). (2005). *Our Constitution: A Conversation* [DVD]. Available from http://www.annenbergclassroom.org/page/our-constitution-a-conversation.

Bridwell, N. (1972). *Clifford the Small Red Puppy.* New York: Scholastic.

Brown, M.W. (1947). *Good Night Moon.* New York: HarperCollins.

Burns, K., & Duncan, D. (1997). *Lewis & Clark: The Journey of the Corps of Discovery.* New York: Knopf.

Cameron, P. (1961). *"I Can't," Said the Ant.* New York: Scholastic.

Charney, S. (2010). *Cool Card Tricks.* Mankato, MN: Capstone.

Cleary, B. (1968). *Ramona the Pest.* New York: HarperCollins.

Cook, J. (2005). *My Mouth Is a Volcano.* Chattanooga, TN: National Center for Youth Issues.

CornshaqGaming. (2009, July 23). "Play It Through—

Platoon." YouTube. Retrieved from https://www.youtube.com/watch?v=N_2tw9ehIwY.

Craig, D. (2012). *Detect Deceit: How to Become a Human Lie Detector in Under 60 Minutes.* New York: Skyhorse.

Crews, D. (1991). *Bigmama's.* New York: Greenwillow.

Crews, D. (1992). *Shortcut.* New York: Greenwillow.

DaveHax. (2016, January 8). "Orange Peel Trick—Life Hack." [YouTube]. Retrieved from https://www.youtube.com/watch?v=s0ZorQ6-qlg.

Deci, E.L., Betley, G., Kahle, J., Abrams, L. & Porac, J. (1981). "When Trying to Win: Competition and Intrinsic Motivation." *Personality and Social Psychology Bulletin,* 7, 79–83.

DePaul Teaching Commons. (2010, March 4). *Teaching Difficult Concepts: Cell Division.* YouTube. Retrieved from https://youtu.be/t-DSExOjTTg.

DreamBigC. (2008, October 15). "Jack Canfield Explains: How to Accelerate Your End Result." YouTube. Retrieved from https://youtu.be/8jS8kn-NjsgQ.

Editors of TIME for Kids Magazine. (2016). *Time for Kids Big Book of Why (Revised and Updated): 1,001 Facts Kids Want to Know.* New York: Time for Kids.

Ehrilich, A. (2015). *When I Was Your Age Volume One: Original Stories About Growing Up.* Somerville, MA: Candlewick.

Excluyente6. (2013, September 4). "Ana Julia Torres y su León Jupiter HD." YouTube. Retrieved from https://youtu.be/yx4bd8OY6iw.

Fisher, D., Flood, J., & Lapp, D. (2005). "Neurological Impress Method Plus." *Reading Psychology,* 26 (2), 147–160. Retrieved from https://eric.ed.gov/?id=EJ692257.

Foehr, U.G., Rideout, V.G., & Roberts, D.F. (2010). "Generation M²: Media in the Lives of 8–18-Year-Olds." *A Kaiser Family Foundation Study. #8010.* Retrieved from https://kaiserfamilyfoundation.files.wordpress.com/2013/04/8010.pdf.

FORA.tv. (2010, October 18). "Writers on Writing: Fiction vs Nonfiction." YouTube. Retrieved from https://youtu.be/xty4QPdXWqk.

Frank, Barbara. [Business Buffet]. (2013, April 20). "How to Read Financial Statements—Painless, Light, Quick and Simple." YouTube. Retrieved from https://www.youtube.com/watch?v=gZOhNZ4MAYw&feature=youtu.be.

Frankels, E., & Heapy, P. (2012). *Dare.* Minneapolis, MN: Free Spirit.

Frankels, E., & Heapy, P. (2012). *Tough.* Minneapolis, MN: Free Spirit.

Frankels, E., & Heapy, P. (2012). *Weird.* Minneapolis, MN: Free Spirit.

Fulghum, Robert. (1991). *Uh-Oh.* New York: Random House.

Gardner, R. (2004). *Light, Sound, and Waves: Science Fair Projects Using Sunglasses, Guitars, CDs, and Other Stuff.* Berkeley Heights, NJ: Enslow.

Gatto, J.T. (2005). *Dumbing Us Down: The Hidden Curriculum of Compulsory Schooling.* Philadelphia: New Society.

Gauvin, L.I., Halliwell, W.R., & Vallerand, R.J. (1986). "Negative Effects of Competition on Children's Intrinsic Motivation." *The Journal of Social Psychology.* 126 (5), 649–656. Retrieved from http://dx.doi.org/10.1080/00224545.1986.9713638\.

Gifford, C. (2004). *Spies.* London: Kingfisher.

Grams, Brandin. (2013, June 12). "WWDC 2013 Stump the Experts." YouTube. Retrieved from https://www.youtube.com/watch?v=60mXJ8SDqqk.

Gutierrez, K. (2014, July 8). "Re: Studies confirm the power of visuals in eLearning." Blog post. Retrieved from http://info.shiftelearning.com/blog/bid/350326/Studies-Confirm-the-Power-of-Visuals-in-eLearning.

Harvard University. (2014, December 1). "J.K. Rowling Harvard Commencement Speech, Harvard University Commencement 2008." YouTube. Retrieved from https://youtu.be/UibfDUPJAEU.

Helmreich, R.L. (1982). "Pilot selection and training." Paper presented at the American Psychological Association Annual Meeting, Washington, D.C.

Helmreich, R.L., & Spence, J.T. (1978). "The Work and Family Orientation Questionnaire: An Objective Instrument to Assess Components of Achievement Motivation and Attitudes Toward Family and Career." *SAS: Catalog of Selected Documents in Psychology,* 8, MS-1677.

Hickman, P. (2008). *It's Moving Day!* Toronto: Kids Can.

Historiasvivas. (2007, May 19). "SANTOS DUMONT e o 14 BI." YouTube. Retrieved from https://youtu.be/vhE7UPOlmeQ.

The Historical Gamer. (2015, March 7). "Vietnam 65—Into the Jungle." YouTube. Retrieved from https://www.youtube.com/watch?v=FW3i7B90cmM.

Hoban, R. (1970). *A Bargain for Francis.* New York: HarperCollins.

Hollingsworth, P.M. (1978). "An Experimental Approach to the Impress Method of Teaching Reading." *Reading Teacher* 31 (6), 624–626. Retrieved from https://eric.ed.gov/?id=EJ177559.

Hopkins, G. (2012, March 5). "Keyboarding Skills: When Should They Be Taught?" *Education World.* Retrieved from http://www.educationworld.com/a_curr/curr076.shtml.

House, L.K. (2014, September 3). "Re: Growing up in the 1950's." Blog post. Retrieved from https://laurakayhouse.wordpress.com/tag/1950s/.

Hughes, S.L. (2008). "Vincent van Gogh: His Biography." On *Rappin' Clappin' Singin' 'Bout Art.* Audio CD. CD Baby.

Humphreys, H. (2014, May 30). "10 Hugely Successful People Who Failed Hard Before Making It Big." Blog post. Retrieved from http://thoughtcatalog.com/holly-humphreys/2014/05/10-hugely-successful-people-who-failed-hard-before-making-it-big/.

Jamison, Anthony. (2013, October 17). "Les Brown Getting Unstuck." YouTube. Retrieved from https://youtu.be/zTNNKUBDNsU.

Jenson, J.A. (1998). *Lost and Found.* New York: Hyperion.

Jet zak. (2012, May 21). "GOPRO gets the BITE from SALT WATER CROCODILE." YouTube. Retrieved from https://youtu.be/2AfG1nww6pQ.

Kahneman, D. (2011). *Thinking, Fast and Slow*. New York: Farrar, Straus, and Giroux.

Keats, E.K. (1998). *Peter's Chair*. New York: Puffin.

Kingwood Garden Center. (2013, July 10). "How to Plant a Butterfly Garden—Kingwood Garden Center." YouTube. Retrieved from https://youtu.be/WJjHQTfkKXg.

Kohn, Alfie. (1986). *No Contest: The Case Against Competition*. New York: Houghton Mifflin.

Krashen, Stephen D. (2004). "The Evidence for FVR." In *The Power of Reading: Insights from the Research, 2nd ed.*, 1–17. Westport, CT: Libraries Unlimited.

Kuo, Albert. (2014, January 30). "How to Peel an Orange the Easy Way!" YouTube. Retrieved from https://www.youtube.com/watch?v=FaR3ofRxjSo&feature=youtu.be.

Kurlansky, M. (2014). *The Story of Salt*. New York: Puffin.

Lansky, V. (1995). *Transparent Tape: Over 350 Super, Simple, and Surprising Uses You've Probably Never Thought of*. Deephaven, MN: Book Peddlers.

Ldonline. (2013, August 26). "When the Chips Are Down—Poker Chips—Richard Lavoie." YouTube. Retrieved from https://youtu.be/Vsl_XiyJupg.

Lee, H. (1960). *To Kill a Mockingbird*. New York: Grand Central.

Lehrman, C.K. (2016, November). "Should My Pillow Become Your Pillow?" *Consumer Reports*. Retrieved from http://www.consumerreports.org/mattresses/should-my-pillow-become-your-pillow/.

Leonard, J. (1995). *Patriotic Medley. On Places and Faces of America*. Audio CD. http://www.songsforteaching.com/judyleonard/patrioticmedley.php.

Lepper, M.R., Greene, D. & Nisbett. R.E. (1973). "Undermining Children's Intrinsic Interest with Extrinsic Reward: A Test of the 'Overjustification' Hypothesis." *Journal of Personality and Social Psychology*, 28, 129–137.

Lester, J. (1968). *To Be a Slave*. New York: Penguin Young Readers Group.

Leveille, V., & Mizner, S. (2017, February 20). "ACLU: Gun Control Laws Should Be Fair." *USATODAY*. Retrieved from http://www.usatoday.com/story/opinion/2017/02/20/gun-control-congress-aclu-editorials-debates/98147914/.

Levine, E. (2007). *Henry's Freedom Box: A True Story from the Underground Railroad*. New York: Scholastic.

Library of Congress. (2010, June 3). "Skating on Lake, Central Park." YouTube. Retrieved from https://youtu.be/E_98EUGWVZ0.

Life_of_mohan. (2015, April 23). "Gandhi Salt March." YouTube. Retrieved from https://www.youtube.com/watch?v=XqEfeEzaulc.

Locke, L. (1992). *Making "Movies" Without a Camera: Inexpensive Fun with Flip Books and Other Animation Gadgets*. Cincinnati: Betterway.

Lovell, P. (2001). *Stand Tall Molly Lou Melon*. New York: G.P. Putnam's Sons.

Lovely Greens. (2014, October 23). "How to Extract Honey from Honeycomb." YouTube. Retrieved from https://youtu.be/ufLnOEoaN-c.

Macaulay, D. (1976). *Underground*. Boston, MA: Houghton Mifflin.

Macaulay, D. (1988). *The Way Things Work*. Boston, MA: Houghton Mifflin; London: Dorling Kindersley.

Macdonald, K. (2013, October). "Survival Stories: The Girl Who Fell from the Sky." *Reader's Digest*. Retrieved from http://www.rd.com/true-stories/survival/survival-stories-the-girl-who-fell-from-the-sky/.

Machinima. (2008, November 13). "COD: World at War—'Jungle Warfare' (Game Trailer)." YouTube. Retrieved from https://www.youtube.com/watch?v=SI2wLgFqRWE.

MahaloPiano. (2012, January 6). "Learn Piano HD: How to Play G Major Scale (Right and Left) on Piano." YouTube. Retrieved from https://www.youtube.com/watch?v=7H4n6P-.

McKay, H. (2003). *Indigo's Star*. New York: McElderry.

McLoyd, V.C. (1979). "The Effects of Extrinsic Rewards of Differential Value on High and Low Intrinsic Interest. *Child Development*, 50, 1010–1019.

MotivatingSuccess. (2012, May 5). "Famous Failures." YouTube. Retrieved from https://www.youtube.com/watch?v=zLYECIjmnQs.

Mueller, C., & Dweck, C.S. (1998). "Praise for Intelligence Can Undermine Children's Motivation and Performance." *Journal of Personality and Social Psychology*. Vol. 75(1), 33–52.

Mundy, M. (2012.) *Sometimes I'm Afraid: A Book About Fear*. St. Meinrad: Abbey.

Nerburn, K. (2009, November 20). "The Last Cab Ride." Blog post. Retrieved from http://academictips.org/blogs/the-last-cab-ride/.

New Jersey 101.5. (2015, March 25). "AAA Video Analysis Provides Shocking Results Among Teen Drivers." YouTube. Retrieved from https://youtu.be/cs0iwz3NEC0.

No Comment TV. (2009, November 10). "The Fall of the Berlin Wall in 1989." YouTube. Retrieved from https://www.youtube.com/watch?v=zmRPP2WXX0U.

Ogle, D. (1986). "K-W-L: A Teaching Model That Develops Active Reading of Expository Text." *The Reading Teacher*, 39 (6), 564–570. Retrieved from http://www.jstor.org/stable/20199156.

Pacific, T. (2001). "The Fundamental Algebra Song." On *Musical Recall Greatest Hits*. Audio CD. Midi Magic Studios.

Page, Wes [YosemiteCCD]. (2009, June 9). "The Barbie Doll Test." YouTube. Retrieved from https://youtu.be/YOHbtM9463c.

Pease, Allan [AllanPeaseLive]. (2010, February 1). "Allan Pease Teaches How to Become a People Magnet." YouTube. Retrieved from https://youtu.be/c_d3W99Hpn4.

Postlethwaite, T.N. & Ross, K.N. (1992). *Effective Schools in Reading: Implications for Educational Planners.* The Hague: IEA.

Prompt Arts. (2014, November 19). "Experiments in Literature—1." YouTube. Retrieved from https://youtu.be/xYLEqEJvtc4.

Quitney, J. (2013, July 10). "Psychology: 'An Experimentally Produced Social Problem in Rats' circa 1940, O.H. Mowrer, Yale U." YouTube. Retrieved from https://youtu.be/A2jS0J86d5U.

Rankin, L. (2007). *Ruthie and the (Not So) Teeny Tiny Lie.* New York: Bloomsbury USA Childrens.

Relay Graduate School of Education. (2014, March 19). "Drs. Carol Dweck and Greg Walton Talk About Growth Mindset." Vimeo. Retrieved from https://vimeo.com/89521168.

The Richest. (2015, February 23). "The Amazing World Seen Through a Microscope." YouTube. Retrieved from https://youtu.be/bSieT0KTfp0.

Rock, B. (2013). *Deductive Detective.* Mt. Pleasant, SC: Sylvan Dell.

The RSA. (2013, December 10). "Brené Brown on Empathy." YouTube. Retrieved from https://youtu.be/1Evwgu369Jw?list=PLmHmICyEzbjZELowSuV5_mM6Xv1kJ_wDc.

Rumorintown. (2010, April 3). "1939 World Series Color Footage." YouTube. Retrieved from https://youtu.be/jMm_GeM4Hhk.

Sanborn, M. (2006). *You Don't Need a Title to Be a Leader: How Anyone, Anywhere, Can Make a Positive Difference.* Colorado Springs, CO: WaterBrook.

Schulz, C.M. (2010). *My Life with Charlie Brown.* Jackson: University Press of Mississippi.

Schwartz, D.M. (1985). *How Much Is a Million?* New York: William Morrow.

Sears, Roebuck & Co. (1897). *Sears, Roebuck & Co. Consumers Guide.* Chicago: Skyhorse.

Seyyah, Rotasız. (2016, October 23). "'Çok Güzelsin' Demenin Etkileri—You Are So Beautiful." YouTube. Retrieved from https://www.youtube.com/watch?v=vAXNREWZ128.

Show Box. (2014, September 30). "President John F. Kennedy Inaugural Address 'Ask Not What Your Country Can Do For You.'" YouTube. Retrieved from https://www.youtube.com/watch?v=8GsLEmZTgFo.

Silver, D.M., & Wynne, P.D. (1993). *The Body Book.* New York: Scholastic Teaching Resources.

Slaughter, Stan. (2010, January 16). "Why Compost?" YouTube. Retrieved from https://www.youtube.com/watch?v=Dwot5IzRpq0.

Smith, F. (1978). *Reading.* Cambridge: Cambridge University Press.

Speer, N.K., Reynolds, J.R., Swallow, K.M., & Zacks, J.M. (2009). "Reading Stories Activates Neural Representations of Perceptual and Motor Experiences." *Psychological Science*, 20, 989–999.

Subsymmetric. (2011, April 23). "Abigail & Brittany Hensel—The Twins Who Share a Body." YouTube. Retrieved from https://youtu.be/K57IcN9DWXo.

Seuss, Dr. (1939). *The King's Stilts.* New York: Random House.

Testervid. (2014, December 3). "Oldest Footage of the Grand National Steeplechase (Horse Racing)." YouTube. Retrieved from https://youtu.be/b554Hvz MM2c.

TED. (2009, October 21). "Itay Talgam: Lead Like the Great Conductors." YouTube. Retrieved from https://www.youtube.com/watch?v=R9g3Q-qvtss.

TED. (2012, March 2). "The Power of Introverts—Susan Cain." YouTube. Retrieved from https://www.youtube.com/watch?v=c0KYU2j0TM4.

TED. (2012, April 26). "The Surprising Science of Happiness—Dan Gilbert." YouTube. Retrieved from https://www.youtube.com/watch?v=4q1dgn_C0AU.

TED. (2013, May 3). "Every Kid Needs a Champion—Rita Pierson." YouTube. Retrieved from https://www.youtube.com/watch?v=SFnMTHhKdkw.

TED. (2015, March 4). "Harry Baker: A Love Poem for Lonely Prime Numbers." YouTube. Retrieved from https://www.youtube.com/watch?v=O6jrLgvCUNs.

TED. (2015, July 6). "Rajiv Maheswaran: The Math Behind Basketball's Wildest Moves." YouTube. Retrieved from https://www.youtube.com/watch?v=66ko_cWSHBU.

TED. (2015, October 12). "How I Stopped the Taliban from Shutting Down My School—Sakena Yacoobi." YouTube. Retrieved from https://www.youtube.com/watch?v=fCKNScHMBGE.

TED. (2017, January 6). "What I Learned from 100 Days of Rejection—Jia Jiang." YouTube. Retrieved from https://www.youtube.com/watch?v=-vZXgApsPCQ.

Tienken, C.H., Goldberg S., & DiRocco, D. (2009). "Questioning the Questions." *Kappa Delta Pi Record*, 46, 39–43.

Tierney, J. (2001, August 5). "Here Comes the Alpha Pups." *The New York Times*, 38. Retrieved from http://www.nytimes.com/2001/08/05/magazine/here-come-the-alpha-pups.html?pagewanted=all.

"Tinkering with Tops." (2017). Retrieved from http://www.tryengineering.org/sites/default/files/lessons/tinkeringwithtops.pdf.

Tunis, E. (1957). *Colonial Living.* Cleveland, OH: World.

The Twisted Trilobite's channel. (2011, August 31). "There Are as Many Creatures on Your Body as There Are People on Earth." YouTube. Retrieved from https://youtu.be/QrmashOX5EU.

VanCleave, J. (1996). *Janice VanCleave's 202 Oozing, Bubbling, Dripping, and Bouncing Experiments.* New York: John Wiley & Sons.

VICE. (2011, October 26). "Inside Darfur—VICE News." YouTube. Retrieved from https://www.youtube.com/watch?v=W66ovZe1-TM.

Vock, J. (2013, August 30). "Courage of Famous Failures—Inspirational." YouTube. Retrieved from https://www.youtube.com/watch?v=Ydeyl0vXdP0.

Walker, S.M. (2006). *Sound.* Minneapolis, MN: Lerner.

Wargin, Jo. (2009). *Moose on the Loose Kathy.* Ann Arbor, MI: Sleeping Bear.

Westervelt, E. (2014, July 26). Interview by E. Westervelt [Radio]. "An Idea That Stuck: How a Hymnal Bookmark Helped Inspire the Post-It Note." NPR West.

What's My Line. (2015, April 20). "*What's My Line?* Phil Rizzuto—Debut Show (Feb 2, 1950)." YouTube. Retrieved from https://www.youtube.com/watch?v=Nw5IwQ2mLX4.

Whildin, Don. (2013, November 29). "The Greatest Hostage Rescue in History: Documentary on the Entebbe Raid." YouTube. Retrieved from https://youtu.be/4acDtx85CBw.

Wiley, K. "Momma, When Do You Use a Comma?" On *English: Sing Your Way to Easy Learning.* Audio CD. http://www.songsforteaching.com/readinglanguagearts/commas.php.

Willems, M. (2005). *The Terrible Monster.* New York: Hyperion Books for Children.

Wood, R.W. (1999). *Sound Fundamentals: Funtastic Science Activities for Kids.* Philadelphia: Chelsea House.

The WWYD Show. (2013, July 24). "Single Mother Can't Afford Food: What Would You Do?" YouTube. Retrieved from https://www.youtube.com/watch?v=ayKv9IeeS_E.

Young, Kevin. (2012, September 29). "'Where Have All the Flowers Gone' written by Pete Seeger and Joe Hickerson." YouTube. Retrieved from https://www.youtube.com/watch?v=LzyfmzfuGyc.

Index